WITHDRAWN

D1116370

SCHUMPETER'S THEORY OF CAPITALIST MOTION

Other books by the author

The Making of Marx's Critical Theory (1983)

Marx's Critique of Political Economy:
Intellectual Sources and Evolution (2 vols: 1984, 1985)

Essays in Political Economics:
Public Control in a Democratic Society by Adolph Lowe – Editor

338.9
Oa4s

Schumpeter's Theory of Capitalist Motion

A Critical Exposition and Reassessment

Allen Oakley

Department of Economics
University of Newcastle
Australia

Edward Elgar

© Allen Oakley 1990

All rights reserved. No part of this publication may be reproduced, stored in a retrieval system, or transmitted in any form or by any means, electronic, mechanical, photocopying, recording, or otherwise without the prior permission of the publisher.

Published by
Edward Elgar Publishing Limited
Gower House
Croft Road
Aldershot
Hants GU11 3HR
England

Gower Publishing Company
Old Post Road
Brookfield
Vermont 05036
USA

British Library Cataloguing in Publication Data
Oakley, Allen
  Schumpeter's theory of capitalist motion: a critical
  exposition and reassessment.
  1. Economics. Theories of Schumpeter, Joseph A. (Joseph
  Alois), 1883–1950
  I. Title
  330.1
  ISBN 1 85278 055 X

Printed in Great Britain by
Billing & Sons Ltd, Worcester

For Renate

ALLEGHENY COLLEGE LIBRARY

90-9105

Contents

Figures

ix

Preface

The year 1983 saw the occurrence of that now well-known and well-worn chronological coincidence of centenaries: the death of Karl Heinrich Marx (1818–1883), the birth of John Maynard Keynes (1883–1946) and the birth of Joseph Alois Schumpeter (1883–1950). At the biennial conference of the History of Economic Thought Society of Australia, held in the same year at the University of Sydney, the opportunity was taken to provide centenary orations about these people.

Peter Groenewegen read the oration on Schumpeter and his presentation regenerated my interest in the Austrian. I re-read Robert Heilbroner's brilliant, but all too brief chapter in *The Worldly Philosophers* (1986) and this further stimulated me to pursue Schumpeter's thought more intensively.

The period 1983 and beyond brought a flurry of secondary literature about Schumpeter and I became aware that many others had also 'rediscovered' the man on the occasion of his centenary. It also became apparent when I compared my expanding reading of Schumpeter's original writings with the contents of this burgeoning literature that, because of its specialized and delimited nature, it was not able to present a full and balanced critical account of the mainline of his economic analyses as a whole. I found that much the same assessment applied to the earlier secondary literature. Throughout all this work on Schumpeter I found many brilliant, and some not so brilliant, pieces about particular facets of the man's thought. There were, though, few comprehensive studies available. One, by Erich Schneider (1975), proved to be a wide ranging, but brief, biographically-oriented work. Another by Richard Clemence and Francis Doody (1966) I found to be rather superficial and far too enthusiastic in its often contorted endeavours to defend Schumpeter against *all* critique. The study by M. S. Khan (1957) was of a high standard of scholarship, but more concerned to 'connect' Schumpeter's work with that of his antecedents and that of later analysts of motion than with any detailed exposition of his thought itself.

My response to this state of the literature was to conceive a research project on Schumpeter originally in somewhat broader terms than what ultimately emerged. I found that as my research proceeded, and the mass of material began to accumulate and grow in its complexity, that to do justice to Schumpeter's wide-ranging output would take me well beyond the themes in which I was most interested and lead me to devote more time to the project than I was prepared to do. I resolved, therefore, to concentrate on a more intensive critical study of his theoretical analysis of economic development and the business cycle, i.e. of those dimensions of the totality of capitalist motion on which he chose to focus his attention.

So, the reader should be aware that what follows in this study is *not* an intellectual biography and is *not* a study of Schumpeter's thought as a whole or even of the whole of his economic thought. There are many fascinating stories yet to be told, but I must leave those to others. We can but hope that a comprehensive record of Schumpeter's life, character and work will have accumulated in the not too distant future. My study is but one part of that record.

A further limitation that I decided to impose upon my study, because of its single-minded purpose and the need to confront the very real and understandable economics of publishing, was to avoid engaging in polemic with other interpreters of Schumpeter. As Schumpeter himself once put it, 'I had my own tale to tell' and I have used up the whole of the space available to me telling it. This should not be taken to mean that I am claiming that my interpretations and critique transcend all others or that they are unique in being either wholly original or exclusively correct. I simply decided that there was a lacuna in the literature that could be filled by the detailed exegetical study that will be found below. The existing literature has not been ignored, but it has been used very selectively on its own terms, mostly for purposes of elaboration on particular themes.

My critical reading of Schumpeter's theory of motion has taken place through an intellectual 'grid' that has particular origins and insists that certain methodological qualities be present in any such theory. My perception of capitalism and its motion has its roots in the works of four great contributors to our discipline: Karl Marx, Michal Kalecki, John Maynard Keynes and Adolph Lowe. It has been my intention, however, that my critique should not be confrontationist. Rather, I have tried to maintain as much empathy with Schumpeter's endeavours as possible along the way – an intention, as readers will, I think, come to realize, that was not always easy to sustain. Ultimately, I wanted to discover the precise dimensions of the legacy that Schumpeter had left for future analysts and to reassess its potential to contribute to the further development of the theory of motion that is gradually being derived from the writers cited above.

Some of the ideas that have been elaborated in this study were first presented at seminars in the Institut für Volkswirtschaftslehre of the Technical University of Vienna, Austria (1985); in the Institut für Volkswirtschaftslehre of the University of Graz, Austria (1985); in the Dipartimento di Scienze Economiche of the University of Bergamo, Italy (1988); and at the Einaudi Foundation in Turin, Italy (1988). Some ideas were also the subject of a paper presented at the third Conference of the History of Economic Thought Society of Australia at La Trobe University in 1985. I thank the participants in all these presentations for their interest and comments. More specifically, I am grateful to the following people for their assistance and comments on these occasions and at other points in the evolution of the project: Riccardo Bellofiore, Helmut Frisch, Harald Hagemann, Gerhard Hanappi, Geoffrey Harcourt, Robert Heilbroner, Ludwig Lachmann, Adolph Lowe, Phil O'Hara, Michael Schneider and Andreas Wörgötter. I am especially grateful to Stephan Böhm of the University of Graz, Austria, for his interest in the project since its inception. Dr Böhm read the entire manuscript and provided several penetrating and helpful comments of a general and substantive nature. In thanking these scholars I absolve them from all responsibility for what has appeared in the final product.

The study was mostly written during my sabbatical leave, on an Outside Studies Programme granted by the University of Newcastle, Australia, in 1988. My hosts for much of this time were Dr Andreas Wörgötter and his colleagues in the Department of Economics of the Institute for Advanced Studies in Vienna, Austria. I am very grateful for the kind hospitality that they afforded me. During my two stays in Vienna while working on the project, I was also helped in a number of ways by Professor and Mrs Herbert Rosenauer and I convey my special thanks to them.

The typing of the manuscript was undertaken very largely by the ever efficient and able Lorraine King, with the assistance of Jenny Hargrave, Elizabeth Williams and Maxine Zerafa. I thank them, too, for their work on the project.

Finally, my wife Renate, to whom the study is dedicated, shared and assisted in the whole process of the research for and writing of the work in too many ways to enumerate. My warmest thanks must go to her for all that she has contributed along the way.

Allen Oakley
Newcastle, Australia

Reference Works

The following works or collections of works by Schumpeter are cited frequently in the text by means of the abbreviated titles given in the list below. Full publication details can be found in the References at the end of the book.

Das Wesen	*Das Wesen und der Hauptinhalt der theoretischen Nationalökonomie*
Development	*The Theory of Economic Development*
Doctrine	*Economic Doctrine and Method*
Wesen des Geldes	*Das Wesen des Geldes*
Cycles	*Business Cycles*
Capitalism	*Capitalism, Socialism and Democracy*
History	*History of Economic Analysis*
Classes	*Imperialism and Social Classes*
Aufsätze	*Aufsätze zur ökonomischen Theorie*
Economists	*Ten Great Economists*
Essays	*Essays on Economic Topics of J. A. Schumpeter*

1 Introduction

1.1 Bibliographical matters

The writings of Joseph Alois Schumpeter (1883–1950), *Doctor utriusque juris*, University of Vienna, 1906, spanned a period of more than 40 years. He entered the lists in 1905 with three brief reports on statistical seminars conducted in the University of Vienna that were published in the *Statistische Monatsschrift*, the monthly statistical bulletin of Austria. When he died during the night of 7–8 January 1950, he left on his desk the unfinished manuscript for *History* along with the incompletely written-up paper 'The March into Socialism' that he had presented at the American Economic Association Meeting in December 1949 (reprinted in *Capitalism*, pp. 415ff.). In this period, he wrote in all some 15 books and pamphlets, about 125 articles and reviewed more than 90 books (see the Bibliography in *Essays*, pp. 316ff.).

It was already made clear in his earliest major work, *Das Wesen* from 1908, that he intended to devote his research in economics largely to the analysis of motion, to an endeavour to comprehend the 'dynamics' of change in the capitalist economic system, rather than to the overwhelmingly dominant 'statics' of orthodoxy. *Das Wesen* itself comprised an elaborate literary synthesis of all those themes and theses, methodological and substantive, of received economic theory that Schumpeter felt instinctively to be important. It contained little that was original, and probably was not intended to as it had an air of self-clarification and preparation for things to come about it — he wrote in the Foreword: 'We want to *understand* and not engage in polemics [about the theories], to *learn* not to criticise, to *analyse* and work out what is correct in every theorem rather than simply to accept or reject' (*Das Wesen*, p. vi, original emphasis).[1] The central objective of the book seems to have been to provide a foundation for the erection of Schumpeter's own theoretical edifice. His intention was to survey the existing body of 'pure economics' in order to elicit 'all starting points that [may] lead to further development. . .' (ibid., p. ix). Most particularly, his survey convinced him that the way ahead in economic analysis was to bring the theoretical 'dynamics' of capitalist development up to the same level of formal analysis as that which had been achieved in 'statics'. He recognized, though, that 'statics' and 'dynamics' are 'completely different fields' dealing with 'different problems' requiring 'different methods and different material'; that they 'are not two chapters of one and the same theoretical edifice but two fully independent constructions' (ibid., pp. 182-3; cf. p. xix).

After referring to the matter of 'dynamic' analysis in the Foreword (ibid., pp. xix-xx), Schumpeter devoted two pieces to the theme in the main text of *Das Wesen*: one comprised a concluding chapter, entitled 'Statics and Dynamics', in the first methodological section of Part II that dealt with static equilibrium analysis; and the other comprised the second and last section of the final chapter of the book, a chapter that carried the title 'The Development Possibilities of Theoretical Economics' (ibid., pp. 176 ff., 614ff.). In addition, there were two particular categories of income distribution theory that he argued to have essential 'dynamic' content, namely interest and entrepreneurial profit (ibid., pp. 414ff., 431ff.). Thus, while the subject of his theoretical exposition in *Das Wesen* was predominantly 'static' orthodoxy, he highlighted wherever appropriate the inherent limitations of that level of theory *vis-à-vis* any endeavour to understand the totality of the economic system. These limitations are 'the most painful of all' for, as an object of theory, 'the pure economic system is essentially non-developmental in nature'. These self-imposed limitations therefore follow 'naturally and ineluctably from the [chosen] nature of our system'. And yet, 'one cannot fail to appreciate that development is the most important of all those phenomena whose explanation we strive for' (ibid., p. 186). Such was Schumpeter's intuition about the potential problems of 'dynamics' that he could foreshadow a difficult time ahead for analysts. The theory of development would comprise 'moments altogether different from those which our ['pure'] system depicts, and the complexity of the relevant relations probably will defy exact treatment for a long time to come' (ibid.). Indeed, as things turned out, his own attempt to meet the challenge of formally analysing motion occupied him for most of the rest of his intellectual life.

Two features of *Das Wesen* should be noted in passing. First, as already suggested, he espoused in the work a more 'exact' conception of economic theory than he would have learnt in Vienna. He allowed himself to be strongly influenced by Walras even though the influence of von Wieser and von Böhm-Bawerk remained evident, especially in the analysis of production costs and income distribution. His own perception was that 'L. Walras and v. Wieser are those writers to whom the author believes he stands closest' (ibid., p. ix; cf. Samuels (1983) and Boehm (1989) on themes in Schumpeter's 'Austrian' connections). However, even though Walras provided the essential framework for the book's exposition, there are few further references to him in the text (pp. 12, 39-40, 261, 275, 300, 336). There can be no doubt, though,

about his admiration for that writer's contributions at this formative
stage of his career, for the obituary article dedicated to the man that
Schumpeter wrote in 1910 is full of emphasis on the original and
fundamental insights that can be found in the *Elements* and other works
(*Economists*, pp. 74ff.). The flavour of his admiration can best be
expressed in his own words.

> Whoever knows the origin and the workings of exact natural sciences knows
> also that their great achievements are, in method and essence, of the same
> kind as Walras'. To find exact forms for the phenomena whose interdepen-
> dence is given us by experience, to reduce these forms to, and derive them
> from, each other: this is what the physicists do, and this is what Walras did.
>
> The theory of economic equilibrium is Walras' claim to immortality,that
> great theory whose crystal-clear train of thought has illuminated the structure
> of purely economic relationships with the light of *one* fundamental principle.
> (*Economists*, pp. 79, 76, original emphasis)

Just what Schumpeter was able to derive from the work of Walras for his
own theory of motion will be considered again in Chapter 4 below.

The second feature of *Das Wesen* to be noted here concerns
Schumpeter's use of mathematics. Perhaps surprisingly for an 'Austrian'-trained economist, he was a staunch advocate of the merits of
mathematical methods in economic analysis. One of his earliest papers
was devoted to that theme: 'Über die mathematische Methode der
theoretischen Ökonomie', published in 1906 (*Aufsätze*, pp. 529ff).
There he outlined the merits of using such methods in the expression of
economic arguments and reflected upon objections that have emerged
as well. His conclusion could not have been clearer: none of the
objections 'has made me waver in my belief in the principle of applying
the method or in my belief that the future of economic theory as a
science rests on this method – as Jevons put it: If economics is to be a
science at all, it must be a mathematical one' (ibid., p. 546). I have
drawn attention to this espousal because it contrasts so strongly with his
own life-long method and style in which mathematics was very rarely
used. *Das Wesen* set the stage for this future of literary expositions, for
in some 626 pages of theoretical text that could well have lent itself to
much more, only about 22 pages included mathematical formulae, and
these comprised quite elementary algebra and calculus (pp. 106–7,
130–1, 213–15, 225, 261–2, 484–6, 488–96). Two possible reasons come
to mind for this contrast: first, perhaps Schumpeter felt that the
resistance to theory alone was great enough in the German-speaking
world outside Austria without jeopardizing any potential of his book to
communicate with 'the Germans' by filling it with abstract mathematical

expressions; and, secondly, perhaps his lack of formal training in mathematics led him to avoid undertaking to write a treatise that depended for its substance on mathematical methods. From this distance in time, it is not possible to be sure whether either, neither or both of these reasons has any foundation.[2]

One final point of interest about *Das Wesen* is the reception that it enjoyed amongst his contemporary economists. Perhaps representative of its 'Austrian' reception was von Wieser's review of the book (1911) in which he praised its achievement of a wide and erudite coverage of the economic theory of the time, even though he did not like much about its emphasis on the 'exact' economics that was espoused by Walras and others (Schneider, 1975, p. 8). The Italian response was more sympathetic and it has been reported that Pantaleoni, given a copy of the book to read by Pareto, wrote to the latter that while the work is 'diffuse, but good' and 'does not contain anything new', it should be 'very useful for the Germans'. He concluded that its author 'must not be discouraged' (ibid.).

And discouraged he was not. Schumpeter's concern to press ahead with the development of a 'dynamic' economics can be seen in two papers published in 1910, one of which dealt directly with the essential nature of, and origins in capitalist motion of, economic crises: Über das Wesen der Wirtschaftskrisen' (Böhm (ed.), 1987, pp. 227ff.); the other of which comprised an extensive discussion of recent work in economic theory in the USA, including contributions to the analysis of motion by J. B. Clark and others: 'Die neuere Wirtschaftstheorie in den Vereinigten Staaten' (Schumpeter, 1910). For my present purposes, the importance of these two pieces centres on the fact that some of the most significant theses of Schumpeter's first *magnum opus* on motion, *Development*, were adumbrated in them. In particular, the former paper provided a summary of these theses at the end in nine points (Böhm (ed.), 1987, pp. 273-4). First, economic processes fall into two distinct categories, the 'static' and the 'dynamic', where, secondly, the centrepiece of the latter is the process of 'pure economic development' that comprises an immanently-generated form of motion. In the main text, he had defined this development as the particular aspect of economic motion that can be attributed to the 'new combinations' affecting production that are implemented by entrepreneurs (ibid., pp. 232ff.). Thirdly, the new combinations cause an existing 'static' equilibrium state to be disturbed, with such disturbance, fourthly, setting off a sequence of reactions within the economy that return it to a new equilibrium. Fifthly, the equilibrium restoration process involves a reorganization of the price system and liquidations of firms that prove to be economically non-viable as, sixthly, the economy passes through a wave of prosperity and depression. That wave may involve, seventhly, 'abnormal' distortions that engender an economic crisis. Eighthly, there may also occur accidental external factors that bring crisis, and, ninthly, these latter causes must be understood separately as not having their roots in the necessary processes of the capitalist economy. As Chapters 6 to 9 below will reveal, this was an accurate preliminary insight into much that was to come in Schumpeter's work on motion.

The rich contents of these 1910 articles is less surprising when it is realized that they were probably by-products of Schumpeter's research for and writing of *The Theory of Economic Development*. The Foreword to the first edition of the work carries the date July 1911, with 1912 given as the date of publication, and he referred to it there as comprising ideas that dated from 1905 (Schumpeter, 1912, pp. VII, VIII). Some confusion has arisen in the literature about these dates, probably due to Schumpeter's sometimes inconsistent references to them. For instance, in the Preface to the English edition, he wrote: 'Some of the ideas submitted in this book go back as far as 1907; all of them had been worked out by 1909, . . . The book was published for the first time, in German, in the fall of 1911' (*Development*, p. ix). The second German edition's Foreword cited it as 'the book from 1911', the fourth edition's as 'the text from 1911' (Schumpeter, 1935, pp. XI, XIII). However, elsewhere he gave a different impression, referring in 1914 to 'my book that appeared in 1912' (Böhm (ed.), 1987, p. 275n) and in 1927 to ideas 'arrived at in 1909, first published in 1912' (*Essays*, p. 24). Readers may form their own opinions about all this.

The Theory of Economic Development is one of the works that is central to the study that follows and its contents will be elaborated upon in due course. For the present, some brief introduction to what Schumpeter set out to achieve in the book will help to situate it within his bibliography of writings in which the theory of motion is the dominant theme. First of all, it should be kept in mind that the book enjoyed widespread popularity over a long period of time. Subsequent to the first edition, he decided to shorten the book considerably (from 548 to 369 pages of text), mainly by omitting the seventh chapter of the first edition with its predominantly sociological themes, a move designed to emphasize to his readers that it was the *economics* of development that he felt represented his main contribution (1935, p. XI). And then, having rewritten Chapters 2 and 6 dealing respectively with the core thesis of development and its business-cycle form, along with making other more minor editorial changes, the second edition appeared in 1926. Third (1931) and fourth (1935–with a new Foreword) editions appeared, but these were but reprintings of the second edition. Translations also began to be published: in Italian, 1932; in English, 1934; in French, 1935; in Japanese, 1937 (with a special and insightful Preface by Schumpeter that is reprinted in translation in *Essays*, pp. 158ff.), together with a second edition in that language from 1950; and in Spanish, 1944.

The second edition of *Development* had added to its title a sub-title that is highly indicative of the book's intentions: *An Inquiry into Profits, Capital, Credit, Interest and the Business Cycle.* Now while Schumpeter did 'inquire into' all of these things to one degree or another, the overall purpose of the book dominates the tenor and direction of these 'inquiries' into individual topics. All contributed to the explanation of economic development (as he defined it) and its form as business cycles, where the 'argument of the book forms one connected whole' (*Development*, p. xi). His rationale for providing such an elaborate subtitle to the revised version of the work is worth quoting in full as it gives some indication of the potential for misreading work on 'dynamic' economic theory that must have been rife at the time.

> Unfortunately, in order to express the fundamental identity of the book in its new form with the book from 1911, I had to retain its title. How inappropriate it is is demonstrated by the recurring questions that come from everywhere about my 'book on economic history'. The new subtitle should counteract this misleading impression and indicate that what the reader will find here has not more to do with economic history than all other economic theory. (1935, pp. xi-xii).

In the Japanese preface he set out the book's objective in the most general terms possible: 'I was trying to construct a theoretic model of the process of economic change in time, or perhaps more clearly, to answer the question how the economic system generates the force which incessantly transform it.' (*Essays*, pp. 158-9).

The second *magnum opus* with which my study will be centrally concerned is the massive *Business Cycles* published in 1939. What is to be noticed straight away here is that the book's object of analysis is set squarely before the reader in the title. It, too, carried a highly indicative subtitle designed to explicate the scope of the work on its chosen theme: *A Theoretical, Historical, and Statistical Analysis of the Capitalist Process.* As Schumpeter put it: 'I have called the book "Business Cycles" in order to indicate succinctly what the reader is to expect, but the subtitle really renders what I have tried to do.' (*Cycles*, p. v). His view was that the analysis of business cycles presents a task of 'formidable dimensions' because it 'means neither more nor less than analyzing the economic process of the capitalist era'. More graphically: 'Cycles are not, like tonsils, separable things that might be treated by themselves, but are, like the beat of the heart, of the essence of the organism that displays them.' (ibid.). Just how 'formidable' the analytical task proved to be when posited in this way is to be revealed in my critical exposition of Schumpeter's endeavours below.

There are several methodological and substantive aspects of the relationship between *Development* and *Cycles* to which I think it appropriate to draw attention. First, at least in retrospect, Schumpeter looked upon *Development* as a foundation for the later book. In the Preface to *Cycles*, he alluded to the seminal work as providing a theoretical 'scaffolding' and to his efforts 'to turn that scaffolding into a house, to embody the results of . . . [his] later work, to present the historical and statistical complement, to expand old horizons' (ibid.). However, this is a potentially misleading assertion and must be interpreted with care. Clearly, he regarded *Cycles* as a continuation of the earlier work that included complementary elaborations that flowed from additional research. There was no suggestion that he either retreated from any of his seminal analyses or that *Cycles* was intended to replace *Development* in his bibliography. Apropos the former point, it is clear that there was a shift of emphasis in the later book away from the detailed analysis of development *per se* found in *Development* towards a much more elaborate theory of the process's business cycle form. He did this in the knowledge that readers could be referred back to the earlier book for any details glossed over in *Cycles* – for example, regarding entrepreneurs (p. 103n), profit (p. 105n), money and banking (p. 109n), and interest (pp. 123n, 124n). That *Cycles* did not replace *Development* in his bibliography is evident from this substantive complementarity, but it is reinforced by the fact that Schumpeter allowed the latter work to be carried through the multiplicity of editions and translations to which I made reference earlier. These were being worked on and appearing during the period that *Cycles* was being drafted, with the Spanish translation not on the shelves until five years after its complement was published.

Besides the shift of emphasis just referred to, there were three other distinctive features of *Cycles* that stand out in any comparison with *Development*. One of these concerns the different readerships at whom the two works were directed. Schumpeter made it clear that *Development* was intended to be in 'aim and method . . . frankly "theoretical"' (*Development*, p. x). This, together with the style and tenor of the prose used, suggests that it was directed at mainly specialists in economics, with few concessions being made for lay readers. In *Cycles* he referred to the earlier book as of no necessary concern to the 'beginner or non-professional reader' (p. v). By contrast, *Cycles* was expressly designed to appeal to and be meaningful to 'the general reader' with the inclusion of 'an introductory chapter, constant attention to the common-sense meaning of technicalities, utmost simplification throughout . . . [being] the chief means to that end' (Cycles, p. vi). This really was an unfortunate decision on Schumpeter's part because the work ended up 'falling between two stools'. Its text in many and crucial places remained well beyond all but the most exceptional 'general reader'. This feature was compounded by the numerous 'schoolmasterly' demands that readers work out for themselves pieces of vital and intricate analytical argument, the natures of which were merely suggested in the text (e.g., ibid., pp. 17n, 133, 136 and n, 150, 158). And yet, at the same time, the lack of any rigorous, detailed and formalized analysis at key points in the development of the theory left professional readers with nothing very substantial to take away from their efforts to wade through the often 'heavy' prose. As I will have occasion to note again in the next section, he ended up apologizing to professional readers for these very lacunae in his argument (e.g., ibid., pp. 36n, 45n). And, on a note of irony, I draw attention to his later hostility to such popular objectives in technical works: he expressed the opinion that economists have, 'much to the detriment of their field, . . . attached unreasonable importance to being understood by the general public . . .' (History, p. 10n) – a case of mea culpa for Schumpeter.

The second distinctive feature of Cycles when compared to Development flows from this attempt to provide a 'popular' accessible analysis. Schumpeter's decision led him to change h:3 analytical strategy in a way that affected the opening gambit of his argument. In the seminal opus, he began his analysis with an abstract and purely theoretical model of the circular flow of economic life in a steady state unaffected by any change. This model was to act as the core reference state for the subsequent analysis of the sequence of disequilibria that constitute development. The construction of the model involved an a priori deductive procedure which built onto the maxims of a Walrasian general equilibrium framework (see below, Chapter 4). Schumpeter's approach in the opening pages of Cycles was quite different. There he began with the same essential idea of formulating a reference state of the economy that could provide a 'centre of gravity' for his analysis of motion. However, the formulation now involved an inductively-derived and impressionistic analysis of the observed characteristics of a 'normal' business situation as it would be perceived by a representative 'business-man'. Then, whereas in Development the use of an abstract circular-flow model upon which to build a theory of motion was not seen as needing defence, the explicit purpose of the inductive approach in *Cycles* was to justify such use by linking it to elements in an observed reality.

The third distinctive feature of *Cycles* is evident in its subtitle, namely the extension of the theoretical approach to include complementary historical and statistical analytical techniques. I noted above how Schumpeter had taken steps in the second edition of *Development* to avoid any assumed association of his analysis with economic history. The point actually went somewhat deeper, for he explicitly eschewed any empirical analyses in the work. There was a hint that he saw their relevance to a more extensive analysis of business cycles (*Development*, p. 212), but for the immediate objectives that he had set himself in the work, no 'historical evolutionary factors' needed to be addressed. He wrote: 'I have taken account not of one factor of historical change [as the cause of development], but none', for he claimed to be 'not at all concerned with the concrete factors of change, but with the method by which these work, with the *mechanism of change*' (ibid., pp. 60, 61n, original emphasis). But, by the time he came to present his theory in English for the first time in a 1927 paper published in *Economica* (*Essays*, pp. 21ff.), he saw more clearly the need for complementary empirical analyses. The 'backbone' tenets of his theory, he said, comprise '*no* theory of the cycle, if we understand by this a complete explanation of all that happens. This can only be found in a reasoned history of industrial life' (ibid., p. 33, original emphasis). There was from then on a progressive rise in the significance that Schumpeter ascribed to the empirical complement to theory until it reached, via the excruciating descriptive detail of *Cycles*, a parity status or beyond in his last paper on business cycles, published in November 1949, entitled 'The Historical Approach to the Analysis of Business Cycles' (*Essays*, pp. 308ff.). Perhaps the ultimate position that he took on this matter came in his well-known assertion in the *History* manuscripts: 'if, starting my work in economics afresh, I were told that I could study only one of the three [analytical techniques – history, statistics, theory] but could have my choice, it would be economic history I should choose' (*History*, p. 12).

Having said all this in relation to the third feature of *Cycles*, though, it is still important to stress that in his analyses of development and cycles as they are extant,there was never any indication that theory's essential role could or should be usurped by history and/or statistics. Rather, the relationship between the techniques remained one of complementarity, delimited by certain logico-expositional priorities. Thus, he wrote in the Preface to the English edition of *Development*, dated 1934: 'Perhaps I think somewhat differently now about the relation between "factual" and "theoretical" research than I did in 1911. But my conviction stands that our science cannot, any more than others, dispense with that refined common-sense which we call "theory" and which provides us with the tools for aproaching both facts and practical problems' (p. x). The point was reiterated in *Cycles*: 'some of our refinements on common sense are logically anterior to the facts we wish to study and must be introduced first, because our factual discussions would be impossible without them' (p. 31). A more detailed treatment of Schumpeter's analytical strategy will be provided in Chapter 3 below.

All in all, the discussion above has been intended to portray *Development* and *Cycles* as *magna opera* that are related by continuity and complementarity in the totality of Schumpeter's writings on motion. The existence of this relationship is reinforced by the fact that he contributed a series of shorter pieces to journals and collections of essays in which similar theses were expounded. These appeared over the years after *Development* was published and enabled him to present his ideas in a more direct and simplified form and thereby, he felt, promote dissemination and improved understanding of them. He made this intention clear in the first of these papers, 'Die Wellenbewegung des Wirschaftslebens', published in 1914 (Böhm (ed.), 1987, pp. 275ff.; see p. 275n). This particular summary version of the *Development* theses was occasioned by Schumpeter's year at Columbia University in New York in 1913-14 where he presented a paper on his ideas that followed the published format. His first foray with his development theory into the English language journals did not come until 1927, as I noted above, while he was still in Bonn. He contributed an invited review article on Pigou's just-published *Industrial Fluctuations* to *Economica* and it was in that context that, as he put it: 'The writer begs .eave to avail himself of the Editor's invitation to start, in discussing Professor Pigou's theory, from his own views . . . [that are] capable of being compressed into a very few propositions . . .' (*Essays*, pp. 24 and ff.). Later in the same paper, he also took the opportunity to provide an exposition of his complementary views on the nature and role of money and credit in a theory of motion. His general ideas on these themes had already been outlined on several occasions in the German-language literature. In *Das Wesen* there was a chapter entitled 'The Bases of the Theory of Money' (pp. 276ff.) and this was followed by a series of four papers that built upon these seminal ideas and upon those worked up in the relevant chapters of *Development* (Chapters III and V). These papers dated from 1913, 1917, 1925 and 1927 (*Aufsätze*, pp. 1ff.; see also Schumpeter, 1956). It is also appropriate to mention here that during the period of the late 1920s, Schumpeter worked at drafting a treatise on monetary analysis. The manuscript was never completed or published in his lifetime, although it was announced as imminent by the German publisher Springer-Verlag in 1929 under the title *Geld und Währung* – the projected 36th volume of an encyclopaedia on law and political science (Reclam, 1984, p. 211). Schumpeter referred to the work's existence from time to time in his other writings, but he never gave it a title. It became available in 1970 as *Das Wesen des Geldes*, the title being adopted from the heading given by Schumpeter to the ninth chapter (see *Wesen des Geldes*). The treatment of money and credit in the theory of motion will be considered more fully in Chapter 7 below.

Two further papers in English on themes in the theory of motion followed soon after the *Economica* piece. One was the methodological work entitled 'The Instability of Capitalism' in the *Economic Journal*, 1928 and the other was a review article about 'Mitchell's Business Cycles' in the *Quarterly Journal of Economics* in 1930 (*Essays*, pp. 47ff., 73ff.). In neither of these papers did Schumpeter set out his theory explicitly. It provided a more or less implicit background to the latter review, while in the former paper he emphasized the methodological distinctions between analysing 'static' models of capitalism and models of capitalism 'in progress'. During the 1920s and 1930s, several other brief pieces were directed at themes pertinent to the understanding of motion (see the *Essays* Bibliography, pp. 319-22), but the next exposition of his 'complete' theory in outline came in the 1935 *Review of Economic Statistics* paper entitled 'The Analysis of Economic Change' (*Essays*, pp. 134ff.). This piece presented in miniature the extended theory that was to appear in *Cycles* a few years later. A decade later, he mounted a defence of his theoretical focus on development as the core mode of change in capitalism rather than on 'pure' economic growth in a 1945 supplement to the *Journal of Economic History*; the paper carried the title 'Theoretical Problems of Economic Growth' (*Essays*, pp. 227ff.). Finally, there is the paper from 1949 that I mentioned earlier, 'The Historical Approach to the Analysis of Business Cycles', in which Schumpeter endeavoured to ensure that the legitimate place of historical analysis in the study of business cycles would be preserved (*Essays*, pp. 227ff.). Each of these papers is drawn upon as and where necessary in my study. But, given that they very largely only repeat what is to be found in Schumpeter's major texts on the themes and theses that are at issue here, they have had mainly only a supplementary role to play in my reading of his work.

There are, of course, many other pieces in Schumpeter's extensive bibliography that deal with themes that have some relevance to his work on motion. The richness and great scope of his coverage of economics and related subjects can only be gleaned by a personal perusal of the list (*Essays*, pp. 316ff.). It has been necessary for me to limit the extent to which I have drawn on this remaining literature and only a few of the pieces will appear from time to time in the exposition that follows. These are mainly concerned with the themes of methodology, capitalism, social classes and entrepreneurship. In no case, though, do I claim to have done anything but make very selective use of some of the arguments that they contain.

There remain two *magna opera* that have not yet found a place in my bibliographical discussion, namely *Capitalism, Socialism and Democracy* (1942) and the incomplete and posthumously published *History of Economic Analysis* (1954). Neither of these will be directly in focus in my study except where their themes overlap with or throw some additional light upon Schumpeter's theory of the economic motion of capitalism. Their chronological situation in his output is such, though, that as far as the mainline of his theory of development and cycles are concerned, they are appropriately treated as containing retrospective and supplementary reflections on what was already established. Their contents will be found to provide some powerful additional insights in this role, mainly on the themes of Schumpeter's concept of vision and his analytical strategy in the case of *History* and on the theme of monopoly-power capitalism in the case of *Capitalism*. I emphasize, hopefully unnecessarily, that the position of these major texts in the present study is in no way indicative of my perception of their stature as individual works or within the totality of Schumpeter's writings. Each warrants independent critical study as an integral part of his thought and perhaps some anniversary of *History* (1994, 2004?) will see it subjected to the same erudite, scholarly scrutiny as that was recently devoted to *Capitalism* on the occasion of its fortieth year in the literature (see Heertje (ed.), 1981).

One final comment of a bibliographical nature. Schumpeter, as is well known, was fond of the adage, adopted from one Wilhelm Ostwald, in which it is claimed that 'the roots of important original achievements, especially those of a theoretical nature, can almost always be found in the third decade of the lives of scholars' (quoted by Haberler, 1951a, p. 28; cf. *History*, p. 388n). Thus he wrote of Carl Menger: 'His gift [to economic theory] was the fruit of his thought and struggle during the third decade of his life, that period of sacred fertility which, in the case of every thinker, creates what is subsequently worked out' (*Economists*, p. 87; cf. p. 240 in connection with the work of Wesley Clair Mitchell). Schumpeter's own decade of 'sacred fertility' occurred from 1903 to 1913 when he turned 30 years of age. In that period, the pattern of his life's work was largely set and his main theoretical achievements were realized in accordance with the adage. *Das Wesen* set the stage of 'static' theory which was to form the foundations and background for the formulation of the 'dynamic' theory that appeared in *Development* after being introduced in outline in the earlier book itself and in the 1910 journal paper on 'Wirtschaftskrisen' (Böhm (ed.) 1987, pp. 227ff.) The publication in 1914 of the historical piece *Economic Doctrine and Method*[3] laid the foundations for *History* many years later, while aspects of the ill-fated seventh chapter of the first edition of *Development* foreshadowed themes taken up again in *Capitalism*.

1.2 Methodological and substantive boundaries

My purpose in this section is to set the scope of the thematic agenda for the critical exposition that follows. Most of the themes and criticisms touched upon in this outline will receive more substantial treatment in the appropriate place in my text. Particular references to Schumpeter's works are, therefore, avoided as far as possible. My hope is that the brief introduction of these themes now will help the reader to know what to expect and, perhaps more importantly, *what not to expect* to find in this book.

Schumpeter's object of study was the capitalist economic system in motion. He had some very particular ideas about what characteristics of capitalism are to be taken as indicative of its essential nature and some equally particular ideas about what dimensions of the system's motion warrant emphasis in a theoretical analysis. At this stage, I want to introduce only a few key points concerning these fundamental premises from which he worked. First, on the subject of capitalism itself, Schumpeter drew two distinctions that require preliminary clarification. He distinguished between capitalism as a *system* and capitalism as an *order* and this has particular relevance for the scope of my treatment of his theory of motion. In the case of capitalism perceived as a system, it is the structural and operational economic characteristics that are brought into focus and motion involves both the preservation of and changes to these characteristics. Now while the term 'economic' has only nominalist boundaries, Schumpeter's intention in separating the economic system from the socio-political order in which it is set is quite clear. The capitalist order comprises the transeconomic structures, institutions and operations that, to varying degrees of efficacy, facilitate the functioning of the economic system. But the order, too, experiences motion in the sense that it is constantly in the process of becoming something else, some other sort of order. In Schumpeter's analyses, the long-term fate of capitalism as an order is to 'turn into' a socialist order by virtue of a socio-political dialectic that was argued out in *Capitalism*. What he emphasized in this latter thesis was that capitalism could not suffer this fate on *economic* grounds. As a system, it is unstable for one reason or another, but that instability cannot impede its survival as a means of economic provisioning. As an order, it is unstable, too, but it is not *economically* unstable. My focus here will be exclusively upon the instability that Schumpeter identified in capitalism as an economic system and that he endeavoured to explain. This choice of theme is not to be taken as indicative of my acceptance of his perception that the capitalist order experiences no economic dialectic. I do not accept such a thesis, but that is another story.

Under the rubric of capitalism, Schumpeter also distinguished two main historical cum theoretical 'stages' of the system's existence. The historical and the theoretical perspectives get rather mixed up in his work, but I think that some valid generalizations can be made about his approach. The two 'stages' concerned are first, that in which market-price competition prevails in the system such that economic equilibrium is more or less assured by virtue of price flexibility and perfect resource mobility and adaptability; and secondly, that in which the forces of monopoly-power prevail such that competition takes the more complex form of interfirm strategies involving price, quantity, growth and innovation decisions, with the result that no equilibrium state is ever automatically assured. The extreme version of the former 'stage' is, of course, perfect competition, but this condition took only a background role in Schumpeter's analyses. However, his overwhelmingly dominant analytical position was that for the period of the history of capitalism upon which he intended to focus, the forces of free-market competition, price flexibility and resource mobility could be assumed, albeit imperfectly, to rule what happened to the system in motion. The position is clouded a little by the adoption of this perception in *Das Wesen* and *Development* as an a priori premise rather than one derived from any apparent historical observations. That is, to begin with, he simply accepted the market-competitive framework that he had served up to him in his student lectures and that he found in his wide reading of the orthodox economic theory of his era. Only later, especially in *Cycles*, was the perception of this 'stage' half-heartedly linked to the historical evidence.

Schumpeter explicitly endeavoured to minimize the economic and social significance of monopoly power as a distorting force in the capitalist system. One facet of that endeavour was to claim that the phenomenon had little empirical status. This was generally the position taken as far as his formal analyses of development and business cycles was concerned. Where he gave any attention to imperfect competition (in its usually understood sense), it occupied a separate 'compartment' in the analysis that was added on to rather than integrated with the mainline of the argument. That is to say, his model of development and its business-cycle form was one in which adjustments to disequilibrium were taken to be dominated by the market-price theoretic forces of supply and demand. Outside of the context of these theoretical analyses, though, he gave somewhat more credence to the relevance of the forces of monopoly power. This became most evident in *Capitalism*, Part II. But, the thesis that such forces are insignificant as negative influences on the system there took on a different guise. In this later work, monopoly power was posited as a means of facilitating a degree of economic stability and material progress that expressly could *not* be realized under conditions of market-price based free competition. The only proviso was that the forces involved must be given free rein, that they be 'unfettered', as Schumpeter put it. Of course, this belated recognition of monopoly power as a force inherent in the capitalism of his time, however we may assess his view of it, left the established theory of development and business cycles unaffected and he made no endeavour to revise his earlier analyses as he might have been expected to.

The motion of any economic *system* through historical time is a multidimensional affair. Schumpeter chose to give emphasis to two of those dimensions, namely what he defined as economic development, essentially the process of motion induced by changes in the conditions under which production takes place, and the instability of that development process that manifests itself in business cycles. This motion was portrayed as centring around the circular flow of economic life in a steady state characterized by the absence of all quantitative and qualitative change. Two dimensions remained relatively neglected in this format. One was the idea of reproduction. He claimed here and there that his steady circular-flow model was representative of the capitalist system in a state of simple reproduction. There is no doubt that in spirit this was true and that he recognized the fundamental need for a system to be shown to have the capacity to reproduce itself as a preliminary step to analysing it in motion. However, the construction of the model mitigated against any explication of the fact that capitalism is a system comprising *interdependent* production sectors between which appropriate flows of commodities must take place if reproductive viability is to be established. This image of the production-exchange structure was not present in Schumpeter's Walrasian-'Austrian' world of fully vertically-integrated production processes and independent final-

ALLEGHENY COLLEGE LIBRARY

commodity markets. The other neglected dimension of motion was 'pure' quantitative economic growth that stems from finance capital accumulation and population growth. Schumpeter explicitly isolated his perception of motion from this process claiming that the simple adjustments that it demanded from the system did not warrant separate theoretical treatment. He recognized that such growth is an integral part of the observed totality of motion and maintained from time to time that he would reintegrate it into his theoretical analysis when the appropriate time came. This did not happen to any but the most desultory extent.

Schumpeter's analytical strategy eventually comprised three main component 'techniques': history, statistics and theory. As I noted in the previous section, this had not always been the case. He began in *Das Wesen* and *Development*, and in the papers published in this same era, with the intention of pursuing 'pure theory' in isolation from any concerns with empirical manifestations of the issues upon which he focused. This emphasis on theory really lasted the whole of his intellectual life, but by the 1930s, in particular in *Cycles*, it had to take its place alongside statistical and historical analyses in a claimed mutually complementary strategy. My reading of Schumpeter's analyses reveals that the necessary unity of this strategy should not be exaggerated. I will adopt the position that his theoretical endeavours must stand up on their own in terms of their consistency with the essential nature of the capitalist system and their logical coherence and completeness. This is not to say that his empirical studies, especially the 800 plus pages of *Cycles* devoted to such studies, do not warrant separate critical investigation. My point is rather that his theoretical analyses cannot be read as standing or falling on the basis of the extent of support or otherwise that they receive from his empirical work. Indeed, there are even grave doubts about all but the loosest of connections between the theoretical and empirical parts of *Cycles*. For this reason, in particular, my study is more or less exclusively about Schumpeter's theoretical contributions.

In any critical assessment of these contributions, though, there are certain aspects of Schumpeter's intentions and objectives that should be observed, for these must temper the scope and foci of the critique. These tenets of his approach were posited only in a series of scattered remarks, but I have tried to assemble them here in some coherent arrangement. In doing so, this part of my argument will stand a little closer to his actual writings than in the more generalized points so far alluded to. I will argue here, most particularly, that Schumpeter never achieved a *complete and definitive* theory of the business-cycle dimension of capitalist motion because he never sought to do so. He was quite candid about this. In the 1927 paper in which he first presented his ideas on motion to English-speaking readers, he urged them 'not to be deterred by what must necessarily look like a highly abstract if not one-sided view of the thing [the business cycle]'. He admitted here, to reiterate a piece quoted in the previous section, that what he had presented comprised '*no* theory of the cycle, if we understand by this a complete explanation of all that happens' (*Essays*, p. 33, original emphasis). On a more general level, Gottfried Haberler quotes Schumpeter as having said in his valedictory speech when leaving Bonn for Harvard in 1932 that 'I never wish to say anything definitive; if I have a function it is to open doors not to close them.' (1951a, p. 46). Schumpeter was soon to make a similar claim in the Preface to *Cycles*. There, as I noted in the first section above, he referred to *Development* as providing a 'scaffolding' for his theory that requires completion. Aspects of *Cycles*, then, represented his endeavour 'to turn that scaffolding into a house', although he immediately added to this the qualification that he doubted 'whether the result warrants that simile' because the 'house is certainly not a finished and furnished one – *there are too many glaring lacunae and too many unfulfilled desiderata*'. On this basis, he concluded that the 'younger generation of economists should look upon this book merely as something to shoot at and to start from – as a motivated program for further research. Nothing, at any rate, could please me more.' (*Cycles*, p. v, emphasis added.) At around the same time, he wrote to the readers of the Japanese translation of *Development* that he hoped that his work would 'stimulate further advance [in Japanese economic theory], at least by provoking criticism' (*Essays*, p. 158). In all of these comments, there is no reason to doubt the sincerity of Schumpeter's intellectual modesty and reservation as the 'lucunae' and 'unfulfilled desiderata' to which he referred are all too evident in his analyses.

What Schumpeter sought in his theoretical construction was the most essential cause of the phenomenon of motion. Once he was convinced that he had discovered it and set it into a primary analytical framework that was logically complete as far as it went, his theoretical progression from there took on a somewhat 'optional' status. That is to say, any extensions to the primary argument could emphasize a variety of additional factors that may bring his theory into closer proximity to the empirical characteristics of particular historical periods of motion. During the years after *Development* was published, research into business cycles gathered momentum and a large body of literature began to accumulate (see, e.g., Hansen, 1927; Haberler, 1964). In much of this research, more extensive causal bases for cycles were established, but there is no evidence that Schumpeter in any way saw the burgeoning theories as any intellectual 'threat' to his own work. He did not make any suggestion that his theory should or could replace any of the others. Rather, he wanted to provide a more essential foundation which would complement the existing theories by bringing a more definite order of priorities to the various causal factors that had been elicited. For instance, he once made the following comment about von Hayek's theory of fluctuations and it is reasonable to take the point as indicative of his general attitude towards much of the work of other cycle analysts: 'the reader knows . . . that the author is not a wholesale admirer of Professor Von Hayek's theory *as far as it claims to be a fundamental explanation* of the causes of the cycle'. But, at the same time, he had no hesitation in recognizing the strength of the theory in accounting for particular inflationary periods in the American business cycle experience (*Cycles*, p. 296n, original emphasis). There was a sense, then, in which Schumpeter's theory 'needed' the work of others to bring it to completion. However, he took few steps himself to establish any such contacts and his main writings are almost devoid of references to other research. And, except for a few passages added to Chapter VI of *Development* in its second edition (pp. 212ff.), he engaged in no controversy over the criticisms of his work that appeared from time to time. This was, it seems, largely because, as he put it in 1934, 'I have never come across any objection [to my theory] on essential points which carried conviction to my mind.' (*Development*, p. x).

It is possible to suggest that Schumpeter's intellectual aloofness stems from arrogance and a presumption of superiority that led him to treat other theories with disdain. There is little evidence of such an attitude. For example, in the two review articles from the 1920s about Pigou's *Industrial Fluctuations* and Mitchell's *Business Cycles; The Problem and Its Setting* (*Essays*, pp. 21ff.; 73ff.), he treated the writers' works with a careful sympathy and sought to give credit where it was due. Only in the former did he take the opportunity to set out his own theory as a preliminary to the discussion. What is more telling, though, is his reputation for a reluctance to make public references to his own work. This applied even to his lectures in Harvard where, Paul Samuelson reports, 'he rarely mentioned his own theories' (1951, p. 52), a recollection shared by Schumpeter's wife: 'J. A. S. hardly ever referred to his own work either in his teaching or in his writing' (*History*, p. xi). Gottfried Haberler's view was that Schumpeter's courses 'all suffered from one defect: by listening to . . . [his] lectures and studying his reading assignments and suggestions, students could have never found out that he himself had ever written anything on those subjects' (1951a, p. 39). Then, from Paul Sweezy we learn that while he was working with

Schumpeter in the mid-1930s, he tried to persuade the Professor to change this practice. The result was that he 'listened sympathetically but never did anything about it' (1951, p. 119n). Further to these sorts of reports, it is also worth noting that when Schumpeter did come to undertake some explicit enquiry into other theories of business cycles in *History* (especially pp. 738ff., 1117ff., 1160ff.), he made no effort to bring his own work into the picture. It is not apparent from his exposition that he had written extensively on the subject, although a familiarity with his work gives the reader an insight into some of the emphases of selection and critique used.

For the purposes of my study, the upshot of all this is that there is little to be gained by any elaborate juxtaposing of Schumpeter's theory with those of his antecedents and contemporaries. Neither the impetus for, nor the substance of, his theses can be traced to any critique of other work. He worked in isolation and devised and reiterated his arguments quite independently of what others were doing, a fact that can be partially explained by the delimited objectives that he set for his own theory. In some ways, he was working at a more fundamental 'level' – toiling, as it were, with the foundations while others worked on more elevated and obvious parts of the construction.

Unfortunately, it will become apparent in due course that this isolationist strategy had its dangers as well as some taint of intellectual arrogance. It led to Schumpeter's decision to ignore certain *alternative essential foundations* for a theory of motion that appeared around him, foundations that can readily be shown to be in more immediate contact with the real-world nature of capitalism. In particular, he chose to ignore the reproduction schema that Karl Marx had developed from the Physiocratic *Tableau économique*; to ignore the applications of the schema to the analysis of motion worked out by the Austro-Marxists with whom he was well acquainted, especially Rudolf Hilferding and Otto Bauer; and to ignore the work of the Kiel School, led by Adolph Löwe (see especially his 1926), that went even further in developing the schema, especially through Fritz Burchardt's path-breaking work on a unification of Böhm-Bawerk's 'stages' model of production with the schema. To have remained convinced, in the face of these developments and contributions, that Walras's general equilibrium model most adequately represented the essence of the production and exchange structures and operations of capitalism revealed a truly unfortunate blind-spot in Schumpeter's intellectual make-up. All this was, however, even further compounded with the appearance of the work of Michal Kalecki and John Maynard Keynes. The contributions that these writers made to our *essential* understanding of capitalism as an economic system, with their roots so obviously reaching back to Marx, soon had an influence on many analysts of motion. But here too, Schumpeter stood aloof and would not allow the ideas to penetrate his work. Indeed, he now actually expressed his objections, perhaps hostility, to the new contributions, but these remained on a quite superficial level and even revealed some lack of comprehension of the thrust of the arguments being presented. In assessing this implicit and explicit resistance to these sorts of alternative bases for understanding motion, it is difficult to avoid the suggestion that some ideological strictures barred Schumpeter's way, whatever may have been his claims, from time to time, to possess the 'Olympian' detachment of the 'pure scientist'. But, whatever the explanation for the intellectual directions that he took, the above choices cost him dearly. In particular, in terms of his failure to set his important insights into the theory of motion in an analytical framework that adequately and immediately encompassed the readily-observable structural and operational essentials of the capitalist system.

There is a further aspect of Schumpeter's approach to his theory that, perhaps, should temper any critical assessment that is to be made of it. As I indicated in the previous section, he chose to compound the restricted ambition for the scope of his theory by imposing the additional requirement in *Cycles* that his ideas should be accessible to lay readers. This intention immediately cut off any possibility that the new exposition of the *Development* theses would be used to raise the level of analytical rigour of the argument. On the contrary, it demanded a reduction in that level for ideas that had been covered in the original version and doomed the important extensions to the theory in *Cycles* to a standard of analytical expression that Schumpeter himself acknowledged to be below that which was professionally acceptable. His decision 'to make sure that the general reader who is willing to take the trouble will be able to travel the . . . [analytical road] mapped out in this book' (*Cycles*, p. vi) meant that he found himself on several occasions in the work apologizing to professional readers for the oversimplified presentation of key theoretical arguments. He proffered the tautological justification that his approach was all that was needed to meet 'the rough purposes of our volume' and what he referred to as 'the level of approximation I had to be content with' (ibid., pp. 42n, vii). But he still remained concerned at giving 'offense' to his peers by using some theoretical tools that were 'antiquated' and by the fact that 'in many points recent progress of analysis has not been sufficiently taken into account' (ibid., p. 36n). Then, to cap off these confessional inclinations, he penned the following, somewhat remarkable statement: 'To the theorist apology is again due for brevity of statement amounting to dogmatism, for failure to supply proofs, and for simplification verging on incorrectness' (ibid., p. 45n). And, perhaps to forestall criticism on these counts, he assured his readers that an analysis of motion more in keeping with professional standards would be presented 'in another book which, in a wider frame, will among other things overhaul the purely theoretic parts of the present argument' (ibid., p. 36n). There is no extant evidence that such a book was ever written or even planned.

All Schumpeter's frankness about the self-imposed limitations of his theory of motion should not be allowed to obscure two points that are central to the *raison d'être* of my critical exposition. First, acceptance of the limitations cannot overcome the fact that *in itself and as far as it goes*, the theory remains a valid target for some of the critical 'shooting' that Schumpeter himself invited. I perhaps do somewhat more 'shooting' below than has been attempted before. What is at issue is the extent to which the theory represents a legitimate and appropriate 'something . . . to start from' in understanding the motion of capitalism. Secondly, whatever admissions Schumpeter made about his theory, he remained absolutely and resolutely convinced of and dedicated to his thesis that economic development and its business-cycle form could not be adequately explained without beginning from the onset of a wave of innovations in and around production and without the complementary thesis that this wave should be funded by bank credit created for the purpose. Whatever turn out to be the strengths of this position, it is appropriate to retain a degree of scepticism lest its possible weaknesses pass us by.

Finally, in these preliminary remarks on the boundaries of Schumpeter's theoretical endeavours, I should draw attention to his conviction that his work was of a purely 'scientific' nature. This conviction manifested itself in his conscious avoidance of any extensive involvement in policy-related analyses that might flow from his mainline theoretical work on motion.[4] In *Das Wesen*, he stressed in his Foreword that 'I keep aloof from practical politics and know no other striving than that for knowledge' (p. vii). More pointedly, in his 1915 monograph on the past and future of the social sciences, he argued that researchers have been far too inclined towards 'preoccupying themselves with questions of the day. For the exclusive or predominant concentration on such practical questions of the day threatens to stifle or overwhelm interest in work oriented towards a purely scientific viewpoint and thereby jeopardises scientific progress' (1915, p. 115). Attitudes such as these continued to dominate throughout his work and only rarely did he allow some mention of policy to enter his discussions (e.g. *Development*, pp. 254-5, where he advocated that policies be designed to mitigate the effects of deep depressions). More generally, his strategy was to 'recommend no policy and propose no plan' for he felt that the foremost 'social duty' of the 'scientific worker' is to provide an understanding of empirical phenomena that are of concern to people and their representatives in government. In this sense, economic theory can be applied 'exactly as one and the same body of engineering or medical knowledge can be used for the most varied of purposes' (*Cycles*, p. vi); that is, in providing a range of solutions to any practical problems that arise in the economy from time to time. Thus, Schumpeter recognized that the purpose of theory is ultimately practical, but that it need not immediately be so. Theory facilitates 'understanding of the process [of motion] which people are *passionately resolved to control*' (ibid., emphasis added), although it does so without any commitment to a particular form of policy response. In his own case, he emphasized, in particular, that his theory 'lends no support to any general principle of *laisser-faire*' and that it 'can in fact be used to derive practical conclusions of the most conservative as well as the most radical complexion . . .' (ibid.). To some extent, he must have had difficulty conveying his 'purely scientific' intentions to his readers and evidence of such misinterpretation surfaced again in the Preface to the second edition of *Capitalism* (dated 1946). There he complained that even though he had stressed 'that this is not a political book' and that he 'did not wish to advocate anything', accusations to the contrary still ensued (pp. x-xi). Most importantly, he took this to reflect a significant methodological misperception that in order to write anything mean-ingful an analyst must espouse something practical. He asked: 'Is it not entirely futile to elaborate inferences from observed facts without arriving at practical recommendations?' and replied simply that there is an inclination 'always [to] plan too much and always [to] think too little' (ibid., p. xi). Schumpeter felt that his theoretical work on motion had always emphasized 'thinking' about the puzzles of the phenomenon as a necessary preliminary to any practical response to them.

1.3   Organizational matters

My task of exposition, critique and reassessment is approached in the following sequence. In the next chapter, I apply Schumpeter's idea of 'vision' as a 'preanalytic cognitive act' in order to establish his percep-tion of the essential characteristics that comprise capitalism as an economic system and his conception of its core category, capital. These formulations provide the foundations upon which he built up his theoretical image of the capitalist system in motion. Juxtaposed to the essentials of Schumpeter's object of analysis is the analytical strategy that he devised in order to work on it. This strategy is investigated in

Chapter 3 where, as already indicated in the previous section, he will be found to have proposed the use of three 'techniques': history, statistics and theory. My focus will be almost exclusively upon the theoretical dimensions of his strategy as it is these dimensions that I consider dominate in his work and ultimately determine the contributions that he made to our understanding of motion in capitalism.

Chapter 4 brings me to the substantive nature of Schumpeter's theoretical object in which the capitalist economy is initially portrayed as the circular flow of economic life proceeding from period to period in the absence of change. I will argue that the particular perception of the steady circular flow that he adopted had its *origins* in the 'static' general equilibrium model devised by Léon Walras. However, it will also become clear that Schumpeter reworked the original model in order to emphasize those aspects that he considered to be most pertinent to his particular purpose, for example, by giving additional emphasis to production. Once some change is introduced into the steady circular-flow state, then the reactions of economic agents are compounded into a complex of processes that constitute the motion of the system through time.

It is the purpose of Chapter 5 to examine in detail the component dimensions that comprise the totality of the observed motion of capitalism and to set out the way in which Schumpeter chose to deal with them. His emphasis was on the generation of what he defined as economic development by means of waves of innovations in and around production. These waves impinge upon otherwise stability-seeking circular-flow processes and the temporal form of the resulting development is the business cycle. I will take the position in this chapter that two necessary conditions must be met if any explanation of motion is to be successful. One is that it must be formulated within a structural and operational representation of capitalism that is consistent with several of that system's most essential observed characteristics. The other is that the mode of explication must centre on the concept of the *traverse*; that is, the temporal sequences of adjustments within the economic structure that are brought about by agents' reactions to the introduced change, and that constitute the motion itself, must be made explicit.

Various aspects of the theory of economic development as the foundation of the explanation of motion more generally are considered in Chapter 6. After outlining the main points of the theory, I focus on the role of economic agents in the process, especially on their actions as innovating entrepreneurs, the access to resources and finance capital that they require in order to facilitate those actions and the entrepreneurial profit which provides the main component of their reward for carrying out successful innovations. A separate chapter, Chapter 7, is then devoted to an analysis of the involvement of the monetary dimensions of the economy in the development process. This analysis includes consideration of Schumpeter's theory of interest and his credit theory of money.

My critical exposition of Schumpeter's business-cycle theory occupies the next two chapters. In Chapter 8, the primary model of the cycle in its two-phase format is explained and is shown to follow more or less directly from the logic of economic development. Then, in Chapter 9, attention shifts to the various secondary factors that bring more complicated dimensions to the primary cycle and give it its empirical form as an historically unique phenomenon. Here the cycle units are argued to have four phases, but I suggest that a three-phase schema is more accurate. The chapter concludes with some critical reflections on the three-cycle schema that Schumpeter devised to represent what he saw as the empirical existence of simultaneous multiple cycles.

The final chapter of the study brings together the main threads of my critical exposition and provides a summary reassessment of Schumpeter's endeavours to explain the unstable motion of capitalism through historical time. I give emphasis to certain selected facets of critique that a rise in relation to the primary business cycle and its logical extensions to encompass the secondary wave effects. The chapter concludes with a summary listing of those particular contributions that are to be found in Schumpeter's analysis and that have some potential for the future development of the theory of motion.

Notes

1. All translations from German language sources are my own throughout the study unless otherwise stated.
2. Readers may be aware that there is listed amongst Schumpeter's works a book entitled *Rudimentary Mathematics for Economists and Statisticians* (1946) with the parenthetical addition 'with W. L. Crum' (*Essays*, p. 317). It may seem that in writing such a book Schumpeter was claiming some competence in mathematical technique. An inspection of the book does give some support to such an idea. In the first place, though, I should point out that the copy of the work that I obtained, a first edition, second impression dated 1946 gives the sole author as one W. L. Crum, Professor of Economics, Harvard University. The Preface, over the name of W. L. Crum, tells us that the work was originally prepared by Crum as a long article for the *Quarterly Journal of Economics* and published as a Supplement in March 1938. It was not, therefore, really Schumpeter's book at all and Mrs Schumpeter's way of listing it in the Bibliography was, to some extent, misleading. His role in the work, together with some interesting insight into Schumpeter and mathematics, was summarized by Crum in the following passage.

> The present volume could not have been completed so soon, nor could it have reflected such marked improvement in content and presentation, had the task of revision not been largely assumed by my colleague, Professor Schumpeter. *His far*

greater experience with the use and teaching of mathematics in economics brings this new revision to a higher level than I alone could have achieved. Although we consulted together about all aspects of the revision, the actual preparation of the new materials, both the minor alterations and the substantial additions to topical content, was mainly the work of his hand. *So great has been his contribution that I have induced him to permit his name to be included equally with mine in the authorship of the present book.* (1946, p. v, emphasis added)

The intended joint authorship was clearly not conveyed to the publisher. Further discussion on Schumpeter's attitudes towards and use of mathematical methods can be found in his own paper, 'The Common Sense of Econometrics', written as the opening *article* in the first number of *Econometrica* in 1933 (*Essays*, pp. 100ff.); and in Frisch, 1951, pp. 8ff.; Machlup, 1951, pp. 98-9.; and Tinbergen, 1951, pp. 59ff.

3. The English translation cites the original publication date as 1912, but this is not consistent with the 1914 listing in the Bibliography (*Essays*, p. 316).
4. There is no suggestion here that Schumpeter was never concerned with economic policy matters. The point is simply that his theoretical analysis was conducted in isolation from any policy implications that it may have. His writings on policy matters were, in fact, quite extensive as a perusal of his Bibliography will reveal. A collection of these papers, all in German, including a number that were written during his time as Finance Minister of Austria during 1919, has recently been put together by Wolfgang Stolper and Christian Seidl and published as *Aufsätze zur Wirtschaftspolitik* (1985). See also Seidl, 1984c.

2 Visions of capitalism

2.1 Defining capitalism

For Schumpeter, the process of defining his analytical object, the capitalist economic system, comprised the formation of what he called a *vision* (*History*, pp. 41ff.).[1] That is, it was effectively a 'pre-analytic cognitive act that provides the raw material for the analytic effort'. The rationale for this act was that 'before embarking upon analytic work of any kind we must first single out the set of phenomena we wish to investigate, and acquire "intuitively" a preliminary notion of how they hang together or, in other words, of what appear from our standpoint to be their fundamental properties' (ibid., pp. 41, 561-2). Schumpeter himself faced this requirement no less than his antecedents about whom he was writing at the time.

He approached the issue of identifying the fundamental characteristics of a capitalist economic system as one involving more than analytical convenience, more than 'our logical right to terminological freedom . . .' (*Cycles*, p. 223). A nominalist perception of the problem of definition would allow for any meaning to be given to a category that suited the purpose at hand – nominalists 'regard *words* merely as *useful instruments of description*' (Popper, 1960, p. 29, original emphasis). By contrast, an essentialist approach to definitions stresses that 'scientific research must penetrate to the essence of things in order to explain them' and that this demands the discovery of 'the real or essential meaning of . . . terms' (ibid., pp. 28, 29). This was Schumpeter's conviction and he treated a definition as 'a statement of fact, namely, that the defining characteristic gives the essence of a definite historical phenomenon' and he added that his definition of capitalism 'belongs to this class' (*Cycles*, p. 223). However, at the same time, he allowed for some nominalist intrusion when he qualified his view so that definitions 'may legitimately differ according to point of view and purpose, and such differences need not, although they often do, imply difference of opinion as to the nature of the phenomenon' (ibid.).

In *Development*, Schumpeter initially defined his analytical object only indirectly as capitalist when he circumspectly referred to it as 'a commercially organised state'. Such a state is characterized by an 'economic mechanism' in which three essential features dominate, namely 'private property, division of labour, and free competition' (*Development*, p. 5). These were, though, only intended to be necessary characteristics for they related to the steady circular flow state that could not, by definition, be capitalist. Schumpeter was always quite clear on this point in that he considered any steady state notion of capitalism to involve a contradiction of terms (see, e.g., *Essays*, p. 193). Thus: 'Capitalism is essentially a process of (endogenous) economic change. Without that change or, more precisely, that kind of change which we have called evolution [development], capitalist society cannot exist, because the economic functions and, with the functions, the economic bases of its leading strata – of the strata which work the capitalist engine – would crumble if it ceased . . . .' More particularly, as I will describe in detail in the chapter on development (Chapter 6 below), 'without innovations, no entrepreneurs; without entrepreneurial achievement, no capitalist returns and no capitalist propulsion' (*Cycles*, p. 1033). In *Development*, the '*differentia specifica*' of capitalism was summarized simply as the existence of credit financing of innovations (p. 69), but this characteristic was carried forward as crucial to any definition of the system in subsequent writings (see, e.g., *Essays*, p. 170 and *Capitalism*, p. 167), albeit with a particular qualification to be noted in a moment.

Some subtle additions and amendments to the terms of the definition followed in Schumpeter's subsequent works, but the essentials were left unchanged. In his 1928 *Economic Journal* paper, 'The Instability of Capitalism', private property was joined by private initiative and the division of labour became the basis for producing for a market (*Essays*, p. 48). Thus, capitalism now appeared as more explicitly a system in which production and market exchange of commodities function as a result of private decision-making. These characteristics were accompanied by 'the phenomenon of credit [as] . . . the *differentia specifica* distinguishing the "capitalist" system from other species, historical or possible, of the larger genus defined by the two first characteristics' (ibid.).

A few years later, these features were made even more specific in *Cycles*. The private property was now to be in the form of means of production and 'salaried workers' appeared as a necessary condition. But it remained the case that a 'society, the economic life of which is characterized by private property and controlled by private initiative, is . . . not necessarily capitalist, even if there are, for instance, privately owned factories, salaried workers, and the free exchange of goods and services . . .' (*Cycles*, p. 223). And, what is more, even economic leadership in the form of the entrepreneurial function as the dominant form of 'private initiative' would not be sufficient to make the system capitalist. Once again, it was to the financing process that Schumpeter turned to close his definition as 'that form of private property economy in which innovations are carried out by means of borrowed money, which in general, though not by logical necessity, implies credit creation' (ibid.).

It is worth noting that by this time, Schumpeter had broadened somewhat the scope of the credit concept that characterizes true capitalism. In *Development*, the emphasis was very much on credit created by banks to fund innovations (e.g. pp. 72-3) and in that context it was, indeed, a 'logical necessity' that this source be available. It was the absence of profit and the consequent absence of savings available *ex ante* in the steady circular flow that made it essential that credit creation be added in order to facilitate innovations, for no existing funds could be borrowed for the purpose (see Chapter 6 below). Only when economic development is underway does 'borrowed money' from savings appear, but in Schumpeter's approach, this could not be assumed to be present initially because it depended upon what was to be explained. This did not make credit creation merely a *deus ex machina*, for it retains both theoretical and empirical significance even when motion is proceeding. Further to this point, when he was called upon to contribute the item 'Capitalism' to the 1946 edition of the *Encyclopaedia Britannica* (*Essays*, pp. 184ff.), Schumpeter reiterated the necessary characteristics as 'private ownership of nonpersonal means of production, such as land, mines, industrial plant and equipment; and . . . production for private account, i.e., production by private initiative for private profit.' And, he went on to add that 'the institution of bank credit is so essential to the functioning of the capitalist system that, *though not strictly implied in the definition*, it should be added to the other two criteria' (p. 184, emphasis added). It is not clear here whether 'bank credit' is meant to imply created credit or all credit; and it is also not clear whether the intention was now to confine the definitional significance of credit to an empirical level rather than arguing it to be essential to the logical framework of the system. That this might have been the intention is indicated by the fact that Schumpeter rarely referred to sources of credit other than banks in his theoretical analyses. However, confusion on this point must be left to reign because in the revised second edition of *Capitalism*, published in 1947, he wrote that capitalist society is a 'special case' of 'commercial society', '*defined* by the additional phenomenon of credit *creation* – by the practice, responsible for so many outstanding features of modern economic life, of financing enterprise by bank credit, i.e., by money (notes or deposits) manufactured for that purpose' (p. 167, emphasis added). Credit was finally left in a sort of 'half-way house' situation when Schumpeter wrote in the *History* manuscript that credit operations 'affect the working of the capitalist engine – so much so as to become an essential part of it without which the rest cannot be understood at all' (*History*, p. 318; cf. *Essays*, p. 194).

As was mentioned above, at one point Schumpeter included in his necessary conditions for the existence of capitalism the phenomenon of 'salaried workers'. When combined with the requirements that production is initiated and managed by private agents using privately-owned means of production, it can be assumed that he envisaged these 'workers' as employed by capitalists. This aspect of capitalism warranted more consistent attention than Schumpeter gave it in his definitions. For, once we reach the 'rock-bottom' conditions for the existence of that system, one thing that cannot be absent from any meaningful definition is a group of people whose income depends upon their being 'voluntarily' employed for a pre-agreed wage (or salary) by a private person or by a legal entity owned by a private person. Any economic system that does not have this characteristic, as Marx long ago made clear, is not a capitalist system in any sense useful for analysis, no matter what other characteristics it may have. Self-'employed' people, state-employed people and, perhaps, even people employed through some form of bondage, may exist in a capitalist economy, but the crucial point is that their absence does not negate its capitalist status. Moreover, while the condition of private property in the means of production must accompany the wage labour for the employment relation to make sense, its presence cannot ensure that the system is capitalist. Both feudal economies and self-employment artisan economies have privately-owned means of production, but they are not capitalist.

2.2 Defining capital

What is glaringly absent from all of the above discussion of capitalism is the concept of capital itself. It seems self-evident that a system alluded to by such a name would be ill-defined without a focus on what part capital plays in it. Schumpeter's approach to the matter was to stand it on its head and look for that definition of capital that flowed from the characteristics of capitalism that he chose to emphasize. What, then, was the concept of capital suggested by his definitions?

Before answering this question, it is appropriate to set out the range of dimensions that may be covered by the category capital. A comprehensive definition would need to include all of the following, preferably as the *basis* for defining capitalism rather than the other way around. First, capital is a financial fund advanced in money (including created credit) form to purchase means of production. Secondly, it is a real stock of means of production, comprising the physical-technical structure of production, valued in some way and expressed as a money sum. Capital is also, thirdly, a basis for facilitating the 'vertical' time-duration of production. Finally, it is a mode of organizing production and income distribution by means of private command over resources and means of production and over what is produced with them. We will find that Schumpeter gave some weight to each of these dimensions, but these weights were not even or consistent over time in his work. In particular, the second dimension was frequently neglected and, at some points, its relevance to the capital concepts was denied altogether (e.g. *Development*, p. 118). There is, of course, a sense in which physical means of production need not be capital. But, it makes no sense to discuss the nature and role of capital without giving due regard to the fact that its productive form must necessarily comprise embodiment in some means of production.

Among Schumpeter's most categorical pronouncements on the nature of capital was the following piece that appeared in *Development*: *'Capital is nothing but the lever by which the entrepreneur subjects to his control the concrete goods which he needs, nothing but a means of diverting the factors of production to new uses, or of dictating a new direction to production'* (p. 116, original emphasis). That he intended this to constitute a definition at the time is indicated by the stark riders attached to the effect that it gives 'the only function of capital, and by it the place of capital in the economic organism is completely characterised' (ibid.). Narrowly considered, this definition ties capital strictly to the innovating entrepreneur and there are places where Schumpeter inferred this. For example, keeping in mind that in the present context he thought of entrepreneurs only as innovating agents, the following passage cannot be read otherwise: *'We shall define capital . . . as that sum of means of payment which is available at any moment for transference to entrepreneurs.'* (ibid., p. 122, original emphasis). I think, though, that it is reasonable to read this as just an overstatement of the point that he was developing at the time, namely that 'capital is a concept of development to which nothing in the circular flow corresponds' (ibid.). He was certainly well aware that finance capital must be continuously advanced by all capitalist agents involved in production and not merely by those concerned to change some aspect of it. In *Doctrine* he attributed the first 'precise theory of capital' to the Physiocrats because they gave due attention to the very point that it comprised advances to purchase means of production and pay for labour power (pp. 53-4). Almost contemporaneously with writing *Development*, then, he gave favour to the view that the 'substance of capital . . . is represented as that part of the social product of preceding economic

periods which maintains the production of the current period . . .'
(p. 54), including any change in the level of the latter.

Schumpeter's refusal to recognize capital as having any physical form
was first argued out in *Development* where he stated quite categorically
that 'concrete goods are never capital' (p. 203). His definition of capital
focused on its financial form and this led him to argue that once the
outlay of funds on means of production is completed, then the capital
ceased to exist as such. The funds are then simply no longer 'available'
in the sense required by his definition, for when 'the necessary
productive means, and . . . the necessary labor services, are bought,
then the entrepreneur no longer has the capital which was placed at his
disposal. He has surrendered it for productive means.' (p. 118). Schumpeter granted that the commonly accepted perception of this act is that
the original finance capital is transmuted into a physical form that can be
used in production. To this idea his response was entirely negative and
he simply maintained his position that 'capital *confronts* the world of
goods' and once the entrepreneur makes his outlays, 'he has acquired
goods which he will not employ as capital, that is as a fund in paying for
other goods, but in technical production' (p. 117, original emphasis).
Capital is but a 'third agent' (along with 'labour' and 'land') that
mediates between the entrepreneur and the goods that he or she needs
in an exchange economy. It takes no direct part in production; 'on the
contrary it performs a task which must be done before technical
production can begin', before the goods can begin 'serving a productive
purpose corresponding to their technical nature' (ibid.).

A rather important insight emerges from this discussion. It is clear
that Schumpeter recognized the separability of the physical-technical
production structure from the institutional and organizational means by
which it is established and run. One option for the latter comprises
advancing finance *capital* and then adopting all the systemic requirements that are entailed thereby. But, the fact remains that *all* modern
economic systems need a production structure and all must set it up by
advancing finance from some source. What Schumpeter wanted to avoid
is the confusion that can arise when the term capital is used loosely
where capitalism is not present. He expressed this when he wrote that
'capital defined so as to consist of goods belongs to every economic
organisation and hence it is not suitable for characterising the capitalis-
tic one . . .' (ibid.). Had he added the equivalent expression for finance,
his insight would have been complete. But, be all this as it may, the
insight was of rather more methodological significance than Schumpeter
realized. The point to which he never gave due attention is that in order
to understand motion in any economic system, the problems of

changing the form of the physical-technical structure of production must receive due prominence. There is a danger that excessive emphasis on the financial form of capital will lead to an impression that 'capital' can be readily manipulated to suit the needs of change and the structural requirements are likely to be ignored as a consequence. This problem is compounded where finance capital is assumed to be invested only in working capital to purchase labour power and natural resource inputs and maintain intermediate goods. So, while Schumpeter's reluctance to link capital to material means of production is soundly based in one respect, it will become apparent later in my critical exposition that this may have contributed to his gross understatement of the complexity of the traverses that comprise the motion he was trying to explain.

Beyond *Development*, Schumpeter wrote little more about his conception of capital. In *Cycles*, the discussion of the topic was confined to one paragraph (p. 129). His inclination there was to continue to espouse 'a monetary theory of capital' because, in the context, it would be consistent with what he thought of as his 'monetary' theory of interest. He reiterated his recognition of the need to keep the financial and structural means of production dimensions of capital separate, but he began to reveal a frustration with the confusing use of the term capital. In order to avoid such confusion, he thought it best to eschew the term altogether and rely on explicit description of what it would have been intended to convey in each case. He was well aware of the contrasting treatments of 'capital' by the Marxists, Böhm-Bawerk and the other 'Austrians' and by other neo-classicals. Ultimately, his reflections on the matter led to the following outburst of frustration in *History*: 'What a mass of confused, futile, and downright silly controversies it would have saved us, if economists had had the sense to stick to those monetary and accounting meanings of the term instead of trying to "deepen" them!' (p. 323). And, he later went on to refer to the 'morass of verbal controversy' that had arisen because people 'kept on asking the meaningless question: What is Capital?' (p. 632). Leaving aside the point that the essentialist Schumpeter, who wanted to define the *essence* of capitalism, would once have found this question highly meaningful, I can only add that while many economists over the years would have sympathized with his frustrations, it is doubtful if many would have been satisfied with his 'monetary' solution. As for his espousal of the 'accounting' valuation version, that must be another story. . . .

2.3   Competitive capitalism and beyond
Schumpeter was aware that whatever definition he devised for the capitalist economic system, he would have to make allowance for the

fact that the system is in a constant state of flux. Some of the changes affect the institutional structure and operations by means of which economic agents carry out their activities. When this occurs, the nature of the overall operation of the system changes and affects the way in which motion and other phenomena are to be explained. Perhaps the most evident form of change to which Schumpeter drew attention is the gradual reorganization of production and market exchange that has reduced the degree of competition between firms over the period since capitalism rose to dominance. As capitalism expanded and advanced in a multiplicity of directions and ways, the progress was accompanied by a rise in the degree of monopoly power that firms could exercise over their market situations and an increase in the importance of inter-firm strategic behaviours for understanding how the system works and changes. What competition then remains between firms is of a very different kind with the result that supply and demand determined price-quantity adjustments lose their dominance over economic events.

To the extent that economic analysis has the objective of maintaining contact with changes in its object of knowledge, this reorganization of capitalism should be reflected in the theoretical models that purport to explain its phenomena. If a very general perspective of the evolution of economic analysis is taken, there is an observable increase in concern with the effects of rising monopoly power, but no overall shift to models in which market-competitive forces are replaced by the interactions of agents with varying degrees of market control on the input and output sides of their production activities.

Schumpeter's *theoretical* work is no exception to this general perspective. He remained very firmly attached to the analytical comforts of a model in which disequilibrium comprises merely a price-quantity displacement from equilibrium market clearing and is more or less automatically corrected for by the appropriate responses from agents. Essentially, he worked close to the perfectly competitive end of the continuum of market models that runs through to perfect monopoly at the other end. At times, he argued as if his model was of a perfectly competitive economy, but he was always conscious of the need to qualify the analysis to take account of the various real-world impediments to its processes. His attitude was that the usefulness of the perfect case did not stem from its *per se* reflection of any empirical system, but rather from the provision of a set of conditions that facilitate the modelling of actual competitive economies as measured deviations from these conditions. In Schumpeter's words, it 'cannot be repeated too often that the case of perfect competition owes the fundamental importance which it always had and still has in economic theory to

certain properties characteristic of it and . . . [not] to any tendency in
the facts to conform to it . . .' The importance of the case has always
come, instead, from the claim that 'by virtue of those properties the
theory of perfect competition . . . remains a useful and almost indispensable background with which to compare, and therefore by which to
understand, any other situation, however far removed it may be from it'
(*Essays*, p. 125; cf. *Cycles*, p. 46n). The bulk of Schumpeter's theoretical work on motion is a testament to his belief in that claim. As I will
detail in a moment, only in *Capitalism* was the essentially market
competitive vision of capitalism replaced by one in which monopoly
power forces prevailed. By contrast, the theory of economic development and business cycles remained set in a model where 'pure' market
forces worked sufficiently well for the correction of any disequilibrium
by them to be relied upon, albeit with some qualification. Any
consideration of monopoly power cases in this context was merely
juxtaposed briefly and never integrated into the mainstream of the
theoretical argument. Beyond the temporary market control acquired
by entrepreneurs by virtue of their innovations, Schumpeter's agents
remained constrained by their relative insignificance in the collective
outcome of actions in their markets.

Outside of the immediate confines of his own theoretical analysis,
though, Schumpeter was much more sensitive to the problems posed by
non-competitive cases. 'For it is not true', he wrote, 'that what can be
proved for the case of perfect competition holds approximately for the
case of imperfect competition . . . On the contrary, it has been proved
of late that in important respects imperfect or monopolistic competition
will produce exactly the opposite of those results which might be
expected from free competition in the theoretic sense.' (*Essays*, p. 122).
Far from being an approximation under monopoly power conditions,
the perfectly competitive model 'becomes a distortion of what it is
meant to describe if its assumptions are not fulfilled exactly' (ibid.,
p. 126). Around 1930, before the drafting of *Cycles*, Schumpeter opined
that there existed 'no other chapter [of economic theory] so full of
inclusive controversy and uncertainty of results as the treatment of all of
those cases which cover the whole of the phenomena between the
limiting cases of perfect competition and "pure" monopoly, i.e.,
practically the whole of the reality of markets.' (Preface to Zeuthen,
1930, p. ix, emphasis added). And, he warned that the reputation of
economic analysis as 'unrealistic' or 'useless' had developed largely
because of the dominance of perfectly competitive models and the
economists' 'habit of brushing aside, as it were, that vast mass of facts
and problems' that are linked to the empirical reality of non-competitive

markets (ibid.). When it came to writing *Cycles*, Schumpeter failed to heed his own warning and allowed an opportunity to raise the standards of non-competitive analysis to pass him by. His defence at one isolated point was to claim that his adherence to the perfectly competitive model was justified by the fact that 'within the period covered by our material it affords a sufficiently close approximation to reality in many cases and that in others the actual patterns, although not fulfilling requirements, yet work in a way not fundamentally differing from the working of perfect competition' (*Cycles*, p. 46n). The contradictions so perpetrated can only be wondered at.

Over the years, when the problem of monopoly power in 'trustified' capitalism was confronted by Schumpeter, the analysis remained quarantined from the mainline of theory. This can readily be seen in *Development* and *Cycles*. In each work, he showed an awareness that the inclusion of monopoly forces in his analyses would bring a formal indeterminacy to the results, although more as a 'friction' due to the loss of price-quantity flexibility than anything else. The consequence upon which he focused was, then, that the adjustment processes towards a restoration of equilibrium when a disturbance occurred would be slowed down and remain incomplete. What little there was on this theme in *Development* was summarily presented when he wrote that the 'progressive trustification of economic life facilitates the permanent continuance of maladjustments in the great combines themselves and hence outside of them, for practically there can only be complete equilibrium if there is free competition in all branches of production' (p. 244). So, rather than any concern with the effect monopoly power would have on the *nature* of the traverse of adjustments that comprise motion, Schumpeter was content with the concession that some minor degree of disequilibrium would remain after essentially the same sort of processes as in the competitive case had worked themselves out. He continued to defend his thesis that 'according to our theory there must always be a process of absorption [of the effects of innovation] between two booms, ending in a position *approaching* equilibrium, the bringing about of which is its function' (pp. 244–5, emphasis added). This concession was not really enough to ensure an understanding of economic motion under conditions of monopoly power.

More space was devoted to the issue in *Cycles*, but the overall result was very much the same in that cases of monopoly power were discussed in isolation. When presenting his steady circular flow model, Schumpeter devoted a section to an overview of the various forms of imperfectly competitive market situations. These included pure monopoly, individual and universal, bilateral monopoly, duopoly, oligopoly and monopolistic competition (pp. 56ff.). His focus was on the question of the potential for self-adjustment towards a determinate equilibrium when the circular flow is disturbed in these cases. The overall result of these deliberations was that such cases were of little significance for his work on motion. Typically, he wrote of oligopoly that while 'we need not deny the occasional occurrence of pure oligopoly and though we cannot deny its logical possibility, we are certainly within our rights in denying the practical importance of the question of its determinateness' (p. 62). Beyond this special section, then, the theory of development and business cycles was worked out along the same lines as in *Development* with only the 'frictional' effects of monopoly power recognized from time to time and the substitution of 'neighborhood of equilibrium' for complete equilibrium.

It was in *Capitalism* that Schumpeter's perception of imperfect competition rose to dominance in his analysis, but there the concerns of business-cycle *theory* were largely left aside. The puzzle remains, of course, that the ideas in the all-important Part II of the book were worked out in the mid-1930s, contemporaneously with the drafting of *Cycles*. And yet, the contrast between the treatments of monopoly power in the two works could not have been greater. In *Capitalism*, it became a central force of capitalism that brings significant economic benefits that are unavailable when strong market competition prevails. Schumpeter was concerned to explain the operations of the burgeoning 'trustified' capitalism and to justify and defend its 'unfettered' operation, free from any government interventions and regulations designed to restore 'competition'. Unfortunately, the implications of such a regime for understanding the periodic instability of motion were not given very much attention and his argument remained more descriptive than theoretical. There were, though, insights in the work that warrant some elaboration.

'The capitalist achievement', Schumpeter wrote, 'does not typically consist in providing more silk stockings for queens but in bringing them within the reach of factory girls in return for steadily decreasing amounts of effort' (*Capitalism*, p. 67). Such material success of capitalism had become especially obvious since the rise of 'unfettered' big business in the United States in the 1890s (p. 81). It was his view that the earlier forms of competitive capitalism could not have delivered any comparable outcome and he cited the automobile, rayon and aluminium industries as evidence for his belief (ibid., pp. 90n, 101n). The key to understanding the source of the benefits flowing from monopoly power was posited as giving due emphasis to the 'dynamic' nature of capitalism. In 'appraising the performance of competitive enterprise, the question of whether it would or would not tend to maximize production in a perfectly equilibrated stationary condition of the economic process is . . . almost, though not quite, irrelevant.' And, he added, 'perfect competition is not only impossible but inferior, and has no title to being set up as a model of ideal efficiency' (ibid., pp. 77n, 106). What emerged as a result of ideas such as these was a broader perspective on the nature of competition in the capitalist economy. The role of supply and demand and their effect on prices as signals for adjustment was extended to include such things as qualitative competition and sales effort. But for Schumpeter this was not enough. He wanted the perception of competition to include pressures on economic agents from 'the new commodity, the new technology, the new source of supply, the new type of organization (the largest-scale unit of control for instance) . . .', a form of competition 'which commands a decisive cost or quality advantage and which strikes not at the margins of the profits and the outputs of existing firms but at their foundations and their very lives'. Under these conditions, 'especially in manufacturing industry, a monopoly [power] position is in general no cushion to sleep on. As it can be gained, so it can be retained only by alertness and energy.' (ibid., pp. 84, 102).

Schumpeter rejected the common interpretation of 'monopolistic practices' as detrimental to economic welfare and progress (ibid., pp. 87ff.). In each case, he argued, the effects of the practice were exaggerated or not adequately balanced against the benefits delivered. Thus, 'price policies that seem . . . predatory and restrictions of output that seem . . . synonymous with loss of opportunities to produce . . . are, in the conditions of the perennial gale [of innovations], incidents, often unavoidable incidents, of a long-run process of expansion which they protect rather than impede' (ibid., p.88). Any 'restrictive strategy' practised by firms with monopoly power, such as erecting barriers to entry, is undertaken in order to ensure that the incentive to innovate is reinforced by the protection of returns generated. In many cases, 'largest-scale plans could . . . not materialize at all if it were not known from the outset that competition will be discouraged . . .' through the existence of various restrictions (ibid., p. 89).

Moreover, Schumpeter denied that large-scale firms would use their monopoly power to prevent progress through innovation. As far as he was concerned, there was little evidence to support the claim that such firms are conservative in this respect, preferring to maintain their economic positions rather than join in the continual 'creative destruction' that innovative competition brings. On the contrary, these firms often lead the way to change by establishing research facilities (ibid.,

p. 96). All firms that are rationally managed would, he argued, pursue profit-increasing innovations independently of their size and market position (ibid., pp. 97-8).

My conclusion from all of this is that during the 1930s, Schumpeter clearly recognized that the empirically-relevant perception of capitalism was one that makes due allowance for the existence of large-scale firms in small numbers dominating many major industries. These firms possess and exercise varying degrees of monopoly power over the markets in which they operate. Their activities are no longer based only on market-price competition in response to the forces of supply and demand. Rather, they engage in a number of competitive strategies that have become known as 'Schumpeterian competition' because of the emphasis that they give to pursuing the gains from innovations and subsequently trying to preserve them. It must have been clear to Schumpeter that such a capitalist vision cannot be adequately modelled and analysed by maintaining a market-price, supply and demand theoretic framework. And yet, he persisted with such a framework, originally set out in *Das Wesen* and the first chapter of *Development*, as the core of theory in *Cycles*. Granted, a myriad of qualifications were added in order more closely to reflect the realities of the system under investigation, but none of these ever overrode the market-competitive essentials of the explanations he gave for the unstable motion of capitalism.

2.4 Summary

Three main issues have been dealt with in this chapter.
1. Schumpeter's concept of capitalism as his analytical object varied considerably in its detail over the course of his writings. However, at various points he referred to all of the characteristics that are pertinent to a meaningful definition of the system. He gave particular emphasis to credit as the essential means of facilitating change and stressed that a static perception of capitalism is misleading because the system is inherently in motion.
2. The treatment of capitalism gave little immediate attention to the category of capital itself. But, in Schumpeter's analyses, it emerged as primarily the financial means of obtaining command over physical means of production with necessary links to credit creation. Combined with his relative neglect of the physical-technical structure of production as the mandatory embodiment of finance capital, this perception left him with a bias towards representing capital as a flexible and mobile resource.
3. Schumpeter was aware that the degree of competition in capitalist

markets had declined over time and that the monopoly power of producers had risen. He recognized clearly some of the analytical difficulties raised by an imperfectly-competitive model of capitalism. Unfortunately, these were kept in a separate 'compartment' of his work and the mainline of his theory of motion was constructed on the assumption of competitive markets in which the forces of supply and demand, along with flexible prices, dominated events.

Note
1. For a critical discussion of the concept of vision and its relationship to ideology and to Schumpeter's economics more generally, see Heilbroner, 1988, pp. 165ff. On the same theme, cf. Meek, 1967, pp. 196ff. and Dobb, 1973, pp. 3ff.

3 Analytical strategy

3.1 Outline of the strategy

Schumpeter had an aversion to analyses that pursue methodological issues for their own sake or in which any attempt is made to defend substantive positions by means of some methodological premises. He was educated in the period of the *Methodenstreit* at the beginning of this century, a conflict that was most pronounced between the historical analysts of Germany and the theoretical analysts of Austria. As far as he was concerned, the debate was sterile and futile, for every methodological approach could be shown to have its appropriate place in the totality of economic analysis and none could claim universal relevance or coverage. Increasingly over his intellectual life, this eclectic position underpinned Schumpeter's writings as he tried to blend the historical with the theoretical analysis of motion.

His dominant view was that where a writer must include some purely methodological discussion, it should be as a reflection upon already established substantive achievement. Thus, it should come at the end of a work, not at the beginning (*Das Wesen*, p. xv). And, while his first major work, *Das Wesen*, was largely methodological in a broad sense, in that it tried, in part, to establish the essential nature of contemporary economic analysis, the discussion of methodological *strategy* came only in the final Part V (ibid., pp. 521ff.). It must be added, though, that some of his earliest writings did focus on methodological topics, most especially the 1906 paper defending the use of mathematical methods in economics and the 1914 paper on the qualified appropriateness of the 'positive' method in economics, occasioned by the publication of François Simiand's book on the theme (*Aufsätze*, pp. 529ff., pp. 549ff.). In both papers, his desire was to inform and keep open discussion rather than to establish a personal position. These were early examples of what Fritz Machlup so appropriately termed Schumpeter's methodological 'tolerance' (1951, pp. 95-6). In later works, there were occasions where methodological issues came up as a matter of course and were treated then and there. But generally he avoided giving his analysis any methodological 'support' or digressing into polemics on such matters. The pronouncement in the first pages of *Development* was indicative of the position he was to sustain: 'The armor of methodological commentaries I renounce completely.' (p. 4). Some methodological discussion did occur in *Cycles* as a means of bridging the gap between his common-

40

sense introduction to the book and the more formal analyses that followed (p. 30ff.), but the purpose was to assist his readers rather than to espouse or defend a position.

It was really only in the drafting of the *History* manuscript in the 1940s that Schumpeter reflected at length on his methodological ideas. On this occasion, quite appropriately given the theme of the book, the ideas came in Part I rather than at the end . His specific intention was to convey to his readers 'the nature of my subject and some of the conceptual arrangements I propose to use', along with 'some information about the principles I am going to adopt . . .' (*History*, p. 3). Whatever its immediate purpose, though, I consider this part of *History* to comprise the nearest thing we have to a general methodological statement by Schumpeter in his mature years. It came, so to say, at the 'end' of *his* work on the analysis of motion, as he would have thought appropriate. He was concerned to set out some broad principles of analytical strategy that he thought could be applied to an understanding of how antecedent economic analysts had approached their work and delineated its scope. There is no reason that I can see to suggest that these principles were not born of his own extensive experience in a like role. I therefore draw freely upon the piece as indicative of the methodological tenets implicit in Schumpeter's analyses of motion.[1]

He saw analyses of economic phenomena as appropriately built up from three 'techniques' or 'fundamental fields'. These form the basic components of an explanation and the means by which it is 'tested' for consistency with empirical experience. The pertinent 'techniques' comprise a 'science of science' (*Wissenschaftslehre*) which, 'starting from logic and to some extent epistemology, treats of the general rules of procedure in use in the other individual sciences' (ibid., p. 33), where the 'other sciences' included economic *analysis* (see ibid., pp. 6ff. and 1948, p. 96). There were three fundamental 'techniques' in Schumpeter's paradigm: economic history, statistics and theory (*History*, pp. 12ff.; 1948, 113ff.). That these three belonged together as a unity was adumbrated as the subtitle of *Cycles*: 'A Theoretical, Historical and Statistical Analysis of the Capitalist Process'; and at that time, he saw this strategy as nothing novel, saying that 'I have merely moved with the general tendency toward their mutual peaceful penetration' (*Cycles*, p. v).

Complementary to these 'techniques' was a fourth 'fundamental field' which Schumpeter called economic sociology (*Wirtschaftssoziologie*). The purpose of this 'field' was to provide theory with a set of 'stylized social facts' to add to the raw data thrown up by history and statistics (*History*, pp. 20-1). Just what he intended in setting up this complementary 'field' will be considered in section 3.4 below. Before that, I consider in turn the 'techniques' of history and statistics and then theory.

3.2 History and statistics

In his retrospective look at the strategy of economic analysis, Schumpeter gave pride of place to historical technique as the indispensable mode of grasping observed experience. His well-known dictum that, 'if, starting my work in economics afresh, I were told that I could study only one of the three [techniques] but could have my choice, it would be economic history that I should choose' (*History*, p. 12), conveys this predilection well.

He gave three reasons for his preference for history as the most fundamental amongst the 'techniques'. First, the object matter of economics 'is essentially a unique process in historic time' (ibid., p. 12; cf.1948, p. 115) meaning that an understanding of the phenomena of any economic order or period must be predicated upon a factual knowledge of the '*historical experience*' involved and the acquisition of 'an adequate amount of historical *sense*' by economic analysts (*History*, p. 13, original emphasis). Secondly, because historical reports on economic phenomena can never confine themselves to purely 'economic' material, they serve to reveal relevant transeconomic facts and elements that are necessary to complete any understanding of the phenomena. Especially does this apply to the role of institutions and, that there is a direct link from this aspect of history to the complementary economic sociology, will become clear in due course. Thirdly, he asserted, without specific cases being mentioned, that 'most of the fundamental errors currently committed in economic analysis are due to a lack of historical experience more often than to any other shortcoming of the economist's equipment' (ibid.). In Schumpeter's case, though, as I will argue throughout my study, it was indeed his 'equipment' that let him down much more so than any lack of historical knowledge or sensibility.

The primary analytical status that Schumpeter gave to historical 'techniques' entailed that in the process of abstraction that is necessary in order to formulate a manageable theoretical object, it is desirable to maintain as close a contact as possible with 'historical experience', including some aspects that reach beyond the immediately economic sphere. This calls for a particular approach to model building that is inductive at the outset. Then the analyst must have an acutely sensitive talent for simplification that preserves historical-environmental relevance without precluding reasoned analysis due to an overly complex construction of the resulting model. The implication here is that the empirical status of assumptions and premises does matter. My critical investigations will show, however, that in his formative years especially, Schumpeter often strayed into making assumptions and applying premises on the basis of their proven analytical convenience and potential for delivering definitive conclusions. Although these remained largely in the background when it came to the analysis proper, in spite of his claim to be pursuing 'exact' methods, their influence was sufficient to lead him to draw some unwarranted conclusions about the essential nature of capitalist motion.

In addition, Schumpeter himself elicited two 'ominous consequences' of his primary emphasis on historical 'technique', consequences that result in certain limitations to what can be achieved in the 'scientific' analysis of economic phenomena. One he phrased as follows: 'since history is an important source – though not the only one – of the economist's material and since, moreover, the economist himself is a product of his own *and all preceding* time, economic analysis and its results are certainly affected by historical relativity . . .' (ibid., original emphasis). There are two senses in which the analyst is an historical 'product'. First, 'the analyzing observer . . . is the product of *a given social environment* – and of his particular location in this environment – that conditions him to see certain things rather than others, and to see them in a certain light' (ibid., p. 34, emphasis added). Schumpeter's view was that this resulted in the intellectual being 'just a bundle of prejudices that are in most cases held with all the force of sincere conviction' (ibid., p. 37). However, he believed that such ideology penetrated only as far as the formation of the 'pre-analytic' vision leaving established economic analysis *per se* free of any taint (ibid., p. 34ff.). 'Tools' and 'techniques' are 'non-ideological by virtue of their logical nature' and are 'purely instrumental' because in employing them, 'no class interest can have any stake' (1948, p. 104). Thus, 'the rules of procedure that we apply in our analytic work are almost as much exempt from ideological influence as vision is subject to it' (*History*, p. 43). What follows from this is that the sort of economic analysis that Schumpeter had developed was to be read as historically relative in the vision that it worked from, but ideologically neutral in the way it was argued and the explanations that it gave for the phenomena of motion.

The second sense in which an analyst can be considered to be an historical 'product' is an intellectual one. Schumpeter did not make as much of this influence of history on economic analysis, but he was aware of the importance of the filiation of ideas as the following passage indicates: 'we all start our own research from the work of our predecessors, that is, we hardly ever start from scratch' (ibid., p. 41). History, as such, then, is indeed not the only source of 'the economist's material' and there emerges here an 'intellectual' relativism that is important in understanding the nature of an analyst's work, including that of Schumpeter. What is really of concern in this regard is just which 'work of our predecessors' he chose to begin from and the ramifications that his choice had for the form that his analysis of motion took. I will have much to say about this in subsequent chapters.

Returning now to the 'ominous consequences' that Schumpeter cited, we find that the second one refers to the difficulty that can arise because economic analysts will mostly not be trained historians and will not have access to original sources (ibid., p. 13). The influence that history can have on their work is, therefore, bound to be mediated by their use of secondary reports. History comes to them 'filtered' and demands careful discrimination in its interpretation if it is to be used optimally. Schumpeter's opinion was that this difficulty is not readily overcome and he was probably led to such a conclusion after his extensive historical studies for *Cycles*. However, it is worth noting, too, that this concern for historical accuracy as a criterion for the construction and argument of this theoretical model did not emerge explicit until after he had worked out his main theses. The precise nature and extent of his historical knowledge and concern when writing *Das Wesen* and *Development* cannot be known from extant literature. It is clear that he depended heavily upon his reading of the work of other economists, most probably combined with intelligent and educated observation of the world around him.[2]

Along with the study of economic history went its formalized quantitative expression in the compilation and interpretation of statistics (ibid., pp. 13-14). For Schumpeter, statistics were needed 'not only for explaining things but also in order to know precisely what there is to explain' (ibid., p. 14). The problem to which he drew attention here is similar to the second of the above 'ominous consequences'. In order to get the best out of statistics, the analyst must be an expert in that field, too. Again, he thought it improbable that most analysts could achieve such a status. A reading of Schumpeter's own writings reveals that while he used statistics to a large extent in *Cycles*, the level of sophistication of the presentation and interpretation left him well short of what was considered professionally acceptable in his own era. Moreover, he generally eschewed the use of statistical and mathematical techniques throughout his work on motion, as I indicated in Chapter 1, section 1.1, above (cf. also Chapter 9, section 9.5, below).

3.3 Theoretical technique
Economic phenomena cannot be understood and explained directly from their empirical form. History and statistics provide the raw material for analysis, but Schumpeter rejected as 'Nonsense Induction' the view that 'the right way to go about our task is to assemble statistics, to treat them by formal methods, and to present the results as the solution of the problem' (*Cycles*, p. 32). The 'raw facts are, as such, a meaningless jumble', although they can only be assembled by the analyst in the first place if some 'common-sense understanding of the *modus operandi* of . . . [the] facts . . . ' is applied. Indeed, it must be recognized that 'some of our *refinements* upon common sense are logically anterior to the facts we wish to study and must be introduced first, because our factual discussions would be impossible without them' (ibid., pp. 30, 31, emphasis added). From this process emerge observations of individual cases of the economic phenomena that are of concern to the analyst, 'individual occurrences each of which, as it occurs, reveals peculiarities of its own'. However, Schumpeter went on, 'experience . . . teaches us that these individual occurrences have certain properties or aspects in common and that *a tremendous economy of mental effort may be realized if we deal with these properties or aspects, and with the problems they raise, once and for all*'. Moreover, in analysing each individual case, 'we discover that we are using, in each case, concepts that occur in the analysis of all'. The various economic phenomena, including individual business cycles, can be treated in this way and they will be found to 'display similar features which, and the implications of which, may be treated for all of them together by means of general schemata . . .' formulated particularly for each phenomenon (*History*, pp. 15-16, original emphasis).

The objective of this initial inductive phase of theory formation is to generate a model or schema that can 'portray certain aspects of reality' in a simplified format (ibid., p. 15). Included in the design of the model will have to be certain propositions that are taken as given knowledge. Schumpeter referred to these variously as hypotheses, axioms, postulates, assumptions and principles, although he was suspicious of 'the objectionable term "law"' that has also been used, usually at the cost of some misunderstanding about the epistemological status of the propositions made (ibid., p. 15 and n). For as he stressed, whatever we may call these propositions, and even though they are '*suggested* by the facts' and are 'framed with an eye to observations made', they remain 'in strict logic . . . [the] arbitrary creations of the analyst' (ibid., p. 15, original emphasis). The propositions so created join 'other gadgets' devised to generalize certain elements of economic reasoning, such as 'marginal productivity', 'multiplier' and 'accelerator', in an assembly of 'instruments or tools framed for the purpose of *establishing* interesting results'. It is this assembly that Schumpeter defined as an 'economic theory', citing 'Mrs. Robinson's unsurpassably felicitous phrase, economic theory is a box of tools' in support (ibid., original emphasis). Then the 'interesting results' may be established by applying 'admissible procedures' to the model, although he never elaborated upon just what these 'procedures' might comprise. Certainly, the essence of the problem is to apply deductive reasoning to the logical structures and relations of the model in order to elicit reasoned arguments that explain the existence and form of the originally observed phenomenon. These arguments he called 'theorems' or 'explanatory hypotheses' that '*embody* final results of research' (ibid., original emphasis).

In *Cycles*, Schumpeter was quite explicit that what must be sought in these results are *causal* explanations for the phenomena. The immediate purpose of 'the analytic tools or a schema or model' may be 'to measure . . . and to describe. . . [the] mechanism' of a phenomenon of interest, but the understanding that this may provide cannot be the end point for the serious analyst (p. 33). While Schumpeter expressed some trepidation about using the 'questionable term' *cause* at all, he was convinced that 'the question of causation is the Fundamental Question . . .', although he granted that 'it is neither the only one nor the first to be asked' (pp. 33n, 34). On this basis, he summarized his views on the ultimate objective of theoretical analysis: 'our mind will never be at rest until all our measurements and descriptions of mechanisms and propositions about relations are linked to the causes indicated in such a way that they may be understood to follow from them or, to put the same thing in our language, until we have assembled in one model causes, mechanisms, and effects, and can show how it works'. And, more particularly, the mechanisms should reveal how the relevant phenomenon is generated in the model '*by its own working*' as a theoretical representation of the processes of reality (p. 34, original emphasis). Such, then, was the challenge for theoretical analysis and my critical exposition will enable us to assess how well Schumpeter met it in his own work on the theory of economic development and the business cycle.

3.4   Economic sociology

In *History*, Schumpeter recorded his ambivalence about the benefits that are claimed to flow from co-operation between different intellectual disciplines in the social sciences when he noted that an unnamed 'eminent economist once observed . . . [that] cross-fertilization might easily result in cross-sterilization' (p. 27). However, Schumpeter considered it to be quite legitimate and beneficial for economics to draw upon the methodological and substantive achievements in other sciences without any commitment to cohabitation. This was especially so in the case of sociology for, because of the nature of economic matters, it is 'impossible to tell . . . where economics ends and sociology begins'. As a result, the 'intermediate field of economic sociology . . . has come into existence *via facti*' (1948, p. 111).

He argued the rationale for an economic sociology by referring to the fact that while history 'alone can tell us what sort of society it was, or is, to which the theoretical schemata are to apply', there is a need to include in economic analysis 'social facts that are not simply economic history but are a sort of generalized or typified or stylized economic history' (*History*, p. 20). More particularly, the sociological connections that appear in economic-historical observations are 'first, the facts of economic behavior from which economists forge certain assumptions and second, the institutions that characterize the economic organization of the societies to be studied' (ibid., p. 544; cf. *Essays*, pp. 286–7). Two aspects of economic sociology were, then, on the agenda for Schumpeter's analysis of motion. One is the need to confront and organize coherently the observed behaviours of economic agents so that they may be included as an explicit component in the explanations devised. In this regard, he attributed to Gerhard Colm the following 'felicitous, if not completely synonymous, turn of phrase': 'economic sociology deals with the problem of how people came to behave as they do at any time and place; and economics with the problem of how they do behave and what economic results they produce by behaving as they do' (*Essay*, p. 287; cf. *History*, pp. 21, 219). The other aspect of economic sociology to be considered is in direct conjunction with the treatment of economic agents because it concerns the institutional structure and organization of society *through and on which* the agents act individually or in groups and, consequently, generate observed economic phenomena. Now, although he gave no explicit attention to the matter at the time, Schumpeter had, in his all too brief discussion of economic sociology, broached some fundamental questions of social theory with significant ramifications for understanding economic motion. I think it is worthwhile to reflect on these issues before we proceed to the more substantive analyses of subsequent chapters.

As human agents are the elements of any social and economic organizations that make it operational, some understanding of their behaviours is mandatory in any endeavour to explain the resulting events. There are two extreme ways of dealing with agent behaviours in socio-economic modelling. One is to treat agents as wholly subjectivistic and voluntaristic in their decision making and actions. The other is to regard what they do as wholly determined by either their structural (or class) positions in the social and economic organization or their functional positions within the necessary operations of the organization. In the latter two deterministic perceptions, institutions and the operational needs of society in the light of its objectives, act to direct and constrain the actions of individual agents, whereas in the former perception, the institutions and operations consist in and only in the independent behaviours of the individuals that comprise them. A compromise theoretical position that avoids these extremes would allow for a balanced view of agents as pursuing subjectivistic, but rational, decisions and actions *within* the confines of a defined institutional-structural entity that facilitates as well as containing and directing their activities so as to realize some social purpose. The image is then one of mutual interaction and interdependence between voluntaristic economic agents who know and understand their environment and their positions in it. Their understanding enables them to maximize their *individual* benefits by means of appropriately constrained creative and responsive actions that are consistent with socio-economic reproduction. Conscious and active individual agents can, therefore, be said to work *in, through and on* the structure of their environment, including its physical-technical and institutional dimensions. There is a 'duality of structure' and the understanding of agent action must involve structures as 'the medium of its production' and, at the same time, as 'its outcome in the reproduction of social forms' (Giddens, 1977, p. 130). That is, economic agents are to be perceived as operating through the structures available to them in order to achieve their individual ends. But, as an integral part of these operations, structures are created, preserved, modified and/or destroyed on a continuous basis in accordance with the needs of their constituent members or owners. Such structural-operational interdependence should be an integral part of any explanation of motion.

Schumpeter's treatment of agents was initially built up around his concept of 'methodological individualism' that was introduced in *Das Wesen*. It should be recalled that his concern in this early work was with 'pure' or 'exact' microeconomic analysis of the static equilibrium model. For the purposes of this analysis, the constituent agents were appropriately treated as individuals endowed with one or more exchangeable commodities whose actions are determined by behavioural premises that require no further explanation and are independent of any social or structural factors (*Das Wesen*, pp. 94ff., *passim*). Thus he wrote in his 1909 paper 'On the Concept of Social Value' that for theory, 'it is irrelevant *why* people demand certain goods: the only important point is that all things are demanded, produced, and paid for because individuals want them. Every demand on the market is therefore an individualistic one . . .' (*Essays*, p. 4, original emphasis). But, he was aware that this concept of the agent could not be applied outside of the 'pure' economic model. It had nothing to do with 'political individualism' (*Das Wesen*, pp. 89–90). And, for all economic and social analysis other than the 'pure' case, sociological dimensions of life must be allowed to influence how agents behave (ibid., pp. 86, 91, 94–5). The most obvious manifestation of this step was Schumpeter's development of a social-class analysis. I consider this analysis below only to the extent that it informs us about his treatment of classes in the theory of economic development and business cycles.

Schumpeter's concern with social classes dates from some of his earliest work. The main ideas of his theory were first presented 'as a lecture course for laymen on the subject of "State and Society" ' which he gave in 1910-11 at the University of Czernowitz (*Classes*, p. 101). Later, in 1913-14, they were presented again in a course entitled 'The Theory of Social Classes' at Columbia University. His concern with the themes slipped into 'second place to other interests', especially after 1916, although he never gave up work on them completely. Then, in November 1926, he delivered a lecture at the University of Heidelberg entitled 'Leadership and Class Formation'. This gave him the opportunity to rework his ideas and to publish them for the first time during 1927. The title that he gave to the paper was then 'Social Classes in an Ethnically Homogeneous Environment', with the latter qualifying phrase designed to forestall any expectations by readers that race and ethnicity would enter into the theory, although he did not rule out their relevance for a broader picture (ibid., p. 102). At the time, he also noted that according to his research plans, the ideas would be able to be developed 'only years from now, if at all' (ibid., p. 101). As things turned out, the 'if at all' phrase proved to be prophetic.

For Schumpeter, the 'ultimate foundation on which the class phenomenon rests consists of individual differences in aptitude', whether they be natural or acquired (ibid., pp. 160, 162). As his text reveals, this amounts to an 'élitist' perception of class formation, for the dominant class or classes in any historical era have comprised those individuals whose talents were most socially valued. Various aspects of leadership received considerable emphasis in his perception of relevant talents (ibid., p. 163). The form of leadership that was relevant was to be 'in keeping with those functions' considered to be most 'socially necessary' and 'the relative social significance of a function always . . . [has been] determined by the degree of social leadership which its fulfillment implies or creates' (ibid., p. 160). The circularity of the argument here only serves to emphasize the profound significance that leadership aptitude had in Schumpeter's perception of social history. Classes below the 'ruling' leadership élite were couched in simple functionalist terms: 'Each class is linked to . . . a special function . . . which it must fulfill according to its whole concept and orientation, and which it actually does discharge as a class and through the class conduct of its members.' It follows, then, that 'the position of each class in the total national structure, depends, on the one hand, on the significance that is attributed to that function, and, on the other hand, on the degree to which the class successfully performs the function' (ibid., p. 137).

The most appropriate class membership unit according to Schumpeter is the family, even though it is the talent and success of a particular individual that determines the status achieved by *his* family (ibid., p. 160) – the paternally-ruled nuclear family was Schumpeter's model, it seems. This view of class composition was posited thus: *'Coordinate families . . . merge into a social class, welded together by a bond . . . . This relationship assumes a life of its own and is then able to grant protection and confer prestige'* (ibid., p. 167, original emphasis). Once in a class, a family's position tends to become entrenched and take on 'a life of its own', with class membership persisting even though the original basis for it may have disappeared. This entrenchment is reinforced by the fact that initial class success 'generally paves the way for further success' (ibid., p. 166), with the prestige of members bringing other related positions and functions to perform that strengthens the family's grip on membership. But, at the same time, classes exhibit an historical 'dynamic' that sees families rise into and fall out of a class as well as classes themselves rise and fall in prestige. No family or class has a permanent hold on its social position, however prestigious or entrenched (ibid., pp. 113ff., 134ff.). The 'dynamic' has two elements: first, the success of family members in performing the functions of the class may decline and, secondly, the status of the functions themselves may decline. Over time, both of these elements contribute to the movements of families and classes up and down the social hierarchy, an aspect of social-class history that dominated much of what Schumpeter wrote in *Classes*.

More important for the purpose of the present study is that the discussion of class formation and 'dynamics' is indicative of his departure from the 'methodological individualist' perception of agents in society that he applied in setting up the 'pure' model of economic equilibrium. That a class has 'a life of its own' reinforced his view that no individualist theory of agency can provide a legitimate foundation for a theory of society. Class is not simply a 'resultant phenomenon'. It is 'something more than an aggregation of class members' where 'this something cannot be recognized in the behaviour of the individual class member' (ibid., pp. 105n, 107). The effect of this is that classes should appear in social analysis as separately identifiable social entities: 'every social class is a special social organism, living, acting, and suffering *as such* and in need of being understood *as such*' (ibid., p. 105, emphasis added). Of course, classes still have individual members whose participation in social and economic events cannot be ignored. But in a class environment, as Schumpeter so clearly recognized, the individual must now be perceived as 'a *social* fact', with his or her class position 'limiting the scope of his [or her] behaviour to a characteristic pattern' (ibid., pp. 161, 113, original emphasis; cf. p. 125). Recognition of this fact effectively does away with much of 'the empty contrasts of the individual vs. the social, the subjective vs. the objective' in social theory (ibid., p. 161). The unfortunate thing is that Schumpeter never gave any further attention to the vital matters raised in these pregnant passages: What is the precise nature of the limitations that social structure imposes on an individual agent's actions? What is the extra something that the separate existence of classes brings to our understanding of society? and, How are the mixes of individual-social and subjective-objective elements in social analysis to be balanced?

So far, I have only pursued Schumpeter's analysis of certain principles of class formation and change. It is reasonable for us to seek some more specific taxonomy of classes in his work as well. What this search reveals is a disorganized jumble of scattered remarks. He made little attempt in *Classes* to particularize the class structures of the historical periods that he studied and contemporary capitalism was no exception. And, when an effort is made to delineate his views about the appropriate perception of classes in a capitalist society by reading his widely scattered remarks in other writings, there are some confusions and contradictions to contend with.

In the *Classes* essay, the only taxonomic references to the class structure of capitalism are in terms of a 'capitalist bourgeoisie' and a 'working class' (pp. 117, 129, 130, 133). No analysis of the rationale for or implications of such a dichotomy was undertaken at that time. Some years later, in a 1943 paper, he reiterated this perception when arguing that while a 'purely capitalist society' is an empirical improbability, if it did exist it would consist of 'nothing but entrepreneurs, capitalists, and proletarian workmen . . . ' (*Essays*, p. 172). Just why he included 'entrepreneurs' here as a *class* alongside the other two must remain a mystery, for one of the crucial points made about such agents in *Development* and *Cycles* is that they *never* constitute such an entity in relation to their defining role as innovators. However, be this as it may, what it is important to go on to notice here, is that although Schumpeter was prepared to use this way of structuring the classes of capitalism as a matter of passing convenience, he was also prepared to condemn it in the work of one of its main advocates, Karl Marx. When writing about Marx in *Capitalism*, one of the few references to the *substance* of his class analysis, as distinct from the critique of its implications, dismissed it as 'the crippled sister of the economic interpretation of history' (p. 13; cf. p. 15). And, at around the same time, Schumpeter wrote in his *Encyclopaedia Britannica* article on capitalism that he judged this dichotomy of classes as 'next to valueless for purposes of analysis' (*Essays*, p. 195). The basis for this assertion was not given, although he did go on to imply that it was simply not detailed enough. He suggested as an alternative 'at least' the following *analytically* unwieldy collection: 'classes associated with the control of large, medium and small businesses; the farmers . . .; the *rentier* class ("capitalists" in a narrower but more useful sense); the professional class; the clerical ("white collar") class; the skilled workers; the unskilled workers', with the rider attached that the borderlines between such classes are ill-defined and they should be seen only as '*zones*' of transition (ibid., p. 196, original emphasis). Nowhere in his writings was it ever made clear to what analytical use this classification could be put and what advantages it would bring over the simpler divisions that had been rejected.

In fact, what is found in his writings on motion most often is that classes receive little attention at all in the analysis. Beyond specific functional references to agents as entrepreneurs and bankers, there is not much about the role that any group affiliations of agents plays in understanding development and business cycles. So, while Schumpeter was concerned to discuss *some* aspects of classes as a sociological phenomenon in history, they did not find a place in the analyses of economic motion with which I am dealing here. I will have more to say on his treatment of agency in the chapter on economic development below (Chapter 6).

3.5 Summary
Several main elements of Schumpeter's analytical strategy, along with some related methodological concerns, have been brought together in this chapter.
1. Although he did not avoid methodological matters altogether,

    Schumpeter was resolute that they should not be given any promi-
nence as the foundations for his substantive analyses.

2. It was clear, though, that he found it appropriate to separate the
theoretical dimensions of his work from those with a mainly
empirical orientation, namely historical and statistical analyses, and
from the broader field of 'economic sociology' in which economic
phenomena should be situated.

3. Schumpeter pursued a 'pure' economic theory, even using the 'box
of tools' analogy, but he always combined his approach with an
historical consciousness. The effect was that in spite of his intentions, his theoretical developments were less than strictly general as
the 'impurities' of particular historical and institutional circumstances continually intruded into his argument.

4. While conscious of the sociological setting of matters economic,
Schumpeter's somewhat desultory attention to relevant matters of
social theory was never integrated with his analysis of motion.
There was some functional classification of human agency, but the
legacy of his methodological individualism steered him away from
any class-related sociological perceptions in economics, even
though he wrote at length on class as a separate issue.

Notes
1. I also refer to the recently discovered alternative version of the introductory part of
   the *History* project, published as Schumpeter, 1948. For a penetrating analysis of this
   piece see Jensen, 1987.
2. For some insights into the intellectual and other influences on Schumpeter's thought
   see März, 1965; Streissler, 1982; Samuels, 1983; and Boehm, 1989.

4   The circular flow of economic life

4.1 Some methodological principles

In formulating his analysis of economic motion, Schumpeter applied three methodological principles. The first was that the most appropriate way formally to analyse motion, especially at the theoretical level, is to begin from, and to relate the subsequent explanations to, some core state of the capitalist economic system in which motion in the form of change is assumed to be absent (*Development*, pp. 3ff.; *Cycles*, pp. 35ff.). In this state, the same quantitative and qualitative conditions are reproduced period by period, but motion is not absent in the sense that certain processes with a time dimension must be completed in order for reproduction to be realized. For this reason, there are some difficulties with the terminology that is to be used to refer to such a state. 'Static' and 'stationary', both of which Schumpeter used from time to time with somewhat confusing effects (see, e.g., *Development*, p. 82n; *Essays*, pp. 24ff, 159), convey the wrong impression because 'movement' is present in the circular flow. And, there were times when he seemed sensitive to the problem (*ibid.*, p. 59 and n). I will avoid both terms and refer to the core state as one of *steady* circular flow.

The second methodological principle that underpinned Schumpeter's analysis was that motion involving quantitative and/or qualitative change in the system can be adequately represented and understood by taking the steady circular-flow model, 'adding in' the causes of change and tracing their logical consequences (see, e.g., *Development*, pp. 64, 68, 72, 73, 195). An implication of this procedure is that the substantive and temporal *form* of motion can primarily be attributed to the particular cause (or causes) that induces it. The third principle then follows as the presumption that it is meaningful to analyse the observed totality of motion into separable components that may be dealt with in isolation from one another (*Essays*, pp. 58–9). The components are separated according to the fundamental cause with which they are associated; in particular, Schumpeter's economic development, with its temporal business-cycle form, is induced only by waves of innovations. He placed great weight on these latter two principles, but I will argue in my critique that unless used properly, they have the capacity to mislead in the way motion is to be explained.

4.2 Antecedent sources

Schumpeter considered the development of the circular-flow model of economic life to be one of the most significant advances in the history of economic analysis. He attributed this advance to the original work of Richard Cantillon and François Quesnay and the Physiocrats. The latters' *Tableau économique* was later to influence the formation of the model that Schumpeter admired so much, Walras's general equilibrium system, although it is evident that what caught Walras's attention was not the circular-*flow* idea itself but the *Tableau format* as an expression of simultaneous economic interdependencies (Walras, 1954, pp. 393ff.). And, what is more, Schumpeter's own earliest references to Walras's *Eléments* gave emphasis to it as containing the first coherent and exactly-formulated expression of static general equilibrium (*Das Wesen*, pp. 139–40, 261; *Doctrine*, pp. 174–5) and to its marginalist treatment of price and distribution theory (*Das Wesen*, pp. 12, 17, 275, 336; *Doctrine*, pp. 182, 194n, 195ff.).

In *Doctrine*, the 'discovery' of the circular-flow idea was attributed only to the Physiocrats (pp. 42ff), although they were given no credit for it in *Development*. The latter work focused on Walras as its source, especially when Schumpeter reflected on these things in the Preface to the 1937 Japanese edition. There he referred to having studied 'the Walrasian conception and the Walrasian technique' when he first began his economic research, with the following tribute providing the rationale: 'To Walras we owe a concept of the economic system and a theoretical apparatus which for the first time in the history of our science effectively embraced the pure logic of the interdependence between economic quantities' (*Essays*, p. 159). At the centre of this Walrasian influence was claimed to be analytical 'technique': on this Schumpeter wrote that 'I wish to emphasize that as an economist I owe more to it than to any other influence' (ibid.). Just what he meant by 'technique' here was not explained and it cannot be gleaned immediately from his own analyses. He cannot have meant Walras's *mode* of analysis because, in spite of his espousal and defence of mathematical methods in economics, he rarely used them himself and the distance between the *Eléments* and *Development* in this respect could not have been greater. As we saw in the first chapter above (section 1.1), even in *Das Wesen*, the most purely theoretical of his texts, there are only seven short pieces of algebra and elementary calculus in 626 pages of text. In his main texts on motion, mathematics hardly appears at all and, when it does, it is used to facilitate expositions of the ideas of other, mathematically-inclined theorists (see, e.g., the piece on Kalecki in *Cycles*, pp. 185ff.). Most probably the 'technique' referred to included the use of the general equilibrium concept itself and the *ab ovo* method that Walras had used (*Development*, pp. 10, 82n).[1]

Already the reader may be wondering why Marx has not been referred to in all this discussion of the circular-flow idea. The simple fact of the matter is that Schumpeter found no place for Marx's reproduction schema in the intellectual line from Quesnay to Walras. Nowhere in the whole of Schumpeter's extant writings was the *Capital*, II schema (Marx, 1971) accorded any status as a central contribution to the revival of the *Tableau* and to our understanding of the circular flow of economic life. Its conception was never discussed, even in Schumpeter's most detailed treatment of Marx (*Capitalism*, pp. 5ff.) or in his explicit analyses of Marx on motion (ibid., pp. 30ff.; *History*, pp. 747ff., 1131–2). Only passing references were made to its existence (ibid., pp. 242, 562, 565–6). The chapter of *Doctrine* on the 'discovery' of the circular-flow idea made no reference to Marx's schema and in the only sustained discussion of his work in the book, an absurdly long footnote almost four pages in length (p. 119n), Schumpeter emphasized the theory of value and distribution and mentioned only as a passing thought that the Physiocrats had some unspecified influence on Marx (cf. p. 46). The importance of this neglect of Marx's reproduction schema is that Schumpeter failed to give it due recognition as, at least, an alternative way of presenting the circular-flow model that may have been worth serious investigation.

It cannot have been that he was unfamiliar with the potential of the schema, even though that potential had never been fully realized by Marx himself. For in his university days, and for some time afterwards, he had much contact with the Austrian Marxists, especially Rudolf Hilferding and Otto Bauer. The latter two wrote major pieces of analysis in which motion was treated as a reproduction-related problem: Hilferding's *Finance Capital* was published in 1910 (1981) and Bauer's two part article, prompted by the publication of Rosa Luxemburg's book on the same themes and with the same title (1951), 'The Accumulation of Capital' appeared in *Die Neue Zeit* in 1913 (1986). Both works were, therefore, available during Schumpeter's intellectually formative years. It is also possible that he had already heard ideas along these lines expressed by Hilferding and Bauer when they participated in Böhm-Bawerk's seminars at the University of Vienna during 1905 and 1906 (see Haberler, 1951a, pp. 26–7, 30–31).

So it was, then, that Schumpeter chose by default to adhere to the Walrasian-styled conception of the circular-flow model. I will pursue further below the idea that had he recognized the particular and contrasting merits of the reproduction schema instead of allowing Marx only a belated general influence on his work – as admitted more directly in the Japanese Preface to *Development* more than 25 years after the book was first published (*Essays*, pp. 159, 160–61, but cf. *Development*, p. 59n) – he could have provided much deeper insights into the realities of the unstable motion of capitalism. Had he also chosen to give Kalecki's and Keynes's work their due, even more might have come of his analyses. And all this could have been done with every other aspect of his methodological and analytical strategies left as they were designed.

4.3 Introduction to the circular-flow model

My focus in setting up an exposition of Schumpeter's circular-flow model will be the version devised in the first chapter of *Development* and left substantially unchanged in all editions of the book through to the fourth German edition of 1935 and all translations beyond (p. ix). The same sort of model provided the core of the analysis in *Cycles* as well, albeit with some points of variation in methodology, substance and emphasis. I will make particular reference to these variations towards the end of this subsection and where appropriate afterwards.

A problem that arises in any endeavour to interpret Schumpeter's main texts is that there exists in them a constant 'tension' between two contrasting approaches to analysis: one is a common-sense inductive and descriptive approach in which the observed nature of reality is kept to the fore and the other is the logico-deductive approach that generates a formal analysis that follows the assumptions and tenets of orthodox theory as he had expounded it in *Das Wesen*. In the latter case, his idea was that his move into 'dynamics' must remain couched in terms that provide 'cogs to grip the wheels of received theory' (*Development*, p. 4). However, he found that in building up his theory of motion, 'only a few of the results of theory are necessary for our purpose' and that as a result, he 'gladly used the proffered opportunity to convey what . . . [he had] to say as simply and non-technically as possible' (ibid.). This 'opportunity' was, as he recognized up to a point, a mixed blessing. He knew that it meant 'the sacrifice of absolute correctness' (ibid.), a cryptic assertion that can only have meant a 'sacrifice' of exactness and determinateness in the outcome of the argument. The overall result of this half-hearted approach to the use of theory was a peculiar mixture of formal analysis and empirical description with neither component dominating the argument for very long. *Development* is a much more theoretically oriented book than *Cycles*, which probably accounts for its greater success as a professional treatise. But the difference is only one of degree as the 'simply and non-technically' remark above indicates. *Cycles* ended up pleasing no one because it tried to be 'popular' and yet its argument and style would have still made difficult reading for lay people. In the context of the present exposition, my intention is to try to reflect this ambivalence of approach while bringing rather more coherence and organization to Schumpeter's often rambling and shifting analyses.

In working out his circular-flow model, Schumpeter claimed to be concerned only with that dimension of human existence usually understood as economic life. His concern was with those structures, institutions and operations through which the 'economic conduct' of agents is carried out, where that conduct 'is directed towards the acquisition of goods [and services] through exchange or production' (ibid., p. 3). That is, he emphasized that economics is essentially about the material provisioning of human agents by a process of production and exchange that mediates between 'nature' and 'needs'. At the same time, though, economic activity is modal in that it facilitates all those other aspects of life that people pursue: this led Schumpeter to write that such activity 'may have *any* motive, even a spiritual one, but its *meaning* is always the satisfaction of wants' (ibid., p. 10, original emphasis). Focusing on the economic dimension of life is an abstraction, for the 'social process is really one indivisible whole' and any 'fact is never exclusively or purely economic'. But, it is an abstraction 'forced upon us by the technical conditions of mentally copying reality', with 'the classifying hand of the investigator artificially . . . [extracting] economic facts' (ibid., p. 3; cf. pp. 4–5 and *Cycles*, p. 36). The effect of this delimitation of the analytical object was to confine the terms of the explanations to those within economic range, leaving other related aspects of the social whole as external and given.

As I have already indicated, the central tenet of the circular-flow model is the absence of change of any sort. The presumption is that the structural environment and the situation of each economic agent within it are well established by past experiences and actions. Schumpeter began his common-sense outline of the model with the microcosm of an individual farmer who produces corn (ibid., pp. 5ff.). This example illustrates certain particulars of the economic problem which he proceeded to generalize into a model of the otality. The primary decision to be made by the farmer, given his or her commitment to corn production, is how much to produce. It is a decision that is *ex ante* to price and demand realization, but in the competitive and established world of the circular flow it can be taken without uncertainty because the absence of change means that a sound memory ensures complete commercial success for all economic agents. In addition to the demand side of the calculus, the farmer knows well the established pattern of his or her input costs and the technical relations involved in the production process. Furthermore, stability on the supply side is assured because all the farmer's suppliers enjoy similar positions of economic certainty. Thus, over time, the farmer has become 'entangled . . . in a net of social and economic connections which he cannot easily shake off. They have bequeathed him definite means and methods of production. All these hold him in iron fetters fast in his tracks.' The past can be said, therefore, to 'govern the activity of the individual', but the result is that 'the mechanism of the exchange economy operates with great precision' (ibid., p. 6).

On the basis of this specific micro-case, Schumpeter 'generalized' and 'refined' his perception of the circular flow by arguing that all economic agents can be taken to be in the same position as the farmer. Each operates with certainty and buys and sells in established and stable markets. Leaving aside possible disturbances to the circular flow, that 'may occur for all sorts of reasons', across the whole economy 'all products must be disposed of; for they will indeed only be produced with reference to empirically known market possibilties.' (ibid., p. 7; cf. pp. 43, 45). Realization of these price and quantity 'possibilities' in each economic period will ensure that agents are individually able to 'maintain their consumption and their productive equipment in the next economic period at the level so far attained . . .' and that 'the circular flow of economic life is closed' ibid., p. 8).

There are implicit in the above introductory discussion of the circular-flow idea some points of analysis that have problematical implications for the subsequent development of Schumpeter's theory. First, the circular flow set up is said to involve in each period an inherited stock of 'definite means and methods of production' which serve to hold each economic agent 'in iron fetters fast in his tracks'. Here we have a clear recognition of the empirically-obvious fact that the structures and operations of production are inflexible, especially from the short-period perspective adopted in the model. Schumpeter made the point even more plainly in *Cycles*: 'Inasmuch as . . .

substitution [between inputs] is possible only according to certain rules and within certain limits, the production function which embodies these rules and limits may be looked upon as a condition or constraint imposed by the technological horizon and the structure of the economic environment on economic decision or on the maxima of economic advantage or profitableness which economic decision strives to attain' (p. 39). Now any retreat from this perception of short-period rigidities in production in order to facilitate the formal analysis of change must mean a loss of some contact between the real-world object and its theoretical reflection. Just to give the flavour of problems to come, I quote the following footnote that was penned as a qualification to a reference in the text of *Development* to 'initial stocks of consumers' and producers' goods': 'As every reader of J. B. Clark knows, it is strictly speaking necessary to consider these stocks, not in their actual shapes – as so many ploughs, pairs of boots and so on – but as accumulated productive forces which can at any moment and without loss or friction be turned into any specific commodities wanted' (p. 10n). This provides us with just one example of the sort of resort to 'pure' theory that was all too often indulged in by Schumpeter at the cost of weakening the explanatory power of his argument.

A second problematical implication concerns the requirement that economic agents 'maintain . . . their productive equipment in the next economic period at the level so far attained'. Even in the total absence of change, as assumed in the circular-flow conditions, this requirement imposes certain well-known difficulties concerning the concept of depreciation and the time phasing of replacement investment. But, more important for Schumpeter's analysis, is the claimed presence of 'productive equipment' itself and the suggestion that it lasts for more than one period in the use of the term 'maintain'. The 'productive equipment' then has both stock and flow dimensions to contend with in the analysis of production and income distribution. But, while he was aware of the stock-flow distinction (*Development*, p. 46n), it did not find any place in his theory of motion for reasons that will become clear as we proceed. A further aspect of this same 'productive equipment' issue is that in an industrialized economy, the replacement process (and eventually the expansion process, too) requires the identification of a sector of production whose output is 'equipment'. Once again, in his common-sense argument, Schumpeter often recognized this requirement and the increased complexity that its inclusion brings to the processes of motion. His formal analysis, though, was not designed to give due weight to it at all and the following passages are again indicative of the problems to come.

He expressed the view that 'produced means of production are nothing but transitory items' and went on from there to draw the conclusion that even though 'very many produced means of production last through a series of economic periods . . . this is not an essential element, and we alter nothing fundamental if we limit the use of such means of production to one economic period' (ibid., pp. 44, 45). I will argue at various points in my critique that this was a profound error of judgement on Schumpeter's part because it can readily be shown that the existence of durable produced means of production makes a very marked difference to the way motion is to be interpreted.

When we consider the decision making process concerning production that economic agents are called upon to make, a third problematical point emerges from the common sense discussion of the circular flow. In the 'perfect' case, *ex ante* decisions about production are made with certainty about the outcome. It is interesting to recognize first of all that this assumption *as it stands* is not dependent upon the existence of any particular state of competition in the markets. The requirement is simply that markets clear and they do so here because of perfect foresight born of experience and the absence of change. Realization of supply and demand equality is not conditional upon price flexibility, for the precise pattern of demand, given the established vector of relative prices, is known in advance. Flexibility is not at issue at all, as each seller is effectively a monopolist in his or her market niche.

In contrast to this 'perfection' of the steady circular-flow state, the introduction of any change, however slight, means that one or more economic agents must react by changing their decisions and behaviour. Then, in order to interpret the nature of the changes that ensue, the state of the markets must be known. With perfect competition throughout, the market clearing outcome is always ultimately assured and the *ex ante* output decisions by producers are relevant only as the determinant of the overall scale of economic activity. Full capacity utilization can be assumed. But, once we move away from this situation and introduce some degree of monopoly power, the *ex ante* production decisions of agents at some locations must be made in the face of uncertainty, perhaps on both the demand and supply sides of their calculus. Expectations immediately have a role to play and the agents' situations are further complicated over and above the rigidities of the production structure with which they must operate in the short period. Formal analysis here faces severe intractabilities that demand a retreat to assumptions that overcome them. Schumpeter often beat such a retreat, as we shall see.

To conclude this introduction to the circular-flow model, I want to draw attention to a pertinent difference between how the analysis was approached in *Development* as compared with *Cycles*. The later work opened with an 'Introductory' chapter that was not present in *Development* and in which the problem of understanding motion was tackled at the level of the common-sense experiences of 'business-men' (reading men and women as included in 'businessmen' in what follows). The centrepiece of the discussion is the general notion that motion is reflected in sequences of 'business situations' that are deviations from what experience and other information have established as 'normal'. Thus: 'business situations sometimes approach and sometimes draw away from these normals in a characteristic way . . . [and] our concept [of the normal is] . . . indispensable as a standard by which to diagnose and, if possible, to measure the actual states of the economic organism' (*Cycles*, p. 4). Schumpeter's idea in positing the 'businessman's' approach initially was that it would provide an effective entrée for the general reader into the more formal arguments concerning motion.

The 'businessman's normal' foreshadowed by analogy the steady circular-flow state of the theoretical analysis that was to follow. In the 'normal' state, there are no events that induce the businessmen to do anything differently and their best interests are served by repeating their current actions. Put more pointedly, a firm has a 'normal year' when it succeeds 'in earning enough to cover current expenditure, depreciation, contractual interest on its debt, plus such remuneration of the owners' services and capital as is sufficient and not more than sufficient to induce them to go on without either increasing or decreasing their investment'. And, a collective 'normal' exists when 'all firms not working under advantages or disadvantages peculiar to them' experience the same conditions and the same rates of return to their owners (ibid.). The analogy is weakened by the fact that in the 'pure' circular-flow state, there can be no 'remuneration of . . . capital' as profit and the rate of profit are argued to be zero and there can be no 'interest on . . . debt' because there is no credit used for productive purposes and the rate of interest is zero. By contrast, Schumpeter's common sense told him that even in a 'normal' state, owner-'businessmen' would receive some rate of return on their 'investment' and have debt obligations to meet. But, be this as it may, the implication that he wanted his readers to draw from this reasoning was that the transition could readily be made in both directions between the theoretical world of the steady circular-flow and the real world of the 'businessman'. He concluded with the argument that there is a 'theoretical norm, however distant it may be from actual life . . . [that] renders to the theorist the service which to the businessman is rendered by the idea of a normal business situation. *Logically purified, the latter concept merges into the former*' (ibid., p. 45, emphasis added).

4.4 Constructing the Model

4.4.1 *Resources and agents*

Consider first the general structure and organization of resources and agents that Schumpeter assumed to be given. The resource picture is by no means clear initially in *Development* and I will have to say more about it progressively in other chapters below. He specified that the physical-technical resource base comprises 'initial stocks of consumers' and producers' goods' (*Development*, p. 10), but this proved to be a misleading opening gambit because the ensuing argument ultimately led to an express denial of the relevance of such stocks. And, although there were frequent references to produced means of production in the circular-flow analysis, they were never satisfactorily integrated into the schema (ibid., pp. 24, 30, 44, 45, 46). The position in *Cycles* was much the same (pp. 38, 40). As I will soon show in detail, Schumpeter's theoretical construction required that resources be represented only by the presence of a 'stock' of natural resources called 'land' and the various capacities of human agents potentially to perform labour. At some points, he referred to the latter using Marx's felicitous term *labour power*, but he did not always make the capacity and the flow of services delivered therefrom distinct (*Development*, pp. 46, 203; cf. 17, 22-3). The availability of these basic resources was taken as given, with both being scarce relative to demand.

The structure of agency assumed in the circular-flow model calls for rather more initial comment than the resource base. Schumpeter followed traditional theory, especially in *Development*, by dividing economically-active agents, as defined by their having a market function, between those endowed with 'land' and those endowed with labour-power, i.e., between 'land' owners and workers. The mode of participation in economic activity of these two groups must be seen as very different in fact, even though orthodox theory treats them as each merely 'supplying' the service of their respective resources. Schumpeter overlooked the fact that the so-called 'service' of owning and supplying 'land' to production is quite different from a *human* perspective from the provision of labour services as the activity of performing work. He placed them on an equal analytical footing in his application of the marginal-productivity theory of income distribution (ibid., pp. 24-5). Indeed, in most of his argument, the ownership of a resource was treated as economically identical to the services the resource provides.

As a further development of the role of the labour-power resource in the circular flow, Schumpeter distinguished between 'directing' and 'directed' labour services. The former, which constitutes effectively 'a third productive factor', involves performing two key functions, namely that of supervising the delivery of directed labour services and that of executive decision making about the 'direction, method, and quantity of production', and perhaps about price setting as well (ibid., pp. 20, 21). These two functions may be carried out by different agents, but this would mean that a 'fourth' would have to be added to the 'third productive factor' in that each would require a separate market-determined wage. Beyond this functional distinction, the appearance of directing labour is identical to that of directed labour in the analysis, for the latter delivers its services in exchange for a wage just the same as the former does. No social difference between the two (or three) forms of labour service was relevant to the economics of the situation. Moreover, all forms of labour service in the circular flow situation are routine and no talent for doing anything creative or new is required, even though in the case of directing labour some degree of leadership ability would appear to be necessary. Schumpeter wanted to minimize this impression, though, in order to preserve the idea of leadership talent for his entrepreneurs later on. Therefore, his directing workers in the circular flow are just as much automatons as those they direct (ibid., pp. 21-2, 45; cf. *Cycles*, p. 40).

One thing that is absent from this discussion of agency in the circular-flow model is any group that owns *produced* means of production and claims an income share by virtue of that ownership alone. This was a conscious and explicit exclusion by Schumpeter in conjunction with his abstraction from any use of durable produced means of production *as stocks* in the production process and any ownership income other than 'land' rent (*Development*, pp. 45-6). Although these abstractions bring a measure of simplification to the model, they also jeopardize any claim that it has adequately to reflect the properties of a *capitalist* version of the circular flow. Production is not organized by or on behalf of capitalist means of production owners; indeed it is not clear how this is done at all in the model unless it is assumed that 'land' owners are the buyers of labour services, the employers of labour, in effect. Or perhaps workers with only their labour power to use buy the services of 'land' and become the employers of 'land', in effect. The analytical structure of the model does not make any distinction in this respect except that as Schumpeter cited certain labour-power owning agents as having the 'directing' talent, the latter of the two scenarios seems to be the more appropriate. This amounts to what Robert Heilbroner has so aptly labelled a 'bizarre' version of capitalism! (1988, pp. 171-2).

However, it should be recalled that for Schumpeter a steady circular-flow model of *capitalism* is a contradiction of terms (see chapter 2 above). On this basis, it does not seem to matter much what characteristics are specified for the model, provided only that they can be complemented by the necessary capitalist features once motion is introduced. But, as I shall argue in due course more fully, this strategy left him with just as 'bizarre' a version of the business cycle in that its periodic circular-flow 'equilibrium' states between fluctuations are *non-capitalist*. If it be suggested that given the *ab ovo* approach adopted by Schumpeter, it is only the nature of the *'first'* circular-flow state that does not matter because the states during the business cycle will retain the capitalist features that appear as a consequence of motion, then the difficulty is only shifted. There is still no model to represent *this latter state* in his analyses. The simple fact of the matter is that all of the problems could have been avoided had he chosen a *steady* circular-flow model that is explicitly capitalist in the first place. There may be no real-world capitalism without motion that involves change, but change is the only feature that need be abstracted from in setting up the model with which such motion will be analysed. Marx's simple reproduction schema is a case in point that, as we have seen, Schumpeter chose to avoid.

4.4.2 Production

Schumpeter gave considerable attention to the nature and organization of the production process as the essential 'base' upon which the other dimensions of the circular flow are established. The rationale for this was his view that economic actions are directed primarily at material provisioning. Other processes that complete the circular flow must be consistent with the production requirements dictated by resource constraints and available technology in the short period. From a long period perspective, there will be a 'dynamic' interdependence between all the processes with independent changes in each demanding complementary changes elsewhere. In Schumpeter's theory of motion, the key changes that generate motion occur in the sphere of production.

There is a 'duality' in production that Schumpeter recognized, albeit in an indirect way. First and foremost, production is an engineering problem in the sense that it is about the physical, chemical, biological and locational transformation of natural resources into goods and services that human agents 'need' in some sense. The process is carried out by means of agents working with a given physical-technical production structure that embodies the technology in use. At one level, the organization of the working agents' actions is also dictated by the structure and technology. But here we begin to shade off into the second dimension of production comprising those operational characteristics that are determined by the socioeconomic system in which the production structure is situated. These must be consistent with the physical-technical demands of the structure, but beyond that, their format may vary widely. It is the capitalist mode of organizing production with which we are concerned here.

Schumpeter's analysis of this 'duality' was built into the *first* of what he referred to as the two 'sides' of production (*Development*, pp. 11ff.). The first 'side' comprises two dimensions that are 'data' for the analysis of production in the sense that they are 'outside the domain of economic theory': one is 'the physical properties of material objects and natural processes' and the other consists of the 'facts of social organisation' (ibid., p. 11). It is clear that 'natural processes' are given and can but be harnassed such as to 'make the most of them'. Schumpeter's position on physical means of production beyond those provided by nature was more ambivalent: 'How much of the realm of physical fact may be relevant to economics cannot be stated once [and] for all' (ibid.). Maybe so, but the immediate difficulty here is that the view of *produced* 'material objects' as 'data' cannot be carried beyond the steady circular-flow situation. Schumpeter's explanation of economic development depended upon innovations, including those that bring technological change to production requiring physical-structural alterations to be made. He was never really able to overcome the ambivalence referred to, even in this crucial context of innovation processes and the consequences that they entail.

The second dimension of 'data' for the analysis of production, the 'facts of social organisation', has been dealt with in some detail in Chapter 2 above on Schumpeter's vision of capitalism. For the purposes of all of his analyses of motion, the nature of the capitalist *order* remained as 'data', albeit with some internal 'evolution' of the system away from competition towards a dominance of monopoly power.

The other 'side' of production to which Schumpeter referred, focuses upon 'the concrete purpose of every act of production', namely 'the creation of useful things, of objects of consumption' (ibid., pp. 11, 12). He correctly considered this ultimately to be the reason 'why there is any production at all', although he did not note at this point that the reason may be made operational by different sorts of motivations in different socio-economic orders: in capitalism, the provisioning problem is solved as a means of generating profit. This aspect of production 'puts its stamp clearly on the method and volume of production' and is 'determining for the "what" and the "why" of production within the framework of given means and objective necessities' (ibid., pp. 11-12). What Schumpeter intended here was to separate the 'economic problem' of what commodities are effectively demanded and 'the purely technological problem' of the means whereby they will be produced (ibid., p. 12).

It is important to add, though, that he carefully considered the economics of the 'technological problem' as well. The existence of a particular mode of production can only be explained if its choice is understood as both a technological and an economic issue, with the latter concerns usually being dominant where any conflict between the two aspects is to be resolved. Whatever 'the half-artistic joy in technically perfecting the productive apparatus . . . in practical life we observe that the technical element must submit when it collides with the economic' (*ibid.*, p. 13; cf. *Cycles*, pp. 38-9). As a consequence of this overriding concern with the economics of production, the 'economic best and the technologically perfect need not, yet very often do, diverge . . . because methods which are technologically inferior may still best fit the given economic conditions' (*Development*, p. 15). The distinction was drawn by Schumpeter between two further agent functions in order to emphasize the way in which production choices are made. 'Managers' may look after 'technical' or 'commercial' matters, but the concerns of the latter are what must decide the choice of technology (ibid., pp. 12-13). In the present context of the circular-flow model, however, the introduction of the choice of technology problem is artificial, for once the model is operational, there are no choices to be made and no functions for the two 'managers' to perform. The matter does become important in the process of economic development when technological change is an integral part of the operations going on. But there, care is needed to avoid forgetting about the 'technical manager's' role altogether and treating the change as a purely economic matter for analytical convenience. What should not be overlooked is that the 'commercial manager's' ultimate decision must be implemented by the 'technical manager' and the latter's tasks are very much part of motion itself. The key presence of the entrepreneur may also tend to obscure these separate functional considerations. Technological change often means that structural and organizational adjustments must be made. That these take time and require particular inputs to be produced was not always given due prominence in Schumpeter's argument.

To return to the present concern with production *per se*, we note that Schumpeter perceived it as a process of transformation: 'Technologically as well as economically considered, production "creates" nothing in the physical sense.' Its purpose is rather to bring about 'all kinds of locational changes and changes . . . [through] mechanical, chemical, and other processes'. And, as the process can be described by the inputs that are used and the way they are combined, he posited the idea that 'to produce means to combine the things and forces within our reach' (ibid., p. 14; cf. *Cycles*, p. 38). The importance of this simple passage is that it gives expression to the idea of 'technology' as 'combinations' of inputs. Schumpeter was to make much use of this perception subsequently in his treatment of innovations as 'new combinations', broadly considered.

Table 4.1

$$n_{a1} \text{ U } t_{a1} \qquad \rightarrow \quad w_{a1}$$
$$n_{a2} \text{ U } t_{a2} \text{ U } w_{a1} \rightarrow \quad w_{a2}$$
$$n_{a3} \text{ U } t_{a3} \text{ U } w_{a2} \rightarrow \quad w_{a3}$$
$$n_{a4} \text{ U } t_{a4} \text{ U } w_{a3} \rightarrow \quad a$$

Schumpeter chose to adopt the 'Austrian' schema of production, attributed mainly to Böhm-Bawerk, when detailing the operational form of the process. This schema envisages the progressive 'vertical' transformation of 'higher order' inputs into 'lower order' goods. The integrated stages include natural 'land' inputs together with successive additions of labour services producing a final output of consumer commodities, with each producing unit fully self-contained and independent (*Development*, pp 16–17). Table 4.1 sets out the schema in physical terms.[2] A unit of final commodity a is produced over four stages from two inputs, 'land' services t and labour services n. Along the way, each stage is marked by the transitory appearance of a different intermediate good w. The symbol U means 'to combine with' and the arrows mean 'produces'.

There are some important characteristics of this schema that warrant careful scrutiny. First, it requires the assumption that it is somehow meaningful to 'resolve all [produced] goods into "labor and land" in the sense that we can conceive all [such] goods as bundles of the services of labor and land' (ibid., p.17). The practical difficulties of applying such an idea to the representation of a complex industrialized production system can be readily imagined. One defence for the use of such an approach is that it provides a model that is highly tractable for the application of mathematical methods. Because it avoids the need to include durable means of production, all changes in scale and technology can be readily dealt with in algebraic terms. There are no durable embodiments to deal with and any change to be analysed takes the form of reorganization. As Schumpeter did not constrain his analysis by imposing mathematical requirements, he could not have resorted to this defence. A further defence is that production does, in fact, involve time-consuming stages and intermediate goods and should, therefore, be portrayed as doing so. Certainly this is true, but for reasons that I will argue in a moment, this is no reason to exclude durable means of production from the analysis. There were, of course, occasions when Schumpeter's common sense led him to make explicit reference to such durable means (e.g. ibid., p. 45), especially when analysing motion proper. However, the model at the core of his analyses never wholly integrated them, and their extensive implications were never dealt with adequately.

Another problematical characteristic of the vertically-integrated model of production is its exclusive focus on final consumer commodities as outputs. No means of production, durable or otherwise, are produced for exchange and the fact that some inputs to all production must be bought outside the firm in a modern industrial system is thereby overlooked. Firms and industries are interdependent in this sense and an adequate model of the totality of production must make this clear. Again, the effect of avoiding this fact is to simplify the responses and adjustments that change brings. All aspects of change are made internal to the firm and no external ramifications need be traced. The result is an analysis of motion that profoundly understates the complexity of the traverses that comprise it.

What must remain a matter for speculation is the reason for Schumpeter's failure to discover in Marx's reproduction schema, and in the literature that applied and developed it, an alternative framework for the analysis of production that is immediately more in accordance with the common sense of an industrialized capitalist economy. I have already made reference to his contact with the Austrian Marxists and the lack of impact that their analyses had on his circular-flow model (see section 4.2 above). In 1926 Adolph Löwe (later Lowe) published a critical survey of the business cycle literature of the period (Löwe, 1926). Included was a critique of Schumpeter's own work (ibid., pp. 171, 180, 193–4, 197 and n). But, more importantly here, this was accompanied by some suggestive discussion of how the reproduction schema could provide a more appropriate alternative to the orthodox equilibrium model as the basis for working out a business cycle theory (ibid., pp. 185ff.). There can be little doubt that Schumpeter knew of the paper. He was aware of Löwe's work, having referred to a 1925 paper (Löwe, 1925) in the second edition of *Development* (p. 213) and the 1926 piece was published in one of the leading German journals of the era, *Weltwirtschaftliches Archiv*. A few years later, Löwe's insights were developed further by his colleague at Kiel University, Fritz Burchardt. In his 1931–32 two-part article published in the same journal, Burchardt worked out a reproduction schema that drew on the production models of Marx and Böhm-Bawerk (Burchardt, 1931–32). Once again, we cannot be sure that Schumpeter read the piece, but the probability must be high that he did. Later in his life, he referred to Burchardt's work in the *History* manuscript and even gave the paper cited here a passing mention (pp. 906n, 908, 927n). Burchardt's ideas were taken up by Ragnar Nurkse and published in the *Review of Economic Studies* in 1934–35 (Nurkse, 1934–35) and this is another source of potential influence that probably crossed Schumpeter's desk. All of these contributions appeared before the drafting of *Cycles* was complete, but he remained unimpressed. The circular-flow model at the core of the work retained the vertically-integrated view of production with all the same limitations that emerged in the *Development* version.

The sort of schema of production and reproduction that Schumpeter had available to him from the sources just discussed is shown in Table 4.2 and Figure 4.1. The former of these revises the Böhm-Bawerk version of Table 4.1 in one crucial respect. Along with the other input services and intermediate goods, there is now a flow of fixed means of production services f included at each stage. These latter originate in a 'depreciating' stock of durable means of production with which the a-producing firm operates. The last row in the table contains the four-stage 'aggregates' of the inputs required to produce a *unit* of a. Figure 4.1 situates the four-stage production process for a and two other commodities, b and x in a *physical*

Table 4.2

$n_{a1} \cup t_{a1} \cup f_{a1}$	$\rightarrow$	w_{a1}
$n_{a2} \cup t_{a2} \cup f_{a2} \cup w_{a1}$	$\rightarrow$	w_{a2}
$n_{a3} \cup t_{a3} \cup f_{a3} \cup w_{a2}$	$\rightarrow$	w_{a3}
$n_{a4} \cup t_{a4} \cup f_{a4} \cup w_{a3}$	$\rightarrow$	a
$n_a \cup t_a \cup f_a$	$\rightarrow$	a

reproduction schema.[3] Production is now represented at the industry level. The a industry produces means of production that will be used to produce other means of production; the b industry produces means of production that will be used to produce consumer commodities; and the consumer commodities are produced in industry x. The number of stages in the production process of each industry is maintained at four only for simplification. Replacement flows of fixed means of production are assumed to coincide with periodic depreciation rates. In this schema, the meaning of N_i should be read as the amount of x needed to sustain a flow of N_i labour sevices ($i = a$, b, x). I_i and Q_i are the inputs and outputs respectively. The T_i inputs of 'land' flow in from 'outside' the system, as it were, and the F_i means of production flows are produced in the appropriate industry and 'exported' in exchange for the required consumer commodities to sustain industry labour-power needs. The b industry 'imports' too much of the consumer commodities for its own use, but just enough to exchange the extra amount with the a industry for its F_b replacement needs. The a and x industries 'export' internally part of their own product.

The most obvious advantage of this alternative circular-flow schema is that it makes explicit the *physical* reproduction requirements in terms of input and output flows. It gives due prominence to the interdependence of the industries and sets the task for the socio-economic order of turning these requirements into operational objectives that must be met if steady circular flow is to be realized. In a capitalist economic system, this must be done through markets for each commodity and a vector of relative prices at which the required exchanges will be carried out. The use of money prices means that a 'dual' of the physical schema can be worked out in value terms, thus setting compounded conditions to be met. At least, a 'socially acceptable' commodity wage for labour power must be set by some institutional means, and its corresponding nominal value must be consistent with a rate of return on finance capital advanced in each

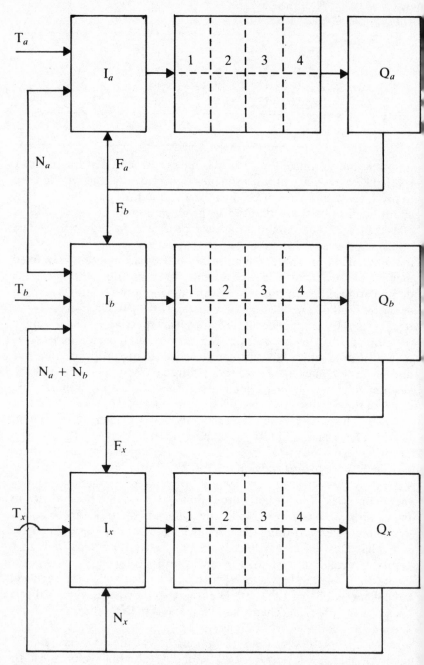

Figure 4.1   A physical circular-flow and reproduction schema.

sector that 'satisfies' the capitalists concerned. The latter will ensure that no inter-sector shifts of funds are induced. Under these conditions, the circular flow of reproduction can proceed at a constant scale over time. Beyond the steady circular-flow situation, the introduction of change into one industry of this model is shown to involve a reverberation of responses and adjustments in other industries. Motion can only then be explained fully by tracing out the traverse sequence of adjustments that ensues. By contrast, with full vertical integration in production, the introduction of a change will have much less complex traverse implications because most of its effects will be internal to the firms and only the relative values and/or quantities of consumer commodities will be affected externally, *cet. par.*

Sometimes Schumpeter sensed the need for some *elements* of this alternative perception in his analyses. In particular, at one point he made reference to two industries in the following passage: 'It . . . makes no difference to an individual firm whether it produces consumption or production goods. In both cases it disposes of its products in the same way. . . ' (*Development*, p. 45). Such an assertion makes no sense in terms of the vertically-integrated, consumer-commodity production schema that is at the base of his circular-flow model. 'Production goods' in that schema are *not* 'disposed of' in any way similar to what happens to consumer commodities. He nonetheless saw the existence of these two industries as consistent with 'the principle of a trading economy with division of labor' and he noted that production must be followed by an appropriate exchange and circulation of the commodities produced if the circular flow is to be maintained (ibid., p. 43). In the piece of analysis referred to here (ibid., pp. 42–3), the idea of the reproduction schema can be perceived very clearly. However, it was not Schumpeter's purpose to set up any alternative model of the circular-flow process. Rather, he wanted to reinforce his common-sense argument about the need for the continuous synchronization of output and consumption so that the 'element of time plays no part' in any explication of the circular flow, thus avoiding any need to analyse the 'period of production' idea or the problem of 'waiting' in the context of income distribution.

4.4.3 Income distribution

In Schumpeter's circular-flow model, the processes of income distribution and commodity exchange and circulation are facilitated by highly competitive markets. Both resource rents and commodity prices are set by the forces of supply and demand and individual agents are price takers in all markets in which they participate. The steady circular-flow state corresponds to a continuous clearing of all markets. Prices are a reflection of marginal utility and rents a reflection of marginal productivity, an assumption that Schumpeter stated quite explicity: 'all household prices must be proportional to marginal utilities of consumers' goods and . . . for all firms prices of producers' goods must be proportional to their marginal productivities' (*Development*, p. 41). Strictly speaking, the 'producers' goods' referred to here can only be the resources 'land' and labour power. I will consider income distribution as a resource rent issue in this subsection and turn to commodity pricing and circulation in the next.

Schumpeter initially sought to establish the relative status of 'land' and labour services as contributors to production and the implications of that status for valuing each in the process of income distribution. He reasoned that because neither is demanded for its own sake, these services can only be valued by their contribution to the production of commodities that do have value. That is, their values must be *imputed* to them, giving rise to an imputation theory of the demand price for 'land' and labour services (ibid., pp. 23ff.). And, 'on the basis of this imputed value they receive their place in each economic scheme' (ibid., p. 24). As far as their relative status in the process of imputation is concerned, Schumpeter argued that neither had any claim to precedence: 'productive factors practically always operate together', they are 'equally indispensable in production' and, as they are both 'economised' in the face of scarcity, the fact that labour is 'active' while 'land' is 'passive' is irrelevant (ibid., pp. 23, 19). How can each be valued separately, then?

The key to the solution of the imputation problem was, for Schumpeter, marginal productivity. He saw this proposition as 'hardly a controversial one in modern theory' and states its import quite explicitly: in the established steady circular-flow situation, 'under free competition landlord and laborer receive the product of their means of production' as their respective shares in the 'total social product' (ibid., p. 25). From this perspective, the prices realized for each commodity must be 'equal to the prices of the services of labor and nature embodied in them' and, therefore, 'no product can so far show a surplus value over the value of the services of labor and land contained in it' (ibid., p. 30). Thus, because all realized commodity value can be traced back to 'land' and labour service inputs in accordance with the imputation principle, 'production "creates" no values, that is in the course of the productive process no increase in value occurs' (ibid., p. 29).

Quite clearly, this sort of approach to input valuation and income distribution was in accordance with Schumpeter's concept of production in the circular-flow model. In particular, there was no scope for any income that could be called profit because no agent provides the 'service' of owning produced means of production. Even the need for working capital is avoided by the argument that outlays on inputs by those 'workers' doing the 'directing' of production are fully co-ordinated with the revenue flows from commodity sales: 'the circular flow, once established, leaves no gaps between outlay or productive effort and the satisfaction of wants' and there is no need for producers to '"wait" for the regular returns, since one receives them as a matter of course just when they are needed'. Schumpeter explicitly denied that capital is required to bring about this 'synchronisation' of outlays and returns, *contra* J. B. Clark's argument. But, just how this can be brought about '*automatically* . . . under the accelerating and retarding influence of profit and loss', as Schumpeter cryptically asserted, was never made clear (ibid., p. 38 and n, original emphasis; cf. *Cycles*, p. 40).

So it was, then, that Schumpeter found himself confronting the apparent paradox that his circular-flow model of capitalism 'in its most perfect condition should operate without profit' (*Development*, p. 31). He contrasted this with the empirical observation that it 'seems obvious that producers do as a rule receive more than wages for their labor and rent for the land they may possess' and asked as a consequence: 'Will there not be a general rate of net profit in the sense of a surplus above costs?' (ibid.). A possible response, he thought, could be: 'Competition may wash away the particular surplus profit of an industry, but it could not destroy profits common to all branches of production' (ibid.). But what this amounted to was really a 'straw man' to be knocked down, for Schumpeter had assumed away any grounds for expecting such a profit in his circular-flow model, whatever may be the real-world position. There were simply no durable produced means of production, no capitalist agents to own them and so, no ownership income to be derived from any claim to a share in the value 'produced'. Had these been included, as we could reasonably expect in a *capitalist* circular flow, then the so-called 'paradox' would have disappeared. One does not have to be a Marxist to face up to the fact that if finance capital is outlaid to establish a means of production stock, the capitalists concerned will expect and receive some 'satisfactory' rate of return in a *viable* steady circular-flow state. Schumpeter was led to bypass this logic of capitalism because of the design of his model.

The remaining component of capitalist income distribution, namely interest on borrowed finance capital used for productive purposes, was treated by Schumpeter as quite a separate issue. Its origin is to be found in the money market and it is paid out of profits that are generated as a result of the processes of motion. In the steady circular-flow state, there can be no accumulation of funds and there is no need for credit from any source. The rate of interest is thus either zero or, perhaps better, simply treated as non-existent. Schumpeter's theory of interest will be dealt with more fully as part of the analysis of the monetary dimension of economic development in Chapter 7 below (see section 7.1).

4.4.4   Commodity circulation

Commodity exchange and circulation, together with the counterflows of money revenues, comprise the most obvious manifestations of the circular flow in operation: they 'constitute in their totality the external form of the circular flow of economic life' (ibid., p. 41). As *real* phenomena, their purpose is to mediate between production and consumption to ensure the delivery of commodities to their appropriate destinations in accordance with the effective demand pattern generated by tastes, technology and income distribution (ibid., p. 45). It was in *Cycles* that Schumpeter gave most attention to the details of this side of the processes.

In the circular-flow model, 'the prices and quantities of all goods and services are *interdependent* and form a *system*' and it is the 'first and foremost task of economic analysis . . . to explore the properties of that system' (*Cycles*, p. 41, original emphasis). Moreover, proof that this system can exist in a state of general equilibrium and thus realize a steady circular-flow state 'is the magna charta of economic theory as an autonomous science, assuring us that its subject matter is a cosmos and not a chaos' (ibid.). It was particularly the Walrasian form of general equilibrium that Schumpeter referred to as 'the only strictly correct one' for his version of the circular flow (ibid., pp. 42–3).

The existence of such a general equilibrium manifestation of the circular flow he realized was dependent upon some quite strict conditions and constraints. It is necessary that the economy comprise a large number of agents who act wholly independently of each other and without being able consciously to affect commodity prices or resource rents. All resources must be mobile across the entire system and fully adaptable to any line of production without friction or cost. Household and firm outlay budgets and incomes from full-employ-

ment market rents must exactly balance and all produced commodities must be sold thereby leaving no effective demand unsatisfied
(ibid., pp. 42–3, 46). Schumpeter was aware, though, that he was
only outlining some necessary conditions for general equilibrium and
that the sufficient conditions in the context of the simultaneous-
equation expression of the model were much more stringent than
Walras had realized. At the same time, he warned against reading
only mathematical conditions into the model without adequate
concern for their economic meaning (ibid., p. 46n).

Schumpeter was also concerned to analyse the *monetary* 'dual' of
the real commodity exchange and circulation flows. 'Thus', he wrote
in *Development*, 'corresponding to the stream of goods there is a
stream of money, the direction of which is opposite to that of the
stream of goods, and the movements of which, upon the assumption
that no increase of gold or any other one-sided change occurs, are
only reflexes of the movement of goods' (p. 55). The focus here is on
money as a medium of exchange and a means of circulation. And,
while in principle any *form* of money – metal (commodity), fiat or
credit (bills of exchange) – could equally well perform these functions, Schumpeter concentrated only upon the use of metal money as
the least complicated means available (ibid., pp. 47ff., *passim*). His
idea was to emphasize that in the circular-flow state, facilitating
commodity flows is the only function performed by money. The effect
of using money is only one of increased convenience because 'it is
clear that the essential lines of our picture are not altered by the
insertion of intermediate links, that money only performs the function of a technical instrument, but adds nothing new to the phenomena . . .'. He concluded that 'money *thus far* represents only the
cloak of economic things and nothing essential is overlooked in
abstracting from it' (ibid., p. 51, emphasis added; cf. pp. 49n, 53).

The emphasis on *'thus far'* is to indicate that Schumpeter was well
aware that this was not the limit to money's role in the capitalist
economic system. Beyond the circular-flow state, money exists also as
'non-circulating' stocks accumulated for the purpose of lending and
transferring ownership of assets (ibid., pp. 52ff.). These do not
appear in the circular flow because there is no access to accumulation
where all income is assumed to be spent immediately on consumption
commodity purchases. He reasoned, though, that the essential nature
of the established circular flow would not be changed by including
some saving that would facilitate transfers of land ownership and
consumer credit transactions. However, the important argument is
that accumulations and advances of credit for *productive* purposes are

not required in order to maintain the steady circular flow as Schumpeter perceived it. Only when motion due to change is introduced do money as an asset and credit money become necessary parts of the operations. Money in this context will reappear in my exposition at the appropriate point below (see Chapter 7, section 7.2).

4.5 Summary

The model of the circular flow of economic life was central to Schumpeter's theory of motion. In this chapter, the nature and construction of the model have been considered.

1. Three methodological principles applied by Schumpeter provide the analytical setting for the model: first, motion is appropriately analysed by devising a steady-state representation of the capitalist system in the absence of any change; secondly, changes that induce motion can be added into this steady state and their particular effects traced; and thirdly, the totality of motion can be formally represented as separable dimensions isolated according to their causal origins in the particular changes introduced into the steady state.

2. While he recognized the Physiocratic origins of the circular-flow idea, Schumpeter chose to overlook Marx's reproduction-schema version of it in favour of using the Walrasian general equilibrium format as the centrepiece of his theory of motion. This decision will be argued to have placed unnecessary impediments in the way of the realization of the potential insights of the theory.

3. Schumpeter's circular-flow model was worked out around a fully vertically-integrated conception of the production process, in which 'raw' labour power and 'land' inputs are progressively transformed into final consumer commodities via stages in which intermediate goods are produced and fully used up. He neglected the specialized status of different sectors of production and their interdependence as manifested in the inter-sector circulation of both produced means of production and consumer commodities. The consequence of his approach was that he went into his theory of motion with an analytically convenient core model, but one which grossly understated the complexities with which any realistic theory would have to contend.

Notes

1. See Goodwin, 1988, for some recent thinking about the Walras-Schumpeter relation.
2. This table format was devised by Adolph Lowe: see Lowe, 1976, pp. 27–8.
3. The suggestion that some important analytical insights could come from dividing

the means of production producing sector into the two subsectors shown was made by Adolph Löwe in his 1926 paper (1926, p. 190n) and developed in two important contributions to the structural analysis of motion in the 1950s (1987, Essays 1 and 2). The fullest exposition of a model of motion based on this production structure is in Löwe, 1976.

5 The nature of economic motion

5.1 From circular flow to motion

When I introduced the circular flow model in the previous chapter, I argued that Schumpeter applied three methodological principles in his analysis of motion. The effect of these principles was to facilitate the move analytically from the circular flow context into the processes of economic development and business cycles and to enable this to be done more clearly by keeping the component dimensions of motion as an observed totality separate when working up the analysis. In particular, the steady circular flow state in which change is absent has been isolated and the conditions for its viable reproduction over time considered. It is now time to analyse the nature of motion by applying the second and third principles to the effect that the generation of motion can be represented by adding a particular change into the circular flow and that the particular dimension of the total process that will result can be linked directly to the form of that change.

Schumpeter effectively isolated three dimensions of motion induced by change. First, he identified the strictly *quantitative* expansion (or contraction) of economic activity as a separate dimension attributable to saving and capital accumulation and/or to population growth. This 'pure' economic growth phenomenon was largely abstracted from in his analysis for reasons that I will discuss in due course. The primary focus of his theory was rather the second dimension that can be isolated namely economic development (called evolution in *Cycles*) that flows from *qualitative* changes that affect the input- and/or output-related operations of production. These changes he referred to as new combinations or innovations. It was the isolation of this second dimension of motion that effectively entailed the separation of the third. Schumpeter's argument was that the realized *form* of economic development is unstable over time due to the discontinuous impact of waves of innovative activity. This instability manifests itself as distinct business cycle units that follow each other in temporal succession. It is clear that Schumpeter understood that this stylized dissection of the empirical motion process could only be a preliminary analytical step. The mainline of the reintegration requirement more or less took care of itself in his analysis because the steady circular-flow, economic development and business-cycle dimensions were worked up in a sequence with the final stage embodying the other two. This left the first dimension economic growth, in isolation, but this was a result that he could justify by reference to the consciously incomplete nature of his theoretical analysis (see Chapter 1, section 1.1 above). From time to time, though, he did approach the problem of integrating growth into his main analyses, but with no formalized result. In my critique, I will argue that in any endeavour to comprehend motion, this step should not have been treated as optional and that Schumpeter's so doing stemmed from his gross underestimation of the complex and potentially destabilizing nature of 'pure' growth.

There is possibly more to this isolation of the different dimensions of motion than is expressed by making it a methodological point as I have done above. In his most recent book, that erudite scholar of the essentials of matters economic, Robert L. Heilbroner, draws attention to what he calls the 'clash of two opposing and indeed incompatible depictions of the capitalist process' in Schumpeter's work (1988, pp. 167 and ff.). One is the circular flow of economic life in which the essence of capitalism is routine and stability. In this 'depiction', agents do not pursue advantage and their behaviour is directed towards maintaining and preserving the collective economic status quo. As a stark contrast to this, there is the 'depiction' of capitalism that centres on the 'perennial gale of creative destruction', as Schumpeter so aptly put it (*Capitalism*, p. 84; quoted in Heilbroner, 1988, p. 170). Now some of the constituent agents act to gain an economic advantage over their fellows by innovating. They thereby disturb the otherwise tranquil circular flow and cause stresses and strains that reverberate throughout much of the economic system leaving it forever changed. A new steady circular flow may be restored, but only to be disrupted again by the 'perennial gale'.

The point to be emphasized about this dual perception of capitalism is that it brings a substantive aspect to the separation of the circular flow from development and business cycles and, to some extent, to the separation of economic growth from development. As Schumpeter noted, there is in the former separation a reflection of the practical decisions and behaviour of 'businessmen'. He wrote in *Cycles* that: 'Every businessman realizes that running his plant in the customary way, going through all the motions of daily business routine, is one thing and that setting up the plant or changing its set-up is another. He approaches these tasks with attitudes which differ characteristically from each other' (p. 37). The implication for analysis of this substantive distinction is that even though often in 'real life' these two aspects of business behaviour must be handled by the agent simultaneously, there would be 'no object in trying to fuse into one schema the things to be done and the behavioristic types [of agents] encountered in the two cases . . .' (ibid., cf. p. 50n).

More broadly perceived, the actual structures and operations of the system can also be seen to comprise the juxtaposition and integration of the circular flow and development. A basic requirement for the continuing viability of the capitalist economy is that its essentials must be reproducible both in the absence and presence of change. Where change is going on, some purely reproduction processes must still proceed to the extent that the diffused effects of change do not reach into every corner of the system. That is, some agents and their environment will be left untouched by a particular episode of change. But, more significantly, one facet of the process of change itself must be the preservation of a core of continuity within the economic entities affected. The interaction of reproduction and change is highly complex. Schumpeter largely avoided addressing the problem by arguing that the initiators of change, the innovating entrepreneurs, enter the circular flow as isolated *additional* agents who establish *new* operations in order to implement their new combinations. The effects soon spread, though, and the problem referred to here must then be confronted by the analyst. Schumpeter's analysis did not often reach into the details of these diffusion processes.

Along much the same lines, it is possible to perceive economic development and economic growth as forms of motion that are juxtaposed and must, therefore, be managed consistently. They have different, albeit simultaneously occurring, causes and effects and may well be independent of each other in reality as the methodological separation applied by Schumpeter suggests. Firms do make decisions to undertake investment in purely quantitative capacity expansions that involve little or no qualitative change. And, marginal and separate productive capacity may be established through decisions that pursue purely qualitative change. The extent of such separation is an empirical matter, but whatever it is, the analyst is faced with explaining how the two phenomena, growth and development, interact as they proceed.

In the end, whether the multi-dimensional treatment of motion is purely a methodological device or a reflection of the reality of the total phenomenon itself, what has to be explained is an observed empirical unity. The statistical time series of aggregate economic performance, however measured, is a compound outcome of all dimensions. Analytical dissection for the purposes of explanation cannot be an end in itself and a complete theory will include argument about how the components can be re-integrated to represent the totality of motion. As I will make apparent in later chapters, Schumpeter left this as unfinished business for his successors to deal with.

Analytically, what was of most direct concern to Schumpeter was the separation of the steady circular-flow state from the process of economic development that reflects the distinction that he drew between the nature and degree of possible adjustment demands placed on the system by different sorts of change. On one level are more or less continuous changes of a limited degree and extent. These, he argued, are capable of being absorbed by means of incremental adaptations and adjustments within the circular-flow model without great disturbance. Routine administrative behaviours by economic agents can be modified suffi-ciently to respond to the needs of change and the structures and operations of the existing circular flow are left essentially intact. Such changes, according to Schumpeter's often repeated assertion, requires no special analytical treatment beyond that possible within available orthodox equilibrium models (e.g. *Development*, pp. 8–9, 22, 40, 61, 62–3, 81n; *Essays*, pp. 59–60). This led him to conclude that this level of changes can be of little interest to an analyst concerned to comprehend and explain the unstable motion of capitalism that manifests itself as business cycles. And, as a consequence, he personally ruled out any detailed interest in economic growth originating in capital accumulation and population increases (e.g. *Development*, pp. 63, 68; *Cycles*, pp. 98–9; *Essays*, pp. 25, 59–60, 136) or in the effects of minor and continuous cases of technological change (e.g. *Development*, pp. 65–6, 81; *Essays*, p. 32).

By contrast, on another level altogether, are changes of an extensive and discontinuous nature that have sufficient initial and cumulative impact on the circular flow to disrupt and distort its structures and operations beyond marginal repair. In these cases, the tenets of received equilibrium theory cannot cope. Schumpeter found that its tools 'fail . . . where economic life itself changes its own data by fits and starts' and that it is 'unable to predict the consequences of discontinuous changes in the traditional way of doing things . . .' (*Development*, p. 62). A revised approach to theoretical argument was needed, he thought, to deal with 'revolutionary' forces that generate a disturbance 'which forever alters and displaces the equilibrium state previously existing' to the extent that a new equilibrium '*cannot be reached from the old one by infinitesimal steps*' (ibid., p. 64 and n, original emphasis). His view that received theory 'can only investigate the new equilibrium position after the changes have occurred' (ibid., p. 63) suggests that what is of concern in the analysis of these disturbances as the bases of motion are the *transition processes* that carry the economy from one

steady circular-flow state to the next, altered one. The fundamenta
sequence that we will find Schumpeter developing is, then, stead
circular-flow state → disturbed disequilibrium state → adaptive anc
adjustment processes → new, revised steady circular-flow state.

Reference to this sequential form of analysis suggests that ideally
Schumpeter should have centred his argument around the phenomeno
of the traverse. A traverse can be most generally defined as a set o
sequential and parallel processes of adjustment that take place when a
economic system changes from one state to another through real
historical time. It involves quantitative and qualitative changes o
varying degrees, extents and durations and it involves and affects th
structural and/or the organizational cum operational characteristics o
the economy. Its constituent processes can follow any temporal patter
that results from the reactions of human agents to the change or change
that impinge upon the initial state of the economy and generate th
traverse. Two particular abstractions involved in setting up a travers
analysis should be noted. First, the initial and final states of th
economy must be specified in analytically manageable terms, either a
equilibria of some sort or as clearly defined disequilibria. Secondly, th
time period of the traverse must be specified such that all the relevan
adjustment processes are completed within its limits. These two require
ments force what is essentially a continuous process of flux comprising
constantly overlapping sequences of events into a very restricted 'box'
Confining the duration of the processes to a prescribed limit and arguing
them all to be complete at the end of the period are extreme
abstractions made necessary by the needs of analytical tractability. It i
also worth noting that there is no definable empirically-representative
traverse *ex ante* because the end state is a function of the path taken tc
reach it. That path will be affected by a myriad of factors about which
we can only form expectations, at best, and can know nothing at all, a
worst, before they appear. The traverse framework suggested above i
only suitable in certain particular circumstances: first for *ex post*
explanations when the final state is defined; secondly, for plotting
alternative imaginary scenarios for realizing a given (perhaps desired)
end state from a given initial state; or thirdly, for devising the imaginary
end state that would result from a particular traverse when the initia
state is given.

Schumpeter's analysis comprises a confusing mixture of the first and
third of these. He sets out from a 'neighborhood' of steady circular-flow
equilibrium to argue his way towards a new, undefined similar state with
different characteristics via a disequilibrium period. The general 'direction' of the traverse (or sequence of traverses if some interim 'end'

states are specified, as may be the case in a multi-phase business cycle unit) is known and the constituent events to be analysed can be identified on this basis, but the new near-steady state can only have its details specified once the *particulars* and *emphases* of the traverse arguments are known. As he put it, the initial circular-flow state provides an '*apparatus of response*' which will 'determine how any given change in data will be absorbed by the economic system and what final results will eventually emerge' (*Cycles*, p. 68, original emphasis). This emphasizes the point that the causality runs from the absorption traverse to the end state that emerges (cf. ibid, pp. 48, 49), but it leaves indefinite much of the particularity of the traverse detail that would be required if the explanation of the motion dimension involved is to be complete. It will become apparent from my critique in later chapters that most of Schumpeter's business cycle theory is characterized by this imprecision in the handling of the traverse phenomenon.

5.2 Equilibrium and motion

It is appropriate here to consider more carefully the epistemological status that Schumpeter ascribed to the equilibrium steady circular-flow state that always remained at the core of his analysis of motion. His belief was that to be useful, the concept had to be, at least potentially, a reflection of an equivalent real-world state. The point of contact that we have already seen him argue is between the theoretical version and the 'normal' business situation (Chapter 4, section 4.3 above). To reiterate, his claim was that the 'theoretical norm, however distant it may be from actual life, is what renders to the theorist the service which to the businessman is rendered by the idea of a normal business situation. Logically purified, the latter concept merges into the former' (*Cycles*, p. 45; cf.p. 4). Moreover, the theoretical logic that ensures that the circular-flow equilibrium will be restored if it is disturbed should also replicate, at least, a real-world *tendency*. The common sense of this idea in relation to the business cycle was posited by Schumpeter as the fact that because, at times, business conditions are 'abnormally high' and, at other times, 'abnormally low', there must be somewhere in between that can be considered 'normal'. Thus, periods of deviation away from the 'normal' must be followed by periods in which there is a drawing back to the 'normal' (ibid., p. 70). 'What matters to us', he concluded, 'is precisely the presence or absence of an actual tendency in the system to move toward a state of equilibrium: if this concept is to be useful as a tool of business-cycle analysis, the economic system must strive to reestablish equilibrium whenever it has been disturbed or . . . it must tend to move, in reaction to every disturbance, *in such a way as to absorb the change* [that caused it]' (ibid., p. 47, original emphasis). Indeed, in actual fluctuations, the restoration of full equilibrium 'may fail to come about at all and . . ., therefore, new disturbances [may] always impinge on an imperfectly equilibrated system'. Schumpeter claimed that for his purposes, this does not matter as 'the existence of a tendency toward perfect equilibrium . . . [will] serve to explain many actual processes, even if . . . [the system] never reaches its goal – which is all we want' (ibid., p. 48). In these passages, the rationale for the 'neighborhood of equilibrium' idea to which he switched in *Cycles* is made clear.

For Schumpeter, the relevant theoretical equilibrating mechanism was that embraced in what he called 'the Walras-Edgeworth schema' (ibid., p. 50, cf. pp. 47, 49). The general premise of this schema is that under conditions of perfect competition, the price and quantity responses of agents affected by disequilibrium are such as to lead collectively to a correction of the situation (ibid., p. 47). Taking off from this premise, Schumpeter was quite comfortable with its extrapolation, *with qualifications of various sorts*, to the real world in which it is assumed some 'adequate' degree of competition is maintained (ibid., pp. 47ff). That is, the qualifications that he saw it appropriate to make were not of a kind that negate the effectiveness of competitive market-theoretic forces – it should be recalled that his treatment of imperfect competition and the accompanying monopoly power of economic agents was largely separated from the mainframe of his concept of capitalism (see Chapter 2, section 2.3 above). As far as he was concerned, our common sense 'tells us that this mechanism for establishing or reestablishing equilibrium is not a figment devised as an exercise in the pure logic of economics but [is] *actually operative in the reality around us*' (ibid., p. 47, emphasis added). The common sense alluded to here was probably the fact of the recurring restoration of 'normal' business situations in response to 'abnormal' deviations. That is, for all its observed instability, the capitalist economic system should, Schumpeter thought, be perceived as maintaining some degree of order at its core. This applied especially to the empirically-relevant form of capitalism on which he claimed to be focusing in *Cycles*: 'within the period covered by our material . . . [perfect competition] affords a sufficiently close approximation to reality in many cases . . . in others the actual patterns, although not fulfilling requirements, yet work in a way not fundamentally differing from the working of perfect competition' (ibid., p. 46n).

The qualifications which the real world imposes on an otherwise perfectly competitive environment were cited by Schumpeter as various sorts of 'frictions' and 'lags' in the market mechanism along with some 'stickiness' of certain key variables and the phenomenon of uncertainty. There could be frictions and lags in the adjustment processes if, for example, there are inflexibilities in the technology of production, if producing agents do not respond immediately to price signals or if there exist adjustment costs in the shifting of resources required by change (ibid., pp. 48–9). The coordination problem involved in restoring equilibrium is compounded when, as is likely, these frictions and lags apply unevenly across the economy (ibid., pp. 50–51). Stickiness of key variables, especially prices, sometimes ranging up to short-term rigidity, can arise from any source that gives individual or group agents some control over the market. In particular, 'willful stickiness' is evident when governments control prices or where firms with monopoly power set the ruling price in a particular market. Such interference in free markets could also bring a stickiness to resource rents, especially wages, and result in unemployment that persists (ibid., p. 52).

It is worth noting, though, that Schumpeter distinguished these impediments to market adjustments from the time lags inherent in the normal processes of adaptation and adjustment that are required to restore equilibrium. The latter do not represent any dysfunction of the market system (ibid., p. 51 and n). In drawing this distinction, perhaps he recalled some of his 'Austrian' heritage with its emphasis on markets as *processes*, the constitution of which affects the temporal and quantitative profiles of the adjustments towards equilibrium as well as the precise format of the equilibrium realized (ibid., pp. 48–9). His expressed preference, though, was for Walras's *prix crié par hazard* and *par tâtonnement* and Edgeworth's recontracting as mechanisms for restoring equilibrium. These were somewhat more precise than the 'Austrian' processes, but also less practical in their relevance.

Once we leave the world of the steady circular-flow state, Schumpeter realized that economic agents are forced to cope with uncertainty about future events and the course of the effects of their actions. The significant point is that '[u]ncertainty of the future course of events gives rise, to be sure, to many phenomena that are very important for any realistic study of business cycles . . .' (ibid., p. 54). Uncertainty leads agents to form expectations as one of the inputs to their decision making. The results then may be positive or negative *vis-à-vis* the market equilibration process. Thus, while in some circumstances, 'expectations may open up a shortcut toward a definite (though possibly different) equilibrium state', in others it is 'obvious from common experience, that action on certain types of expectation may be disruptive and helps to drive the system away from equilibrium' (ibid.). For the analyst, the problem raised by the need to identify carefully the effects of expectations is twofold: how do agents form them; and how are the expectations so formed to be included in economic analysis? Schumpeter's reading was that more often than not, where expectations were recognized in analysis at all, they were treated as 'ultimate data', a solution that partially answers only the second question. In some cases, the first question was addressed by citing expected values 'which simply project into the future the actual rate of change of some quantity . . .' (ibid.). As a more sophisticated version of this projection method, Schumpeter specified close to what would today be referred to as an 'adaptive expectations' mechanism: in making a decision affecting the future, agents are said to 'take account of the past, present, and expected future values of any economic variables they believe to be relevant, weighting those values by weights that in general rapidly decrease to zero in function of distance from the time of the decision' (ibid., p. 55). A generous (or ungenerous, as the reader wishes) reading may even allow here a hint of 'rational expectations', for the weighted variables taken into account extend beyond the dependent variable itself to others that the agents 'believe to be relevant', perhaps in some functionally defined way.

The most significant thing about Schumpeter's reflections on the problem of expectations is the general methodological insight that he formulated. It underpins modern 'rational expectations' endeavours, but its relevance goes beyond to the whole unsolved (unsolvable, more probably) problem of expectations in economic analysis. He first outlined his view in his review of Keynes's *General Theory* in 1936. There is one piece that is worth quoting at length here.

> The emphasis on *expected* as against *actual* values is in line with modern tendencies. But expectations are not linked by Mr Keynes to the cyclical situations that give rise to them and hence become independent variables and ultimate determinants of economic action. Such analysis can at best yield purely formal results and never go below the surface. An expectation acquires explanatory value only if we are made to understand *why* people expect *what* they expect. Otherwise expectation is a mere *deus ex machina* that conceals problems instead of solving them. (*Essays*, p. 154n, original emphasis.)

He repeated the argument in *Cycles* (p. 55) and at the same time warned that the introduction of expectations as an endogenous variable would 'change the whole character of . . . [the analyst's] problem' and make it 'technically . . . difficult to handle.' Perhaps for this reason, together with the general intractability of the problem of explaining expectations formation and his reluctance to repeat what he saw as Keynes's shortcomings in the matter, Schumpeter had little more to say about it. In particular, he made no attempt to bring uncertainty and expectations formally into his analyses of motion in the way that the above passages suggested.

5.3 The causal origins of motion

I have argued above that one of the methodological principles applied by Schumpeter in his theoretical analysis was that the generation of motion can be represented by 'adding' some change to an existing steady circular-flow equilibrium (Chapter 4, section 4.1). The form of the traverse that ensues, as the effects of the change are diffused and absorbed by the system, is then primarily a *function of* the particular change that is introduced, *cet. par.* In order to implement this principle and to target the particular forms of motion that he wanted to explain, Schumpeter first worked through a taxonomy of causal categories.

At the most general level, he distinguished between changes that arise from *external* sources and those that arise from *internal* sources. His reading was that in most of the extensions of orthodox theory to a consideration of motion, only the former category of causes is considered. This reflected the assumption that 'economic life is essentially passive and merely adapts itself to the natural and social influences which may be acting on it . . .' As a result, economic theorists 'cannot say much about the factors that account for historical change but must simply register them' (*Essays*, pp. 159–60). From amongst his antecedents, he recorded that Marx was one of the few exceptions (*Development*, p. 59n) and his intention was to emulate Marx's focus on internally-generated changes as the 'source of energy . . . propelling the economic system from one equilibrium to another' (*Essays*, p. 160). Indeed, he went on later, 'it stands to reason [that] we must try to abstract from [external factors] when working out an explanation of the causation of economic fluctuations properly so called . . .' (*Cycles*, p. 7).

Two preliminary comments are called for regarding this external-internal dichotomy. First, external factors are predominantly and most obviously of an extra-economic character as signalled by the reference to 'natural and social influences' in the quotation above. This need not be the case, though, for some 'purely economic' forces may not be able to be explained in terms endogenous to any model with analytically reasonable 'economic' boundaries. It all depends upon the *scope* of the circular-flow model that the analyst sees fit to handle and this is the second comment that needs to be made here. The distinction is, then, an arbitrary one (cf. ibid., p. 7n) and it is self-evident that a model with a broad reach will include potential motion-inducing factors that would be classified as external to a model with more limited scope. The arbitrari-

ness is not total, however, because relevant natural phenomena will
stand outside all models. The general point being made here about the
problematics of separating internal and external factors will be found to
be pertinent to my discussion of Schumpeter's treatment of innovations
as the causal basis of economic development in the next chapter.

Schumpeter reasoned that 'social' factors, including psychological
institutional and political influences should be accorded external status
as a consequence of his attempt to maintain a purely *economic* analysis
(*Cycles*, pp. 6ff., 72ff.). Some more specific external factors cited were
business fluctuations in other countries, gold discoveries and produc
tion, discoveries of new countries and inventions. The last two of these
have particular relevance to his classification of 'new combinations' and
they will be referred to again in that context (section 5.4 below). He also
chose to treat population increases and demographic changes as exter
nal factors in spite of their strong economic links and implications.

Schumpeter's rationale for separating off the external factors was not
to reject or diminish their significance as causes and conditions of
motion. On the contrary, he wrote that 'they are always important and
sometimes dominant, and that the *response* of the system to their impact
must always be expected to account for a great part of the economic
changes we observe, . . . [and] also that their occurrence may and often
does *condition* [internal] changes . . .' (ibid., p. 72, original emphasis,
cf. *Development*, p. 223). And here he reinforced his earlier obser
vation that there are 'instances covering considerable stretches of our
[time-series] material, in which effects of external factors entirely
overshadow everything else, either in the behavior of individual ele
ments of business situations or in the behavior of business situations as a
whole' (*Cycles*, p. 12). Already in *Development*, Schumpeter had
assessed briefly the possible effects of external factors and concluded
that they 'very frequently explain crises' and he even granted that 'the
view is conceivable . . . that crises are always effects of external
circumstances' (pp. 220, 221).

But, whatever the impact of external factors may be, I have already
indicated that it was Schumpeter's intention to set them aside. He
wanted to break with the response-centred idea of motion and search
for its causes inside the structures and operations of the capitalist
economic system (*Development*, pp. 222–3; *Essays*, pp. 159–60). Hence
he wrote that 'after discarding all extraneous causes of crises [i.e.,
fluctuations] we find still others which are of a purely economic
character in the sense that they arise from within the economic system
. . .' (*Development*, p. 222). Common-sense observation confirmed for
him that 'there would be economic change even in the absence of any

external factor or, to put it differently, that besides factors acting on the business situation, there are also factors in it which make for what we may call *autonomous change*' (*Cycles*, p. 14, original emphasis).

Three such internal factors were of immediate concern to Schumpeter: consumers' tastes, the quantity (or quality) of factors of production and the method of supplying commodities. Consumers' tastes were rejected by Schumpeter as irrelevant to an understanding of the economic development process. He wrote quite explicitly in *Development* that the internal forces with which he was concerned were the spontaneous and discontinuous changes in the channel of the circular flow and . . . [the] disturbances of the centre of equilibrium [that appear] in the sphere of industrial and commercial life, not in the sphere of the wants of the consumers of final products' (p. 65). His choice here to neglect any spontaneity of consumers' needs that may actually exist, and assume tastes as "given"', meant that tastes, too, joined the growing list of data for the economic system which, when they change, elicit only adaptive responses (ibid.). Tastes are an important input in setting up the circular-flow model, but unimportant when analysing the changes of the type that interested Schumpeter. Consumers, he argued, play essentially a passive role in any process of change in that the producer . . . as a rule initiates economic change,and consumers are educated by him if necessary . . .' (ibid.). In *Cycles*, his argument about consumers was very similar and their tastes remained as data, with any unilateral changes therein being absorbed without significant disruption to the circular flow (pp. 73–4).

The rubric of changes in the quantity (or quality) of factors of production is rather more complex to deal with. Schumpeter divided it up into two components, namely increases in population and increases in the stock of producers' goods (*Cycles*, pp. 74ff.). And, even though he granted that such changes 'might at first sight appear to be the obvious prime mover in the process of internal economic change' (ibid., p. 74), both its components were destined to join the list of *data* with no significance for motion as he was concerned to present it (e.g. *Development*, pp. 59n, 63, 71; *Essays*, p. 160). His decision to give population growth an external status was mentioned above and will not be considered further here. It is the increase of the means of production stock that we must focus on in an endeavour to understand how Schumpeter came to leave it aside in his explanation of motion.

The increase in productive resources involved in the process of economic growth was variously referred to by Schumpeter as an increase in capital (*Development*, p. 59n), the growth of wealth (ibid., p. 63), an increase in savings (*Essays*, p. 160) and an increase in the stock of *durable* producers' goods (*Cycles*, p. 75). The important dimension of the growth process, though, is that it appears as an expansion of productive capacity and final output due wholly to a quantitative increase in the resources used in production. This occurs in isolation from any change in the qualitative aspects of production, most especially from productivity changes due to embodied or disembodied technological change. Here I consider first Schumpeter's general attitude towards growth as a dimension of motion and then turn to his treatment of the associated phenomena of saving and investment.

As was indicated earlier on, Schumpeter adopted the position that growth is a process that can be regarded as adding only small and continuous increments to productive capacity in a way that can be absorbed by means of adaptations and adjustments within the existing structures and operations of the steady circular flow state. Thus he wrote of growth in a 1935 essay, that it comprises 'changes in economic data which occur continuously in the sense that the increment or decrement per unit of time can be currently absorbed by the system without perceptible disturbance' (*Essays*, p. 136). More expansively, in *Cycles* he argued that 'the effects of Growth are . . . capable of being currently absorbed – in the sense that any disequilibrium created by every newcomer in the labour market or every dollar newly saved in the money market could under ordinary circumstances be corrected without giving rise to any visible disturbance – hence cannot by themselves create the alternation of booms and depressions we observe' (p. 84), In the light of such reasoning, he decided to 'exclude [growth] from the fundamental contour lines of our analytic model', adding for the benefit of possibly incredulous readers, especially those who knew their Marx, that this 'decision may well look strange. To many it may seem to exclude the very essence of the matter. A little reflection will, however, quickly dispel that impression' (*Cycles*, pp. 82–3; cf. *Essays*, p. 136).

What, then, should we 'reflect' on in order to understand Schumpeter's position here? In one of the passages quoted just above, he made reference to growth phenomena 'by themselves' not being able to account for the instability of motion. This hint reiterated, albeit cryptically, the following piece of insight argued in *Development*: the appearance of growth 'is frequently *a condition of* [motion in the form of] development' and while such increases 'often *make the* . . . [*development*] *possible*, . . . they do not create it out of themselves' (p. 63n, emphasis added). His position here was that the importance of growth could only be explained as a process that conditions the main mobilizing force of motion as it was identified by Schumpeter.

It is apparent that Schumpeter's stand on growth was more methodological than substantive. Ultimately the 'interaction and interdependence' of growth and innovations would have to be recognized in his analysis. Then the 'actual quantitative importance' of growth can be argued as an integral part of the total phenomenon of motion. But, as his interest was immediately in 'booms and depressions' as manifestations of the instability of capitalist motion, and as he saw growth as not contributing to this dimension, he applied his methodological principle that the components of motion could meaningfully be treated in isolation as an analytical convenience. It remained important, though, to 'call . . . [growth] up again' in order to 'complete' the analysis. So, as we can see, Schumpeter had no intention of neglecting growth altogether. Rather it was a matter of situating it correctly in the structure of his approach to the theory of motion. The question open to investigation is the extent to which he honoured his commitment to reintegrate growth into a 'complete' analysis. Virtually not at all must be the response, according to my reading of his work.

Now in order fully to comprehend Schumpeter's position of giving low priority to any analysis of growth, we must know how he treated the saving-investment nexus that is its source. He analysed the nexus in isolation from any concerns about growth *per se*, but his rather eccentric and anachronistic stance does, I think, help to explain why he failed to identify any source of instability in the latter process. His main treatment of the issue in *Cycles* (especially pp. 75ff.) involved a reliance on *definitions* of saving and investment that simply ensured their interdependence as a matter of logical necessity. On this basis, he claimed that 'saving and investment are interdependent and correspective [*sic*][1] so as to shape each other', and, elaborating a little, he added that 'whether savers save rationally or not, their action in any case influences investment opportunity, which in turn tends as much to adapt itself to the amount and rate of saving as it tends to influence that amount and rate' (ibid., pp. 77, 78). The mechanism brought into play in order further to justify this mutuality claim was interest rate flexibility in the market for loanable funds. And, although he eschewed any formalization of the market in terms of Marshallian supply and demand functions, it is clear that he envisaged a market clearing process that would bring saving and investment into line at just that rate of interest that satisfies both household savers and business investors. One way or another, given the definitions devised and the appropriate operation of the funds market, *ex ante* saving and investment intentions will always be brought into line *ex post* by means of the most 'classical' (pre-Kaleckian and pre-Keynesian) of mechanisms. Nonetheless, with but a few qualifications that may impede the mechanism, but never prevent it ultimately from working (ibid., pp. 77–8), he continued to apply it as central to his analyses of motion. Especially, did he consciously block any intrusion into his work by the ideas of Kalecki and Keynes.[2]

5.4   New combinations or innovations

The third of Schumpeter's internal factors of change, 'changes in methods of supplying commodities', was identified as by far the most important force generating motion in the capitalist economy and it became the central focus of the theory of economic development and the business cycle. If we recall that he conceived of production as a process of combining inputs in accordance with some technologically-determined production function (*Development*, p. 15; *Cycles*, p. 38 and n), then it becomes clear that a change in the method means introducing a 'new combination' of the inputs. This term was used interchangeably with innovation in Schumpeter's writings and I will continue that practice here.

Early on in *Cycles*, we have seen that Schumpeter alluded to two possible factors of change which he grouped together because they had a common trait for his purposes. They were the discoveries of new countries and inventions and when introduced they were placed in limbo beyond the classification code of external and internal factors that he was arguing – indeed, each was perceived as, *in itself*, 'no factor at all' (p. 9). Here Schumpeter made the general point that applied to these phenomena and any others that may turn out to be relevant: no such phenomenon can become an internal factor of change unless and until it is economically exploited by agents. Thus, they acquire significance in new combinations 'only as and when the new possibilities . . . [are] turned into commercial and industrial reality, and then the individual acts of realization and not the possibilities themselves are what concern us' (ibid.). The important thing about these unexploited inventions and new countries and their like is that they provide the opportunity for agents with the required talents to reap economic and other benefits by realizing their nascent potentials as 'means of production', broadly considered. So, with the mediation of entrepreneurial agents, factors that are initially 'no factor at all' are turned into the crucial and only internal factor of change that can explain the unstable economic development of capitalism, namely innovation as 'the outstanding fact in the economic history of capitalist society . . .' (ibid., p. 86).

The relation between inventions and their commercial exploitation as innovations was one which Schumpeter considered only briefly (e.g. *Essays*, p. 64; *Cycles*, pp. 84–6). He set out his rationale for this delimitation in the following passage:

Economic leadership in particular must hence be distinguished from 'invention' . . . [as] to carry an improvement into effect is a task entirely different from the inventing of it, and a task, moreover, requiring entirely different kinds of aptitudes. Although entrepreneurs of course *may* be inventors . . ., they are inventors not by nature of their function but by coincidence and vice versa. Besides, the innovations which it is the function of entrepreneurs to carry out need not necessarily be any inventions at all. It is, therefore, not advisable, and it may be downright misleading, to stress the element of invention as much as many writers do. (*Development*, pp. 88–9, original emphasis)

It is clear that he saw the phenomena as related, but the existence of a particular invention can be neither necessary nor sufficient for innovation to take place. Its presence is certainly not sufficient because the recognition and creation of any economic opportunity and its subsequent exploitation requires agent decision making and action of a very particular kind. As inventive and innovative talents and activities are 'economically and sociologically' quite different, the latter can never be assumed to exist and follow the former (*Cycles*, pp. 85, 86). The activities remain different and demand distinct facets of talent, even if they are carried out by the same agent, but in such cases, that one will follow the other is much more probable.

Moreover, as an innovation 'is possible without anything we should identify as an invention' (ibid., p. 84), there can be no necessary link between the phenomena. Two reasons can be given for this. First, as I will indicate further below, one form of new combination posited by Schumpeter involves only organizational changes and two others may be linked to new-country discoveries. These do not involve inventions as the term is usually understood, although new *knowledge* is required and it may be appropriate to consider the activity of generating it to be an invention. Secondly, the invention concerned may not be new. Rather it may exist in a 'pool' of unexploited knowledge and ideas so that the act of innovation need not be preceded by and immediately linked to a *particular* invention. As Schumpeter put it, 'there has never been any time when the store of scientific knowledge has yielded all it could in the way of industrial improvement . . . [and] there may be, and often is, no scientific novelty involved at all' in an innovation (*Essays*, p. 64; cf. *Cycles*, p. 84). That is, the innovation 'need by no means be founded upon a discovery scientifically new . . .' (*Development*, p. 66) and 'economic phenomena which we observe in the special case in which innovation and invention coincide do not differ from those we observe in cases in which preexisting knowledge is made use of' (*Cycles*, pp. 84–5).

On the subject of the causal origins of invention, Schumpeter had little to say. He did suggest that one possible motivation for invention is some extant and unsatisfied human need perceived by the inventor (ibid., p. 85n), but his more generally applied assumption was that innovators are always able to draw from an unexplained 'pool' of inventions and knowledge that is sufficient to occupy the worthwhile entrepreneurial talent that appears periodically in a particular society (*Development*, pp. 78, 88). There is no evidence, what is more, that Schumpeter ever thought of the extent of innovative activity being constrained by an absolute shortage of its 'raw material'. 'New possibilities', he wrote, 'are continuously being offered by the surrounding world, in particular new discoveries are continuously being added to the existing store of knowledge' and '[i]mprovements can always be made. . . [as] the striving after improvements is always limited by the given conditions and not by the perfection of what exists.' (ibid., pp. 79, 197; cf. *Cycles*, p. 97). However, the *economic* viability of things and ideas to be exploited in any one period remains a decreasing function of the volume of innovation attempted, a fact compounded by the profile of concurrently decreasing entrepreneurial ability among the remaining agents available to take up the opportunities. These factors can place an upper limit on the periodic stimulation to economic activity coming from this source. And, as will become apparent in due course, Schumpeter made much use of this mechanism in explaining the business cycle.

Schumpeter actually constructed his whole theory of motion around the new combinations idea. The core process of economic development that flowed from the disturbance of the steady circular-flow state was attributed solely to the introduction of innovative change. Thus: 'Development in our sense is . . . defined by the carrying out of new combinations', with the proviso, we shall see, that they occur discontinuously in waves of such activity (*Development*, p. 66; cf. *Cycles*, p. 86). But, from the outset, the new combination category was a complex one in that Schumpeter listed no fewer than five *quite different* types of innovative changes that were to be included. They were all concerned with the 'methods of supplying commodities' in one way or another and they were all to be carried out only by entrepreneurs. But there the similarity ended. In describing the five types below, and in analysing their subsequent role in the process of development, it will be appropriate for us to remain sensitive to their considerably different modes of involvement in and implications for the traverse of adjustments that will be generated.

The five types were first outlined in *Development* and I consider each in turn as they were therein presented (p. 66). Much the same ones were specified in *Cycles* (p. 84). First of all Schumpeter listed '(1) The introduction of a new good [or service] – that is one with which consumers are not yet familiar – or of a new quality of a good [or service].' He was to add in *Cycles* that this case of product innovation may even serve as the standard case' of a new combination. While all this appears to be straightforward enough, a couple of complications readily come to mind. One is that this form of innovation will most probably involve changes to *supply* conditions as well as the obvious need to tap or create a change in demand patterns. That is, some innovation in the process of production will need to accompany the new product and appear as a precondition in the relevant analysis. The other complication concerns the nature of the commodity that is subject to improvement. It cannot legitimately be assumed that product innovations will only involve consumer commodities. The quite different implications of new or modified produced means of production, especially when they appear unsolicited, should not be overlooked. In this case, an economically-viable process innovation must ensue somewhere if the new means of production is to be effectively demanded. Fully comprehending the role of product innovations in the development and business-cycle traverses will mean including both these complications explicitly in the analysis as and when they occur.

The second of the new combination types is that just referred to as process innovation. Schumpeter specified it as '(2) The introduction of a new method of production, that is one not yet tested by experience in the branch of manufacture concerned . . .'. Within this 'new method' term he included a considerable range of possibilities. Among them were new ways of handling materials and commodities and the 'Taylorization' of work, as well as 'technological change in the production of commodities already in use . . .'. Unfortunately, regarding the last of these, process innovations proper, he paid no attention at all to the problem of classifying them according to the relative dynamics of the input changes required to implement them. Whether a new process demands relatively more or less input of labour power or produced means of production, together with the details of the *qualitative* requirements involved will vitally affect the traverses that ensue. This really was a glaring lacuna in Schumpeter's analysis and it remained unfilled in his extant works.

The third of the new combination types was posited as '(3) The opening of a new market, that is a market into which the particular branch of manufacture of the country in question has not previously entered, whether or not this market has existed before.' Here we have a type that affects first and foremost the demand side of an entrepreneur's endeavours. There will be supply side effects, too, because the commodities to be sold in the new market must be produced somewhere, most probably by an expansion of the existing output of commodities and/or some physical redistribution of their destinations. However, it would seem that such innovations require agent decision making and action of a 'lesser' order of talent and skill than would be the case for the first two types listed. Moving into a new market and expanding or diverting existing production are actions much closer to the routine behaviour of agents and, what is more, are unlikely to cause the degree of disturbance of the circular flow that Schumpeter defined as the condition for development to exist. It is, rather, more akin to growth that requires only adaptive responses. Not surprisingly, then, the third type of innovation received virtually no subsequent attention in his exposition.

In the fourth type of new combination, Schumpeter returned to a supply side effect: '(4) The conquest of a new source of supply of raw materials or half-manufactured goods, again irrespective of whether this source already exists or whether it has first to be created.' Here, once again, the demands on entrepreneurial talent are not of the same order as in cases (1) and (2). Managers of a 'lesser' order could probably embrace it within their routine behaviours, too, especially where the 'source already exists'. As with type (3), this one was left with little further involvement in the analysis of motion to come. It is perhaps pertinent to note also, apropos the relative neglect by Schumpeter of the two types just mentioned, that both may well involve open-economy considerations as the new markets and sources are likely to be found in another country or colony. For obvious reasons of simplification, he restricted his theoretical analyses exclusively to the closed-economy case and this could also help to explain his lack of further treatment of these types of new combinations.[3]

Finally, the fifth category listed was also one that focuses on the supply side, albeit with somewhat broader implications than those canvassed above: '(5) The carrying out of the new organisation of any industry, like the creation of a monopoly position (for example through trustification) or the breaking up of a monopoly position', to which was added in *Cycles* the idea of 'the setting up of new business organizations such as department stores' as distinct from, say, speciality shops (p. 84). Now the general idea of all new combinations is to give the entrepreneur an effective but temporary monopoly advantage over his or her competitors. In this type of new combination, though, Schumpeter suggested a more or less permanent change in the competitive nature of an industry, which has rather different analytical implications and a longer time horizon when compared to the other cases. It is not a process that individual agents can unilaterally effect and control. Moreover, the example of the department store cited above is not very apt because it really constitutes an organizational form of process innovation and belongs in category (2) when it is introduced by an individual agent. It will then be imitation and diffusion of the idea that leads to the extensive change in market structure referred to here. To include alongside all of this 'the breaking up of a monopoly position' is rather incongruous. Such an event is hardly symmetrical with the setting up of monopoly power positions and it is difficult to see how it could be considered an innovation for the individual agents involved, whatever may be its broader social and economic ramifications.

All in all, Schumpeter's presentation of his list of new combination types was rather casual and cavalier and in no way did justice to the variety of implications for motion analysis that are entailed. As things turned out, probably for some of the reasons already suggested, it was really only types (1) and (2), product and process innovations, that took any part in the formal analysis that followed. 'Innovation', he typically wrote, 'unless it consists in producing, and forcing upon the public, a new commodity means . . . breaking off the old "supply schedule" and starting a new one' (*Essays*, p. 64). Changing the *method of production*, the general rubric under which he introduced this third internal factor, most readily suggests process innovation. Relating product innovation to it requires careful analysis as was indicated above because both demand and supply sides of the firm's calculus are involved. The other three types are more remote from changing the *method* by which commodities are produced. They are concerned with alternative output and input markets for, or with the market structure within which, existing commodities are produced by existing methods. As will become clear in the next chapter, in Schumpeter's *analytical* presentation of the innovation process these latter three types find no ready place. As a consequence, only once did he discuss them any further (*Development*, pp. 133ff.), but then in isolation from his main theory of economic development. The contents of this discussion will be outlined in the next chapter (section 6.4).

There remained, though, even within the effectively restricted scope of type (1) and (2) innovations, an unwarranted casualness of treatment. All too often, Schumpeter shifted ground between product and process innovations as the generators of economic development without due recognition of their quite different entrepreneurial natures and production ramifications. The respective traverses that comprise the motion following their introduction into the circular flow were never clearly separated and identified. There was, then, as I will indicate further in my subsequent critique, a decided lack of precision in Schumpeter's handling of this most crucial of phenomena for his theoretical analysis.

5.5 Summary
The objective of this chapter was to provide a transition between Schumpeter's steady circular-flow model and his theory of economic development and the business cycle by considering some issues of motion in general terms.

1. Schumpeter modelled motion by introducing particular changes into a steady circular-flow state. Such changes were classified either as external or internal in relation to the scope of his economic model and while he went on to grant the empirical significance of the former, he emphasized only the latter in the theory of motion.
2. Three separate dimensions of motion were considered by Schumpeter to be attributable to internal factors of change: first, strictly quantitative expansion induced by saving, capital accumulation and investment, i.e., economic growth *per se*; secondly, qualitative changes to production processes or what is produced by way of new combinations or innovations, i.e., what he called economic development; and thirdly, the substantive temporal form that economic development takes as the business cycle.
3. It was the disruptive and discontinuous processes of economic development and the business cycle that became Schumpeter's theoretical object. He left aside quantitative economic growth as being capable of incremental absorption without sufficient systemic disturbance to warrant theoretical investigation.
4. In the theory of motion, Schumpeter maintained the notion of an economy-wide equilibrium or near-equilibrium state as a 'centre of gravity' about which fluctuations occur. This equilibrium had, he insisted, a real-world status that gave it analytical relevance.
5. New combinations comprised the most essential cause of motion for Schumpeter. He identified five separate forms of such new combinations, but he did not pursue fully their particular analytical ramifications and remained rather casual and imprecise about their respective involvements in the economic development process. Ultimately, only two of the forms, product innovation and process innovation, were included in his formal theory, albeit still without adequate analytical distinctions being drawn.

Notes

1. The word 'correspective' appears to be an Anglicized corruption of the German legal adjective or adverb of Latin origin *korrespektiv* which means, roughly, mutually dependent. There is no evidence, however, of any legitimate English equivalent.

2. Schumpeter had quite a lot to say abut Keynes, much of it with an unduly negative tone (*Essays*, pp. 153ff.; *Capitalism*, pp. 392ff.; *Economists*, pp. 260ff.; 1947; and *History*, especially pp. 1170ff.). Some light is shed on the intellectual relations between the two men in two older papers (Wright, 1950 and Smithies, 1951) and in some more recent works stimulated by the flurry of interest in them associated with the coincidence of 1983 (Seidl, 1984; Bronfenbrenner, 1986; Goodwin, 1986; Minsky, 1986; and Morishima and Catephores, 1988). There is much less about Kalecki in Schumpeter's writings – one piece in *Cycles*, (pp. 185ff.) and, although he did not make the index, there is one passing mention of him in *History* (p. 1144). The tenor of the former piece is similar to that in the writings on Keynes, namely lacking in appreciation and, at times, rather hostile. Considering how a proper understanding of the Kalecki and Keynes *analyses* could have enriched his own, often misguided endeavours to explain motion, the situation was quite an unfortunate development in the history of economics. In Keynes's case especially, it is clear that Schumpeter did not like his *politics*. But really, given his claim to the Olympian detachment of the true scientist, Schumpeter might have done better at keeping the analytical insights in the *General Theory* and elsewhere separate. Perhaps here, his own political predilections, made quite obvious in his surprising 1949 tirade, 'English Economists and the State-Managed Economy' (*Essays*, pp. 296ff.), just got the better of him.

3. There is a link here to Schumpeter's piece 'The Sociology of Imperialism' (*Classes*, pp.3ff.) in that what concerned him there was not the immediate capitalist economics of the phenomenon but its origins in social agency. Entrepreneurs seeking new markets for their commodities and new sources of inputs for their production processes will potentially benefit from the imperialist cause and could, therefore be expected to support it. But, according to Schumpeter, they are not the instigators of the colonial push. Rather it is politically-motivated conquest and expansionism that is given primacy. There is, then, a 'warrior' élite behind it rather than an economic élite. Cf. the 'Introduction' to *Classes* by Bert Hoselitz and Paul Sweezy's 'Introduction' to another edition of the work (reprinted as Sweezy, 1951).

6 The theory of economic development

6.1 Essentials of economic development

Central to Schumpeter's theoretical analysis of motion were the processes that constitute economic development. In this chapter, I present a critical exposition of the theory that he thought explained the phenomenon. It should be kept in mind, though, that explaining economic development, as it was defined by Schumpeter, cannot be an end in itself as it has no immediate empirical manifestation. Rather, it comprises the core of motion that takes the observed form of the business cycle. The theory outlined in this chapter is, therefore, but a step towards explaining a more complex analytical object and a full critical assessment of its form and insights can only emerge in that context.

The theory was presented by Schumpeter on several occasions in his writings with only slight variations in emphasis on some points of detail. I will consider the versions in *Development* and *Cycles* as a unity and draw on each as required to build up a complete exposition (the justification for this having been explained in Chapter 1, section 1.1). Most emphasis will be on the former work as it contains the more elaborate treatment of certain important themes and theses to be considered. There were also three particular journal papers from 1927, 1928 and 1935 in which the theory was briefly outlined (*Essays*, pp. 21ff., 47ff., 134ff.) but these will be of little use as sources for they merely repeat in brief what is available in *Development*.

Perhaps it will be helpful for readers, especially for those unfamiliar with the theory, to have an overview of its main tenets to begin with. This will facilitate a more immediate appreciation of the role and significance of the particular themes argued out in the more detailed and critical sections that follow. Such an outline of the essentials is presented in this section. To some extent, this will involve reference to ideas already considered, but their repetition is now set in a more structured context.

Schumpeter's perception of the immanently generated motion of the capitalist economic system was extremely narrow. It is evident, as we have seen, that he was not concerned with *growth* as a dimension of motion. He believed that saving, capital accumulation and population growth as *quantitative* phenomena could be absorbed by adaptation and adjustment of the system in a more or less continuous manner (*Develop-*

ment, pp. 63, 65–6, 81). For Schumpeter, such processes involved little of interest for the theorist beyond what can be said about the circular-flow model (ibid., pp. 63, 68). Growth involves but an expanding replica of the steady state and received theory can handle the consequences of the mere changes in data involved (ibid., pp. 62–3, 82n).

Schumpeter's interest was in those dimensions of motion that explicitly involve discontinuous and disruptive change to the characteristics of the steady circular-flow of economic life (ibid., p. 223). He argued that orthodox equilibrium analysis could not cope with such changes: 'it can neither explain the occurrence of . . . productive revolutions nor the phenomena which accompany them. It can only investigate the new equilibrium position after the changes have occurred.' (ibid., pp. 62–3; cf. pp. 61, 64n). The challenge was to formalize the *qualitative* as well as the quantitative aspects of non-continuous economic change. That is, to pursue motion that comprises the internally-generated disruption of an equilibrium state of circular flow and the subsequent traverse processes that result in a new equilibrium with different qualitative and quantitative features.

In this type of environment of motion, the participating individuals are called upon to react and act in ways which deviate from the 'normal' (ibid., pp. 79–81). Special talents become crucial and subsequent economic success and stability requires that at least some individuals have the ability to handle the transcendence of routines. Novelty and reactions to it become the essence of motion.

Schumpeter cogently summarized three tenets of his position on motion as 'three corresponding pairs of opposites'.

> First, . . . the opposition of two real processes: the circular flow or the tendency towards equilibrium on the one hand, a change in the channels of economic routine or a spontaneous change in the economic data arising from within the system on the other. Secondly, . . . the opposition of two theoretical *apparatuses*: statics and dynamics. Thirdly, . . . the opposition of two types of conduct, which, following reality, we can picture as two types of individuals: mere managers and entrepreneurs. (ibid., pp. 82–3, original emphasis)

The latter of each of these pairs of opposites characterized what Schumpeter called economic development.

The focus of the analysis of capitalist motion, then, was to be on the 'occurrence of "revolutionary" change' which Schumpeter perceived as 'the problem of economic development *in a very narrow and formal sense* (*Development*, p. 63, emphasis added). Development is an immanently generated phenomenon, independent of any external data changes: 'It is spontaneous and discontinuous change in the channels of the flow, disturbance of equilibrium, which forever alters and displaces the equilibrium state previously existing.' So, for Schumpeter: 'Our theory of development is nothing but a treatment of this phenomenon and the processes incident to it' (ibid., p. 64).

More specifically, the context of economic development as it concerned Schumpeter is the 'sphere of industrial and commercial life'. The focus of economic analysis thus shifts from the ultimate determining force of consumer preferences in equilibrium theory to the sphere of production: 'It is . . . the producer who as a rule initiates economic change, and consumers are educated by him if necessary.' (ibid., p. 65). The site of the generation of development is production and 'production means to combine materials and forces within our reach'. It follows that: 'To produce other things, or the same things by a different method, means to combine these materials and forces differently.' (ibid.). Such changes in production involve what Schumpeter termed new combinations and he went on to define development specifically as 'the carrying out of new combinations' (ibid., p. 66).

Five categories of new combinations were alluded to in the previous chapter (section 5.4), namely (1) introduction of a new commodity, or a new quality of an old one; (2) introduction of a new method of production; (3) opening of a new market; (4) availability of a new source of supply for inputs; and (5) carrying out a new organization of any industry. It has been argued that as a basis for analysing the origins of economic development, this list is highly problematical. Suffice it to repeat here that the five categories are far from homogeneous in their analytical demands and implications. Moreover, a key methodological premise upon which Schumpeter founded his theory of development requires that the new combinations be of *already existing* means of production (ibid., p. 67). But, this is immediately inconsistent with item (4) in the above list, very much constrains the significance and nature of items (1) and (2), and may impede the implementation of item (5). That is, any new combination that involves or may involve the supply side of development cannot be fully analysed under the constraints imposed by Schumpeter unless the only existing means of production are assumed to be homogeneous and adaptable labour power and 'land'. However, it should also be recalled that his actual use of the term innovation is not as wide as the new combinations approach to development would suggest, with product and process innovations being the exclusive focus of the formal analysis.

Three related issues are raised by an analysis of motion that comprises the absorption of new combinations into production: first, who organizes the new combination in production? Secondly, what resources will be used to facilitate the new combination? Thirdly, how does the directing agent involved obtain command over the resources required? (ibid., pp. 67–9). The answers given to these three questions by Schumpeter form the operational essentials of the process of economic development that he analyses.

New combinations are applied by a group of people with the particular talent of *entrepreneurship*. It is the 'enterprise' of the entrepreneur, including his or her abilities of leadership, that represents 'the fundamental phenomenon of economic development' (ibid., p. 74). In the circular flow of the steady state, there exists no need or scope for the exercise of such talents. As we have seen, directing agents under these conditions perform only routine managerial tasks (ibid., pp. 79–82).

Entrepreneurs seize on inventions (a term that needs a wide definition if it is to provide the basis for the new combinations listed above) and through new combinations give them *economic* significance (ibid., pp. 88–9). They do so in Schumpeter's world by setting up a new enterprise, a process which injects a discontinuity into economic development as firms appear and disappear (ibid., pp. 66–7). Entrepreneurs also come and go as the role is non-vocational and does not, *per se*, provide the basis for any 'class' in the structure of society (ibid., pp. 77–9). Moreover, the entrepreneurs need not be capitalists in the sense that they already have command over resources by virtue of possessing a stock of finance capital. And, because they need not advance their own capital, they are not financial risk-takers (ibid., pp. 75, 75n, 137). Their access to resources was taken care of by Schumpeter in a special way and will be considered as the third issue below.

On the question of motivation for the entrepreneurs' activities, Schumpeter seemed anxious to avoid emphasizing the pursuit of profit. Clearly profit is involved, but he suggested non-hedonistic alternatives (*Development.*, pp. 90ff., especially pp. 92, 93–4). Nonetheless, it remained a central part of his thesis that entrepreneurial activity is the *only* means of access to profit under competitive assumptions. The importance of this profit to the analysis of motion will be more evident in the discussion of the third issue below.

The second question raised by new combinations in production concerns where the resources are to come from in order to implement the new operation. One of the conditions of the steady circular-flow state is that all resources are fully employed. Competitive markets ensure that this is so. Then it is a further central point of Schumpeter's analysis of development that the implementation of the new combination should disrupt the circular-flow equilibrium by requiring entrepreneurs to enter resource markets as *additional* buyers. They shift demand functions and raise the market clearing prices of resources (ibid., pp. 68, 106, 108). The consequence of this is that a disequilibrium state is introduced and a process of price adjustment and resource reallocation will ensue under the free-market assumption made by Schumpeter. His argument was that the adjustments will tend to restore equilibrium, but one with circular-flow characteristics different from the original state. At this point, he also granted that he had exaggerated the required changes to restore equilibrium by assuming no spare productive capacity or resources. The methodological justification for proceeding on this basis was that it would reveal 'in bold relief what we hold to be the essential contour line' of economic development (ibid., p. 68). As I will argue in detail later, the ramifications of the assumption go beyond this matter of exaggeration.

A related issue of significance here is the potential difficulty posed by this assumption where resources are locked into durable produced means of production that are functionally specific. This issue was not formally dealt with by Schumpeter, although he sometimes hinted at it in passing (e.g. ibid., p. 71). The reason for his lack of concern probably lies in his perception of production. Recall that directing agents do not *possess* resources but merely hire their services on a continuous basis. Production begins from 'land' and labour power stocks which are non-specific and utilizes their services progressively to fabricate consumer commodities. At the end of each production period, any functionally specific means of production produced along the way in the form of intermediate goods will have been 'used up'. Entrepreneurs are then faced only with bidding for the services of basic resources alongside existing directing agents. The new combination is thus implemented in a perfectly flexible resource environment.

In dealing with Schumpeter's third question about the means by which the entrepreneur obtains command over the resources required for the new combination, we have seen that saving and capital accumulation are ruled out by assumption (ibid., pp. 68, 71–2). Profit, the only source of saving allowed for by Schumpeter, exists in a relation of mutual interdependence with economic development. The latter is the essential cause of the former, but once development is proceeding, he granted that saving out of profit could affect the course of that development (ibid., p. 154). However, Schumpeter intended to emphasize the essence of development and found it convenient to begin the analysis from the steady state where no means of saving exists and where there is no incentive to do so because no way of holding the proceeds exists beyond hoarding money. Note that while there is a market for the *services* of 'land', no 'land' itself is traded because in the steady state no means exist for valuing it. The rate of interest must be assumed to be zero, or alternatively non-existent, in such a state (ibid., pp. 166–7).

The key to the funding of the new combinations is credit (ibid., p. 107). This credit must be found in a steady state with no pre-existing flow of saving or stock of accumulated funds (ibid., pp. 69–72). Here Schumpeter introduced the banking system as the necessary credit *creator* (ibid., pp. 72–4). Correctly, he went on to note that banks have a status beyond a *deus ex machina* in the analysis because they do actually perform the function of short-term credit creation in order to fund new enterprises. Longer-term credit made available as a consequence of saving out of development-induced profit can replace the short-term funding if this is desired by the enterprise (ibid., p. 111). The banker becomes 'a phenomenon of development' and 'the capitalist par excellence' in this approach (ibid., p. 74).

In Schumpeter's analysis of economic development, capital took a particular functional form. It comprised only the funds provided to entrepreneurs to facilitate new combinations. Thus: *'Capital is nothing but the lever by which the entrepreneur subjects to his control the concrete goods which he needs, nothing but a means of diverting the factors of production to new uses, or of dictating a new direction to production.'* (*Development*, p. 116, original emphasis; cf. pp. 117, 119-20, 122).

The allocation of capital is controlled through the 'money market' in which the rate of interest as the price of short-term credit is determined (ibid., pp. 123ff.). Schumpeter explained and defended his theory of interest at some length in *Development* (Chapters IV and V). The details of this discussion are not of immediate concern in the present context (see Chapter 7 below). However, a brief summary is appropriate in order to situate the nature and role of entrepreneurial profit and interest payments in the process of economic development.

In the steady circular-flow state, directing agents receive no income beyond that for the services of their labour power, the 'wages of management' in effect. Entrepreneurs also receive this income, but in addition they accrue a 'surplus over costs' that is linked to production (ibid., pp. 128–9). The most direct source of this 'surplus' is the differential cost advantage that the new combination gives the entrepreneurs over established producers who continue to sell at pre-existing prices. This cost advantage is obvious where the new combination involves increased productive efficiency, the classic case of technical change associated with process innovation, or where a new and cheaper source of inputs is made available. The reorganization of an industry by introducing large-scale production is a new combination of a different magnitude, but it, too, could result in lower costs. In the cases where the new combination produces a new product, a better product, or reaches a new market where the commodity concerned has not been on sale before, entrepreneurs' advantageous position depends on monopoly power and they can appropriate a 'surplus' as profit on this basis. In each case of new combinations, then, a source of profit consequent upon the successful activities of the entrepreneurs can be identified, at least as a matter of principle.

The entrepreneur obtains his or her profit by virtue of bank credit. He or she is obliged, therefore, to pay interest at the rate determined in the money market (ibid., pp. 175, 210). Schumpeter's concern was only with this 'productive' source of interest and he associated it exclusively with economic development. There was no place for interest in the steady state, even where 'roundabout', vertically-integrated methods of production are in use. Where the mere repetition of an established and continuous process is involved, Schumpeter's view was that no profit is generated, no credit required and no interest is paid. The phenomenon of credit, and the profit out of which interest is paid, emerges only with an *increase* in the degree of 'roundaboutness' or period of production involved in the vertically-integrated stages. This increase amounts to a new combination where it raises input productivity and thus generates development (ibid., pp. 158–9).

Now the existence of a capacity to pay interest out of entrepreneurial profit does not explain why it is actually paid. Schumpeter explained such payments in two stages. First, there is the fact that the entrepreneur must obtain command over resources to which he or she does not have immediate access. A characteristic of a capitalist economic system is that resources are owned by individuals. It follows that *property rights* over these resources are at the root of income payments in this system. As Schumpeter pointed out, in a 'communist' (centrally-planned) system, incomes would not be on the same basis (ibid., p. 176). Production as a physical-technical process exists in both systems, but the relations of production that *activate* the process are quite different. If the entrepreneurs could directly command the resources that they need, they would still gain a profit, but not on a capitalist basis. Thus: 'It is only because other people have command of the necessary producers' goods that entrepreneurs must call in the capitalist to help them remove the obstacle *which private property in means of production or the right to dispose freely of one's personal services* puts in their way.' (ibid., p. 177, emphasis added).

Interest, then, is *'the price of purchasing power regarded as a means of control over production goods'*, with the qualification that this 'does not ascribe to purchasing power any productive role' (ibid., p. 184, original emphasis). Here the second stage of Schumpeter's explanation of the payment of interest emerged. Purchasing power commands a price by virtue of the forces of supply and demand in the money market (ibid., pp. 184, 187ff.). Interest as a premium of the present over the future purchasing power of money appears as a consequence of the fact that borrowing facilitates the appropriation of profit and the supply of credit money is relatively constrained. The only individuals who can realize the productive power of loans are the entrepreneurs and they confront the capitalist owners of finance in a free market situation where supply and demand are balanced by the setting of an appropriate premium for control of present purchasing power.

More specifically in Schumpeter's world, the only suppliers of credit are the bankers. The demand side of the money market is unaffected by this specification, but the supply side must be considered slightly differently from the general principles enunciated above. It was Schumpeter's position that even allowing for the flexibility of supply that bank credit creation introduces, the demand relativity will always be such as to ensure a positive rate of interest (ibid., pp. 196–8). He concluded that: 'The demand for capital of itself continually engenders new demand. And therefore on the money market there is a limited effective supply, however big it may be, as against an effective demand which has no definite limit at all' (ibid., p. 198; cf. p. 201). Interest is thus an unavoidable burden for the entrepreneur and will always be present as a 'brake' on economic development (ibid., pp. 210-11).

Entrepreneurial profit is not a permanent source of income under normal circumstances. The effects of competition are felt as more and more new entrepreneurs set up in production, encouraged by the success of the pioneers (ibid., p. 228), and disadvantaged existing producers take up the new combination. Those of the latter group who do not follow suit are eliminated. Progressively, the so-called 'law of cost' is restored and the entrepreneur's position reverts to one of mediating in an established production process as a directing agent whose input resource costs, including the services of his or her own labour power, match his or her revenues. A *new* equilibrium is then established and the steady circular-flow of economic life proceeds again without the generation of profit (ibid., pp. 131, 243–5). Herein lies the essence of Schumpeter's analysis of motion which is developed into a theory of crises and business cycles.

6.2   Entrepreneurial agents

The pivotal role played by the entrepreneur in Schumpeter's theory of economic development is apparent from the above essential outline. It is appropriate, therefore, for me to begin my more detailed exposition of the theory by analysing his approach to and treatment of this central dimension of human agency.

Schumpeter was very particular in defining his concepts here as elsewhere and, in order fully to comprehend his theory of development, we must respect the delimitations that he imposed. The relevant definitions appeared as follows in *Development*: 'The carrying out of new combinations we call "enterprise"; the individuals whose function it is to carry them out we call "entrepreneurs"' (p. 74). His first concern having stated these definitions was to ensure that they not be confused with more common usage. He conveyed this by pointing out that coverage of his version is 'at once broader and narrower than the usual' (ibid.). It is broader because it does not confine its attention to 'independent' business agents whose unilateral actions direct the firms and the economy. The criterion is only that the agents must 'actually fulfil the function by which we define the concept' and in some circumstances this could include 'dependent' agents who are employees of firms, in managerial or other jobs, members of the board of directors or majority shareholders (ibid., pp. 74–5). At the theoretical level though, Schumpeter's entrepreneurs turn out always to be 'independent' in the above sense. The coverage is narrower because 'it does not include all heads of firms or managers or industrialists who merely may operate an established business . . .' (ibid., p. 75). Again he reiterated that the sole criterion is the performance of the 'enterprise' function as defined and while entrepreneurs may be among such commercially-established people, they need not have any supplementary functions at all.

The definition is also significant because it makes clear that the entrepreneurially-based character of the development process comprises two separate dimensions: one is the *function* of 'enterprise' itself and the other comprises the identification of the agents that are to carry it out. It is already clear that 'enterprise' here means carrying into effect new combinations or innovations. The nature of this phenomenon was discussed in the previous chapter (section 5.4). Our attention must now turn to the matter of specifying who is to carry out the function. That is to the question: who are the entrepreneurs in Schumpeter's theoretical world?

He approached this question by seeking to identify the particular qualities or talents that an agent would need in order effectively to engage in 'enterprise' activities. This meant first and foremost that the investigation must begin from human agents *tabula rasa*, for neither their existing economic or social locations or status nor their involvement in any particular economic or social function can be taken as indicative of entrepreneurial potential. From a socio-psychological perspective, because 'the carrying out of new combinations is a special function', it can only be 'the privilege of a type of people who are much less numerous than all those who have the "objective" possibility of doing it' (ibid., p. 81). That is, even though many agents may be faced with enterprise opportunities in an 'objective' sense, only a minority can realize those opportunities. This minority will comprise those agents who have the character traits and ability required to cope with non-routine decisions and actions and are sufficiently motivated to be prepared to do so. At a practical level, Schumpeter put the point thus: 'Every businessman realizes that running his plant in the customary way, going through all the motions of daily business routine, is one thing and that setting up the plant or changing its setup is another. He approaches these tasks with attitudes which differ characteristically from each other.' (*Cycles*, p. 37). Most will see the latter task as beyond them, posing the interesting question of why they should adopt such an attitude?

Consider first the situation enjoyed by economic agents in the steady circular-flow environment. They are able to reach an individual 'equilibrium' state in the sense that their established behaviours and relations with other agents are under no pressure to change. There is no uncertainty as tomorrow will be just like today in all respects other than for those minor variations that can be coped with by marginal flexibilities in routines. In reaching this situation, learning and experience are all important and once established, 'all knowledge and habit . . . becomes as firmly rooted in ourselves as a railway embankment in the earth' so that it 'does not require to be continually renewed and continuously reproduced, but sinks into the strata of subconsciousness' *Development*, p. 84). This is indeed fortunate, for to begin from scratch each day to re-establish the 'equilibrium' would pose impossible barriers: 'every man would have to be a giant of wisdom and will, if he had in every case to create anew all the rules by which he guides his everyday conduct' (ibid., p. 83). Now even though all of this is argued in the artificial and sterilized world of the steady circular flow, in real social and economic life the same general principle applies: none of us could operate without a core of established routine and *relative* certainty about some key aspects of the future. So it is that Schumpeter's argument has important theoretical and practical content for beginning to understand the way that agents relate to the prospect of change.

Once the agents choose or are forced to confront disruptive change and novelty, they will be called upon to exercise quite different reasoning and behaviours. These latter do not just involve some *degree* of difference. Rather they demand qualitatively different responses from agents that some will be able to provide better than others: 'Where the boundaries of routine stop, many people can go no further, and the rest can only do so in a highly variable manner.' (ibid., p. 80). It was Schumpeter's view that in order to meet the challenges of novelty and the uncertainty that it brings, agents must possess the talent of leadership, i.e. the preparedness to step out in front of other agents and take maximum advantage of the new situation and prospects. The leaders in this sense are required to leave the security of 'the sharp-edged reality of all the things which . . . [they] have seen and experienced' and confront 'the new [that] is only the figment of . . [their] imagination.' They must recognize 'the impossibility of surveying exhaustively all the [potential] effects and counter-effects of the projected enterprise . . . [and that] action must be taken without working out all the details of what is to be done'. In this sort of situation, 'the success of everything depends upon intuition, the capacity of seeing things in a way which afterwards proves to be true, even though it cannot be established at the moment, and of grasping the essential fact discarding the unessential, even though one can give no account of the principles by which this is done' (ibid., p. 85). To some extent, most economic agents with decision-making responsibilities are forced to act in such circumstances as non-stochastic uncertainty is a fact of real economic life. For Schumpeter's analytical purposes, though, only potential entrepreneurs choose to give themselves these problems as the option of living a life of pure routine is available.

However, having the required inclinations and talent alone is not enough, according to Schumpeter, to ensure that an agent will do enterprising things. Two potential barriers face him or her: one is psychological and personal and the other is social. Each must be transcended in turn. From a psychological viewpoint, it is not the 'objective' difficulties posed by doing something that is new and different that matters. Rather it is that 'the individual feels reluctance to [do] it and would do so even if the objective difficulties did not exist'. For 'fixed habits of thinking' have an 'energy-saving function' and provide 'proof against criticism and even against contradiction by individual facts' (ibid., p. 86). The leadership qualities must, then, be backed up by a psychological tenacity and self-confidence if the comforts and security of the 'equilibrium' state are to be foregone. Schumpeter's conclusion here warrants full quotation for its graphic expression of what is at issue.

> In the breast of one who wishes to do something new, the forces of habit rise up and bear witness against the embryonic project. A new and another kind of effort of will is therefore necessary in order to wrest, amidst the work and care of the daily round, scope and time for conceiving and working out the new combination and to bring oneself to look upon it as a real possibility and not merely as a day-dream. This mental freedom presupposes a great surplus force over the everyday demand and is something peculiar and by nature rare. (ibid.)

Such 'internal' resistance to undertaking things that are new may be compounded by a social resistance once the decision to act has been made and the required actions are being pursued. Where change and its effects are impeded by political or social sanctions, official or unofficial, or perhaps by legal sanctions, the agent needs a further dimension of strength of character to overcome the temptation to forego the expected advantages and retire to the 'quiet life'. The difficulties that might be met in the case of implementing a new combination could come first, from other agents whose economic position and/or 'quiet life' are threatened by it and secondly, from eliciting the required co-operation from other agents upon whose responses the success of the implementation depends – including lenders of finance, workers and established customers (ibid., p. 87; cf. *Cycles*, p. 100). It is at this point that the riskiness of entrepreneurial ventures may confront the innovator. Schumpeter's view was that entrepreneurs, *as such*, are not the bearers of risk: 'Risk-taking is in no case an element of the entrepreneurial function. Even though he may risk his reputation, the direct economic responsibility of failure never falls on him.' Rather, the 'one who gives credit comes to grief if the undertaking fails'; and 'even if the entrepreneur finances himself out of former profits or if he contributes the means of production belonging to his "static" business, the risk falls on him as capitalist or as possessor of goods, not as entrepreneur' *Development*, p. 137; cf. p. 75, *Cycles*, p. 104). However, it is because the risk of loss *de facto* at least, falls directly on the provider of credit – depending on the contractual form of the borrowing, it is possible that *de jure* the entrepreneur *is* ultimately responsible – that the potential entrepreneur may meet resistance in some quarters to his demand for credit. Hence, while risk 'enters into the pattern in which entrepreneurs work . . . it does so indirectly and at one remove . . .'. That it is more difficult to obtain finance as the riskiness of an innovation project increases, then, 'forms one of the obstacles entrepreneurs have to

overcome and one of the instances of resistance of the environment
which explains why innovations are not carried out smoothly and as a
matter of course' (*Cycles*, p. 104n). The role of banks, as representative
of financial intermediaries generally, in this 'resistance' to entrepreneurs' approaches for credit will be discussed further in section 6.5
below.

It was an important part of Schumpeter's argument about the
leadership abilities of economic agents that they occur in any ('ethni
cally-homogeneous') population in what amounts to a 'normal' distribu
tion (*Development*, p. 81n). Agents at the low ability end of the
distribution cannot participate effectively in any economic activity tha
requires the leadership quality, while those in the middle range are well
able to provide leadership in most more or less routine business roles
The latter group, to which 'practically all business people belong'
'prove themselves to be better in the things which even within the
established channels cannot simply be "dispatched" (*erledigen*) bu
must also be "decided" (*entscheiden*) and "carried out" (*durchsetzen*)
(ibid.). Finally, there is a third group in the upper echelons of ability
'rising in the scale we come finally into the highest quarter, to people
who are a type characterised by super-normal qualities of intellect and
will'. Here in this minority are found all sorts of higher business leader
as well as those agents who have the ability to reach such status b
taking up enterprise opportunities. Schumpeter now referred to wha
was to become an important additional characteristic of the highly
talented group. Within it there exists, he claimed, a further hierarchy o
relative capacities as 'a continuous variety of degrees of intensity i
"initiative"'. He went on to point out in his argument that 'types o
every intensity occur' and gave the following outline of the characteris
tics of three sub-groups involved: 'Many a one can steer a safe course
where no one has yet been; others follow where first another wen
before; still others only in the crowd, but in this among the first' (ibid.)
Here he introduced the idea of a declining degree of leadership talen
amongst the potential entrepreneurial group that he would later apply i
arguing the diffusion of innovations as part of the business cycle. As
will explain again later, the wave of initial innovations results from th
activities of the boldest and most daring of the potential leaders. The
are followed by a group of 'imitators' within which some have enoug
ability to take up their own enterprise opportunities once the righ
'atmosphere' of entrepreneurial acceptance and success has been estab
lished by the initiating group. The rest of this group have enough abilit
only to imitate by taking up, where possible, the innovations that hav
already been proven to some degree. The place of this stylized diffusio

process in the theory of development and the business cycle will become clear in due course.

What, then, in Schumpeter's view, motivates the exceptionally talented agents to adopt a mode of participating in economic life that may strain their abilities to the limit? Most obviously, the expectation of receiving entrepreneurial profit if their new combinations are successful must hold some attractions. About this motivational category, Schumpeter remained ambivalent. In *Development* we read that he refused to adopt any part of the time-honored picture of the motivation of the "economic man"' (p. 90), while in *Cycles* the working of the primary business-cycle model depends upon motivation being 'supplied by the prospect of profit in our sense (mixed as the reader pleases with other stimuli) . . .' (p. 130) – where 'profit in our sense' referred to entrepreneurial profit. The latter work contains no further development of the motivation issue, but in *Development* it was just those 'other stimuli' that Schumpeter promoted as being more significant than profit expectations. However, he remained of the opinion ultimately that: 'Pecuniary gain is indeed a very accurate expression of success, especially of *relative* success' so that in an 'acquisitive' society it is 'very difficult to replace it as a motor of industrial development . . .' (*Development*, p. 94, original emphasis).

He engaged in some extra-economic 'psychologizing' in order to elicit these other, less hedonistic and less materialistic motives. As he saw things, in the steady circular-flow state, the basic economic motivation of material provisioning, the 'satisfaction of wants', dominates what all agents do – it is 'the *meaning* of economic action . . . in the sense that there would be no economic action if there were no wants' (ibid., p. 91, original emphasis). But this motive cannot explain the *extraordinary* actions of entrepreneurs and in going beyond it Schumpeter sought to identify some motives that are not immediately materialist in their basis. His view was that unless we make the extreme assumption 'that individuals of our type [i.e. entrepreneurs] are driven along by an *insatiable* craving for hedonist satisfaction, the operations of Gossen's law would in the case of business leaders soon put a stop to further effort' (ibid., p. 92, emphasis added; re Gossen's law, see *History*, p. 910). He drew this conclusion by virtue of the claim that much more than hedonism must be at stake because entrepreneurs, and the high-ranking executive group that they have the potential to join, cannot be observed to limit their efforts according to some utility-disutility calculus. On the contrary, they appear to make no endeavour to curtail their economic activities in favour of the leisure time that would be needed to maximize the utility that they could derive from the consumption of their material achievements. From a hedonistic perspec tive, Schumpeter concluded, 'the conduct which we usually observe i individuals of our type would be irrational'. Indeed, more often tha not, they reveal an 'indifference to hedonist enjoyments' (*Developmen* pp. 92, 93).

Indications are, then, according to Schumpeter's reasoning, that th prospect of some longer-term payoffs is behind the intensive activities c entrepreneurial agents, payoffs that can only be related to 'anothe psychology of non-hedonistic character' (ibid., p. 93). He propose three such motivational prospects. First, there is the desire to found private industrial or commercial 'kingdom', or perhaps even a 'dynasty' This would enable those with little other effective claim to socia distinction to realize 'the nearest approach to medieval lordship possibl to modern man' (ibid.). There is here, too, the possibility to achiev power and independence, although Schumpeter opined that by thi route, such results would both be 'largely illusions'. He gave no reason for this opinion and it may well be argued to the contrary that simpl observation during and before his own era, and certainly beyond it reveals many prominent cases where entrepreneurial ambitions an subsequent success have been rewarded with significant economic an political power, prestige and independence. In one of his last papers however, Schumpeter explicitly denied that this argument has any rea historical significance (*Essays*, pp. 264–5). The second non-hedonisti motivation suggested by Schumpeter involves an analogy with the driv to fight, to win and to conquer in sport in order 'to prove onesel superior to others' and to 'succeed for the sake . . . of success itsel (*Development*, p. 93). In this case, he added, any financial rewards tha are received as a consequence of success are often used as an 'index' o the achievement and may be turned into conspicuous materialis 'prizes', not for their direct consumption benefits, but rather for thei capacity to convey the message of success to society at large. An finally, the least hedonistic of all motives is that of 'the joy of creating, o getting things done, or simply of exercising one's energy and ingenuity' In this respect, it should be recalled that the entrepreneur 'seeks ou difficulties, changes in order to change, delights in ventures' and show no inclinations towards taking up the 'quiet life' (ibid., pp. 93, 94).

The next aspect of entrepreneurial activity that requires som discussion concerns the origin of the enterprise opportunities that th appropriately talented agents are argued to seize. Most fundamenta here is the question: Are such opportunities merely *perceived* by th agents or are they, sometimes at least, *created* out of an otherwise iner environment of knowledge and technology? This is an ambiguous an

.ricky question that Schumpeter rarely addressed. It is, though, prominent in the matter of the relation between inventions and innovations that take them up for development, a topic to which he did direct some brief attention as I noted in section 5.4 of the previous chapter. My conclusion there was that Schumpeter saw potential entrepreneurial agents as facing a more or less given and unlimited 'pool' of inventions and relevant knowledge. To reiterate: 'New possibilities are continuously being offered by the surrounding world, in particular new discoveries are continuously being added to the existing store of knowledge' (ibid., p. 79). Most especially, though, for analytical purposes, he maintained a clear distinction between invention and innovation as agent activities – although he probably saw this as a reasonable reflection of reality as well. The effect of this distinction is to constrain the scope of any creative ambitions that may be involved in the entrepreneur's psychological make-up to the effectuation of new combinations that are made possible by the available 'pool' of inventions and knowledge. There is some creative responsibility in any innovation, but Schumpeter imposed definite limits on its range as the following passage indicates: 'It is no part of . . . [the entrepreneur's] function to "find" or to "create" new possibilities. They are always present, abundantly accumulated by all sorts of people. Often they are also generally known and being discussed by scientific or literary writers. In other cases, there is nothing to discover about them, because they are quite obvious.' (ibid., p. 88). It should be noted, though, that at one point, the actual creation of opportunities to innovate did creep into the argument (*Essays*, p. 28).

On the other side of the stimulation of innovation activity lies the relation between the development of a new combination and the demand or supply objective that is to serve. Whatever may be the motivations of entrepreneurs, it is *success* that they are immediately after, however it is measured. A necessary condition for that success is that the new combination must meet some economically-effective human 'need' or the entrepreneur must be able to generate the appropriate 'need'. Innovations may be 'the result of conscious efforts to cope with a problem independently presented by an economic situation or certain features of it . . .' and there is a sense in which they always require 'some "objective needs" to be satisfied and certain "objective conditions" . . .' to be present (*Cycles*, p. 85n). However, these pre-existing 'needs' are not sufficient to bring forth the innovation that would satisfy them because they can 'remain unsatisfied for an indefinite time . . .'. It is evident, therefore, that the other 'objective conditions' referred to above are required to complete the sufficient conditions, but just what these comprise, Schumpeter did not specify in any detail, possibly because of their immense variability. He did mention that they are linked to the generation of certain 'business behavior' which may be 'molded not only by general environmental conditions but also by the specific action of other social organs, governments for instance, taken with the intention of calling it forth' (ibid., p. 86n). To this it may reasonably be added that entrepreneurial motivations and expectations will be powerful conditioning factors as well. Schumpeter wisely added to all this the qualification that a subjective element must always remain such as to recognize that there can be no unique correspondence between a 'need' perceived by an entrepreneur and the precise nature of the innovation devised to try to meet it (ibid., p. 85n).

It is possible, too, Schumpeter thought, that the causal relation between 'needs' and innovations could run in the opposite direction. He espoused this thesis strongly in *Development* where the innovating producer was argued to manipulate consumers' tastes and preferences in order to ensure the effective acceptance of a new commodity. That is, it is the producer 'who as a rule initiates economic change, and consumers are educated by him if necessary' (p. 65). The idea was also present in *Cycles* where, in the case of the 'needs' met by automobiles, he wrote that 'any "need" for them that may have existed was certainly sub-conscious and not an element in the then existing system of economic values'. In this case, 'the "need" as far as[it was] economically relevant was created by the industry . . .' (p. 85n). Once again here it should be noticed that Schumpeter remained insensitive to the sphere of produced means of production. His argument consistently focused upon consumer commodities and ignored the potential for entrepreneurs to meet or create the technologically-determined 'needs' that may arise amongst already established industrial consumers. Much the same reasoning can be applied to such cases, although where the 'need' must be created, the entrepreneur may face all the inflexibilities presented by any attempt to absorb new types of durable means of production into existing production processes. But the effect of recognizing this additional avenue of entrepreneurial activity broadens the scope for initiating economic development and may significantly complicate the diffusion processes that are to be detailed in the traverse analysis.

Perhaps the best way to summarize the argument here about the source of innovation opportunities is to say that Schumpeter had his potential entrepreneur looking in two 'directions' when seeking to become active. They look to the demand side in order to perceive extant 'needs' that are not catered for at all, or are judged to be somehow less than adequately catered for, as well as to form ideas about 'needs' that might be created. In these cases, the expectation must be that the demand will meet the entrepreneur's own test of economic viability. As far as the other 'direction' is concerned, it is the availability of technology and other means to satisfy 'new needs' that the entrepreneurs must look for. Here, too, they may need to generate what they require, but Schumpeter's judgement was that more usually satisfying a 'need' becomes economically viable only if the means can be drawn from pre-existing inventions and knowledge with only some limited amount of creative input.

We have seen how Schumpeter's entrepreneurial agents have been analytically isolated from any business functions other than enterprise undertakings. This enabled him to emphasize the precise nature of their role and this objective was further served by his strategy of isolating the firms that the entrepreneurs establish in order to carry into effect their new combinations. According to Schumpeter, this latter step is soundly based empirically for 'new combinations are, as a rule, embodied . . . in new firms which generally do not arise out of the old ones but start producing beside them' (*Development*, p. 66). On the emergence of new firms, he wrote more directly that there 'is obviously no lack of realism about this assumption' (*Cycles*, p. 94), although he provided no real evidence for the claim beyond a passing reference to some unspecified aspects of the industrial revolution and to a monograph study of the theme by one 'Professor McGregor' (ibid., p. 94n). Later, Schumpeter wrote in a 1947 paper that the new-firm embodiment of new combinations may be gradually giving way to 'promotion within the shell of existing corporations', but no precise meaning for this was given (*Essays*, p. 218n) – it could be that he intended to suggest a takeover of such 'shells' by entrepreneurs as a means of establishing their innovation operations.

By restricting innovations to new firms set up for the purpose, Schumpeter introduced a discontinuity into the motion process that is reflected in a 'life-cycle' dynamic for firms. He complained that in extant business-cycle analyses this 'cycle' received insufficient recognition: 'the most serious shortcoming of modern business-cycle studies is that nobody seems to understand or even to care precisely how industries and individual firms rise and fall and how their rise and fall affects the aggregates and what we call loosely "general business conditions" ' (*Essays*, p. 315). The issue is doubly important for a full understanding of motion because it involves a dynamic of the structures and operations of firms and a sociological dynamic of the lives and economic roles of the agents who found and run them.

These dynamics were intended by Schumpeter to be perceived as integral components of the traverses that comprise business-cycle fluctuations. Firms emerge and are sustained by the existence of the entrepreneurial profits received by their founders. They survive in a competitive economic environment only for as long as their operations are not fatally impeded by imitative activities and subsequent innovations that bring new firms to replace them. It was Schumpeter's explicit argument that existing firms by and large cannot, or, at least, often do not, successfully protect themselves by engaging in emulative innovation-based counter-strategies. This view was posited in the following passage with some impressionistic cum poetic empirical support: 'Everyone who looks around knows the type of firm we are thinking of – living on the name, connections, quasi-rent, and reserves acquired in their youth, decorously dropping into the background, lingering in the fatally deepening dusk of respectable decay' (*Cycles*, p. 95). His claim was, then, that this inertia of firms in the face of competitive pressures is the key to 'that process of incessant rise and decay of firms and industries which is the central – though much neglected – fact about the capitalist machine ' (ibid., p. 96).

It is not clear what precise analytical status Schumpeter had intended to give the 'life-cycle' idea. There is an impression that he thought it could be blended with the traverse processes that make up the business cycle, but he provided no analysis to back this up. It is, however, an important insight that he seemed to think needed more research: 'Quantitative information about the life span of individual firms and analysis explanatory of their careers and their age distribution are among our most urgent desiderata. They would be important for many other purposes besides the study of business fluctuations, and throw a flood of light on the structure and working of capitalism . . .' (ibid., p. 95n).

The 'life-cycle' of firms is accompanied by a sociological discontinuity as 'individuals and families rise and fall economically and socially' (*Development*, p. 67; cf. the discussion of social class dynamics in Chapter 3, section 3.4 above). To begin with, the entrepreneurial function as such occupies individual agents for only a limited time: 'everyone is an entrepreneur only when he actually "carries out new combinations", and loses that character as soon as he has built up his business, when he settles down to running it as other people run their businesses' (ibid., p. 78; cf. *Cycles*, p. 103). As theirs is a transitory position in social and economic life, entrepreneurs do not form a social class and the status of being an entrepreneur cannot be inherited (*Development*, pp. 78, 79). Moreover, historical evidence suggests that they do not come predominantly from any particular social stratum or group (*Cycles*, p. 104 and n). Now out of this sociologically heterogeneous group of temporary entrepreneurs will arise *some* successful business people – Schumpeter at one point asserted that their failure rate could be expected to be remarkably high with most never getting their project underway and then nine out of ten failing (ibid., p. 117). The survivors are elevated by their success to the capitalist, means of production owning, class and/or perhaps to the 'land' owning class, depending upon the type of enterprise they are involved in and what they choose to do with any finance capital that accumulates out of their profits (*Development*, pp. 78–9). Thus, 'the position of the typical industrial or commercial or financial family directly originates in some act, or some series of acts, of innovation . . . [and when] their period of entrepreneurship is past, those families live . . . on quasi-rents, often supported by monopoloid situations, or . . . on interest' (*Cycles*, p. 106). The thesis was even more clearly put in *Capitalism*: 'Economically and sociologically, directly and indirectly, the bourgeoisie . . . depends on the entrepreneur and, as a class, lives and will die with him . . .' (p. 134). So it is then that the economic 'life-cycle' of the firm will be intimately related to its contemporaneous social 'life-cycle' as its ownership and administrative patterns change over time, with generations coming and going. There will also be a possible slippage of control gradually into the hands of a managerial-executive group due to the owners' default or through the spreading of ownership with public incorporation. Now while all this sociological analysis always hovered in the background of Schumpeter's economic theory of motion, it received little further development outside of *Capitalism*, Part II.

6.3   New combinations and resources

Earlier on, in my outline of Schumpeter's theory of economic development, I made reference to three issues raised by the analysis of new combinations as the basis for that theory (above pp. 104–5). The first concerning the agents that implement the new combinations has just been discussed in the previous section. In this section and the next, I will focus on the second issue: what resources will be used to facilitate the new combinations?

It should be recalled first of all that according to Schumpeter's methodology, development is depicted as the result of adding innovations into the steady circular-flow state. Under assumed highly (or perfectly) competitive conditions, this state must operate with full employment of all available resources. Furthermore, we have just seen how the entrepreneurs are assumed to be *new men and women* who enter the sphere of production and set up *new firms* in order to implement their new combinations. That is, the new combinations do not depend on, nor are they immediately integrated with, any existing production processes. Also, they cannot be associated with any capital accumulation or investment, for there is no scope for these phenomena in the steady state. So it is, then, that the entrepreneurs are required to furnish their new firms with *new plant and equipment* embodying the innovation and they must acquire the necessary items in the face of a current state of full employment of existing productive capacity and resources. 'As a rule', wrote Schumpeter in this context, 'the new combinations must draw the necessary means of production from some old combinations – and . . . we shall assume that they *always* do so, in order to put in bold relief what we hold to be the essential contour line', which amounts to 'simply the different employment of the economic systems' existing supplies of productive means . . .' (*Development* p. 68, original emphasis; cf. *Cycles*, p. 111 and n). This resource reallocation element of his theory was so fundamental to Schumpeter that he added that it constitutes 'a second definition of development in our sense' (*Development*, p. 68).

Self-evidently, all this rules out any reference to unused capacity or idle resources in the essentials of economic development even though Schumpeter recognized that their use in 'practical life . . . is very often the case'. He realized also that the existence of unemployed workers, excess raw materials stocks and excess productive capacity is, from one perspective at least, 'certainly . . . a contributory circumstance, a favourable condition and even an incentive to the emergence of new combinations' (ibid., p. 67). This appeared to be so to him because no *new* resources are argued to be committed in the innovation process. Were such new resources required, and especially if they were to be embodied in new durable means of production, the state of the economy described by Schumpeter could well be seen as a discouragement to the investment in innovations. As the argument went, though, his position was that such economic conditions could only emerge as a consequence of the development process and could not, therefore, logically be used to help explain the process in the first place.

As already indicated, the resource reallocation mechanism is facilitated by the creation of bank credit which is drawn in favour of the entrepreneurs (above section 6.1, cf. below section 6.5). The credit enables the entrepreneur 'to withdraw the producers' goods which he needs from their previous employments by exercising a demand for them, and thereby to force the economic system into new channels'. It effectively acts 'as an order on the . . . system to accommodate itself to he purposes of the entrepreneur . . .' (ibid., pp. 106, 107). What ollows, then, must be a sequence of economic adjustments that disturb he existing steady-state and begin a traverse towards a new, revised tate in which the resource demands of the entrepreneurs have been net. And, although 'no goods and certainly no new goods correspond to he newly created purchasing power', the 'room for it is squeezed out at he cost of previously existing purchasing power' (ibid., p. 109). It was ;chumpeter's view that the required traverse induced by the entrepre- 1eurs' pressure on the input resource markets could be explained simply »y what happens to relative prices and the assumed quantitative reallocations that follow from the changes in them. Of the entrepre- 1eurs' entry into the markets, he assured us that it '*really is obvious*, that ind *how* this will affect prices and values and produce a string of mportant consequences which are responsible for many characteristic eatures of the capitalist process' (*Cycles*. p. 112, emphasis added). Within the confines of a perfectly competitive general equilibrium nodel the 'how' may be 'obvious', but beyond such a context, the traverse must be seen to involve some changes that are less than obvious' when followed out in their sequential detail.

In particular, it is the precise nature of the quantitative reallocations hat needs to be followed through and, as Schumpeter recognized, this vill depend upon 'the whole business situation' (ibid., p. 123). There vill be unique conditions in each 'neighborhood of equilibrium' that nust be allowed for in analysing the system's response to the added lemand for resources. But, more important as a matter of general orinciple, are the problematics that concern the *nature* of the input resources that are to be reallocated. Two aspects of the problem require attention in the present context: one is the existence of means of oroduction with particular physical-technical forms designed to serve oarticular production purposes and the other is the probable need for *qualitatively* new produced means of production in order to implement he innovations intended by the entrepreneurs. From both perspectives, he term reallocation becomes inappropriate as a description of the orocesses that are to follow the entrepreneurs' endeavours to obtain the nputs they need. Schumpeter was more or less aware of the problem. For example, he wrote of production functions that are subject to restrictions . . . in real life' in the case 'of going concerns for which a 1umber of technological data are, for the time being, unalterably fixed . .' (*Essays*, p. 274). Moreover, he adopted the view, confirmed by :ommon-sense observations, that 'major innovations and also many ninor ones entail construction of New Plant (and equipment) – or the rebuilding of old plant – requiring nonnegligible time and outlay' and added that he would 'reason on the assumption that they always do'! (*Cycles*, p. 93). He even broadened the assumption to recognize that while it is possible that not every new plant embodies an innovation . . . practically all new plant that is being constructed beyond replacement, and much of what is being constructed by way of replacement, either embodies some innovation or is a response to situations traceable to some innovation' (ibid., p. 94). Schumpeter sensed the potential difficulties that this complex of assumptions posed for analysis:

> We move on common and familiar ground when we say that expenditure on plant and equipment is the 'active' factor in producers' expenditure. But if we go on to say that expenditure on the creation of new production functions – innovation – is the active element in total expenditure on plant and equipment, we are leaving this terra firma, and there is every reason for the reader to examine the nature of this . . . step. (ibid., p. 560)

Perhaps, we might think, it is important for *the analyst* to examine the step, too.

There is in all of this some potentially deep insight into the true nature of the traverses that will follow the entry of entrepreneurs into input markets. The intimate involvement of the physical-technical structure of production is evident in the above pieces, as is the idea that innovations require *time-consuming production responses* that may be directly linked to an entrepreneur's demand or emerge as a sequential reflection of it in a sector at some remove from that directly affected. The most obvious difficulty that now emerges is that it is not possible to make these assumptions and insights consistent with the idea that innovations must be carried out using the existing stock of resources. This latter approach would require that at least some of such resources be strategically available as well as highly flexible, mobile and adaptable. These qualities really only inhere in homogeneous 'land' and labour power services upon which Schumpeter focused in the basic, vertically-integrated production model in *Development*. In that context, new combinations could readily be represented as demanding simple reallocations because the only *produced* and *particular* means of production comprise intermediate goods. But even there, he soon allowed the need for other produced means of production to intrude in defiance of the theoretical restrictions he initially imposed. He noted, for example, that if 'somewhere or other exactly such produced means of production as the entrepreneur needs happen to exist, then of course he can buy them . . .' and at another point he referred to these needs as including 'machinery' (*Development*, pp. 96, 116). Then, when linking innovation waves with the business-cycle form of economic development, he argued quite explicitly that 'the causal nexus begins first of all with the means of production which are bought with capital and that the boom materialises first of all in the production of industrial plant, factories, mines, ships, railways, and so forth . . .' (ibid., p. 215). The traverse implications of these perceptions simply cannot be represented by a model of production in which the only 'outside' resources are 'land' and labour power. In neither *Development* nor *Cycles* was the void between Schumpeter's analytical simplifications and the descriptive treatment of the real world of an inflexible physical-technical production structure bridged. The rich, albeit passing, insights to which I have referred above just never received the formal attention they warranted (cf. *History*, pp. 631ff.).

6.4 Particular new combinations cases

In the previous chapter (section 5.4), I referred to the heterogeneous nature of Schumpeter's five types of new combinations. At the time I drew attention to the fact that in most of the theoretical analysis of business cycles that he ultimately developed, only the process and product innovation categories received any formal attention. At one point in *Development* (pp. 129ff.), though, he provided a somewhat broader account of the nature of each of the five in relation to their causal role in economic development, with particular reference to the generation of entrepreneurial profit (see section 6.6 below). Here he included his only extended consideration of the latter three categories in the list of five, but they remained in isolation from the mainline of the explanation of motion. Besides shedding some further light on how Schumpeter conceived of his new combinations in an operational sense, these discussions are also pertinent to the resource input reallocation problems considered in the previous section. He built his main argument around the case of a pure process innovation in the form of the introduction of power looms into the weaving industry that is dominated by hand-loom production. The extended discussion of this first case was followed by briefer pieces on the other four types of new combinations.

The power-looms case of process innovation is a 'classic' in the history of economic analysis – Schumpeter referred to its development by Lauderdale and its analysis by Böhm-Bawerk (*Development*, p. 129). But its significance here goes well beyond its substantive content because it serves to highlight the general limitations of Schumpeter's analysis of the means of production dynamics of innovation-induced traverses that I made reference to above. His hope was that in approaching the analysis of this case, he had 'taken the reader so far that . . . [he] may make use of our analytic tools in their purest form without further explanations and repetitions' (ibid.). This was a forlorn hope, for, as we have seen, his theoretical 'tools' as so far developed were not suitable for dealing with the full implications of this type of innovation. I will reiterate this critical thesis in the present context.

Schumpeter's vertically-integrated model of production with its 'outside' inputs restricted to 'land' and labour-power services, lent itself well to a conceptualization of the initial state of the textile industry. The consumer commodity cloth is produced by hand weaving, with the assumption that the hand looms used by the cloth producers are self-made and 'wear out' fully each production period. They are thus true intermediate goods. Into a steady-state situation of the industry, given its location in a steady circular-flow state of the economy generally, the power loom is introduced by an entrepreneur who, on this occasion, is also the inventor. In order to carry into effect this innovation, the entrepreneur obtains sufficient newly-created credit from a bank to establish a new firm to build and operate the new plant. The presumed basis for this decision to innovate is the expectation that the power-loom process will lower costs by raising labour productivity to an extent necessary to generate a profit revenue that is adequate to cover the interest cost of the credit and perhaps provide some additional 'compensations' for the self-employed weaver.

On the subject of how the entrepreneurial agent obtains the new power-loom equipment and plant, Schumpeter claimed that it is 'completely immaterial whether he constructs the power looms himself or has them constructed by another firm according to his directions in order to confine himself to employing them' (ibid., p. 130). As an economic generalization, this claim is patently false. If the power looms and associated power equipment are to be supplied by another firm, the agents of that firm must first be induced to produce such a one-off set of machinery and have a means of production structure that can be adapted to such a project. But, immediately this is assumed, the vertically-integrated structure of weaving is negated and a two-sector model is required with trade in means of production between the sectors. And, what is more, a question that must immediately be addressed is who *is* this 'other firm'? It cannot be one that has any experience building looms because in the hand-weaving industry the looms were hand crafted as part of the production process itself. Perhaps the innovator here can persuade some other agent to set up a new firm to produce the power equipment, but on what economic basis this would be done is not immediately clear because only one order is so far available. The latter agent would need to be convinced, at least, that power weaving would rapidly replace the hand-loom based industry.

Should we go back and reconstruct the model with two sectors from the start such that hand looms are built in a specialized industry, then the problem still remains that the industry must be able to adapt itself to the new demand and be convinced that it is economically viable to do so. On the other hand, the idea that the innovating agent could build up the required looms and power source himself or herself requires us to imagine a versatile craftsperson indeed.

Be all this as it may, let us proceed on the assumption that the innovating entrepreneur has established the power-weaving facility and has it in operation. According to Schumpeter's example, the innovator enjoys a six-fold increase in unit labour productivity and accrues a net surplus over costs as an entrepreneurial profit, albeit with certain supplementary conditions being applicable (ibid., p. 130). It should be stressed here that the entrepreneur's decision to produce does not imply *replacement* of any existing weaving capacity, but is assumed rather to add capacity in the new-technology form. This is an important point because it affects how the pecuniary costs and benefits associated with the innovation are to be interpreted. One of the supplementary conditions is that the price of cloth must not fall, or if it does, it must be to an extent that does not wipe out the entrepreneur's net surplus. Schumpeter felt that this assumption is consistent with the reality of such situations as one new small-scale supplier would be unlikely to disturb the market (and in the perfectly competitive case, could not do so by definition). A second supplementary condition is that the amortization cost of the power-loom equipment and plant must not exceed the wages of the extra workers that would have been needed to produce and maintain a set of hand looms with the same periodic capacity. Correctly interpreted, this condition ensures the basic economic desirability of the innovation in terms of its opportunity cost. The final condition focuses on what happens to input prices when the *additional* demands from the entrepreneur impact on the markets. Whether only 'land' and labour-power services are allowed for, or a broader perspective of inputs is taken, the availability of the inputs is strictly finite and they are assumed to be already fully employed. Schumpeter expressed the view that here, too, if the scale of added demand is relatively small, then no rise in input prices need be expected, especially under competitive conditions (ibid., p. 130 and n). It is probably more realistic to assume that under all circumstances, the new entrepreneur will have to pay more in order to prise the inputs out of their existing, well-established use patterns. And, as Schumpeter correctly recognized, this means that the entrepreneur's decision to innovate must be based on *expected* values of input prices rather than on pre-existing ones (ibid., p. 130). The decision is thereby made more complicated and the chance of *ex post* failure to realize a net surplus is increased (cf. ibid., p. 85). In the absence of discrimination in input markets, it must be assumed that the new, higher prices will spread and cause some surprises amongst existing producers.

As the next stage of this case example of a process innovation, Schumpeter introduced the 'second act of the drama' in which the power-loom innovation is diffused throughout the textile industry (ibid., p. 131). He did not trace the traverse in detail, being content with the assertion that it would include a 'complete reorganisation of the industry . . ., with its increases in production, its competitive struggle, its supersession of obsolete businesses, its possible dismissal of workers, and so forth' (ibid., p. 131). His promise was that he would return to this analytical issue in more detail later, but in the meantime his readers had to be satisfied with the as yet unsubstantiated assertion that 'the final result must be a new equilibrium position' (ibid.). No detailed analysis to justify such an assertion was ever provided and some common-sense reasoning suggests that it would have to include some extremely unrealistic assumptions about agent expectations, information and general abilities, together with similarly unrealistic assumptions about flexibility in the production structure, if the required co-ordination of actions is to be realized.

The general tenor of Schumpeter's subsequent analyses of the other four types of new combinations implied that they are essentially similar to the process-innovation case. He saw the latter as but 'a special case of all changes in the productive process in the widest sense', to which he added that '[m]any innovations in business organisation and all innovations in commercial combinations are included in this . . . [and in] all such cases, what has been said may be repeated word for word' (ibid., p. 133). However, some critical consideration of the additional cases discussed reveals that the degree of similarity to the power-looms case is rather exaggerated here.

Consider first the example designed to illustrate category (5): 'the introduction of large-scale manufacturing business into an economic system in which they were previously unknown' (ibid.). There can be little doubt that this is a task for which much entrepreneurial talent would be needed, but it can hardly be represented by individual entrepreneurs acting unilaterally on borrowed credit. It would seem much more probable that such a reorganization would be a gradual process centred upon some existing firms in an industry undertaking takeover and merger activities. Schumpeter's conclusion is misleading in ts simplicity: 'these individuals have done nothing but employ existing goods to greater effect . . .' (ibid.).

The next case explored by Schumpeter was that of a new 'commercial combination' in the form of 'the choice of a new and cheaper source of supply for a means of production, perhaps a raw material' (ibid.). In order for such a choice to rank as an innovation for his purposes, he quite correctly stressed that the new source must be demanding and hazardous for the entrepreneur to get at – remote location being a case in point. And, quite clearly, the successful innovator in this case will be able to produce the commodity concerned at lower cost provided only that he or she can obtain all the other means of production required to set up the new firm and plant in 'local' markets at prices that are not so high as to negate the benefits of the new source (ibid., p. 134). The post-innovation traverse implied here will be less complex than in the process-innovation case because, strictly speaking, this new combination does not involve any change in the qualitative characteristics of the production process in use. Moreover, the process of imitation and diffusion will be more rapid and complete once the initiating entrepreneur has shown the way, unless he or she can exclude others from the new source by some means. But, there is no justification in this case, either, for taking the traverse to a new steady-state equilibrium for granted. If motion is to be understood, the resource reallocation sequences would still have to be traced in detail and the co-ordinating forces identified.

Schumpeter turned next to the case of product innovation: '(1) The introduction of a new good . . . or of a new quality of a good.' His treatment here was based on the claimed 'analogous' status of this category *vis-à-vis* the process innovation exemplified in the power-looms case (ibid.). However, there is much more to the proper analysis of this type than was ever recognized by Schumpeter and the analogy can only be carried so far. Product innovation has both demand and supply side effects for the analyst to contend with. On the demand side, it is self-evident that a successful innovation requires either that some independent change of tastes or technology, and the associated change in effective demand, is perceived by the entrepreneur, or that he or she must confidently expect that some invention or idea, once innovated, will be able to be effectively promoted in order to create the effective demand needed. The complicating factor in this latter case is that the promotion costs must be estimated *ex ante* thus complicating the calculation of net revenues to be expected from the new commodity.

It is also important in understanding the demand side of the product innovation type to distinguish between a commodity that serves a totally new purpose and one that serves an existing purpose 'better' by virtue of an improvement in some facet of its quality. The reason here is that in the former case, the appropriate unit price that should be set, and the relevant price elasticity of demand, will have to be estimated by cost analysis and market research more or less from scratch, while in the latter case, all that is needed is some modified price that can be established with much less effort and expenditure and with more certainty that it is apt. It should be noted immediately that in this latter case, the requirement that the price of the commodity concerned in the innovation should not rise makes little sense, for the profit of the entrepreneur depends upon the new qualities of the commodity enabling him or her to lift the price above that at which the existing form sells. The only alternative is that the new product costs less to produce even with its new qualities, but the relevance of this possibility depends upon the particular item involved. The result of these distinctions is that there will be four sorts of demand-side contingencies possible, in principle, at least: a totally new commodity for which effective demand appears automatically; a totally new commodity that must be promoted; a modified commodity for which effective demand appears automatically; and a modified commodity that must be promoted. Overall, the automatic emergence of demand seems less likely than the need for promotion, especially in the first case. Schumpeter himself only considered cases where promotion is needed (cf. ibid., p. 65).

Still on the demand side of the product innovation, a further distinction to be made is between products that will serve as means of production and those that will serve consumer needs directly. The main immediate difference between the two is that the promotion procedures suitable for the latter may not be useful for the former. What is more important, though, is that the traverses induced by each cannot be expected to be the same. Product innovation in a means of production has more complex implications for the process of diffusion and absorption than those that follow from launching a new consumer commodity. Moreover, the new means of production will be associated with some technological change in the processes of production into which it is absorbed and from this perspective, its consequences can be expected to be similar to those of a process innovation. Quite evidently, it makes little sense to try to maintain a common analytical treatment for these two new-product types as Schumpeter seemed wont to do (ibid., p. 134).

On the supply side of the product innovation, there are other complications that affect its consequences to consider. In particular, these concern the fact that the new commodity must be produced and it is probable that this will require some modification of the existing process or the establishment of a totally new process. That is, in this case, the new entrepreneur is faced with a double-sided decision problem involving his or her perception of the nascent demand opportunities and then his or her ability to obtain the necessary means of production and set up the required production plant. There is here a double lot of uncertainty to contend with, too, as the demand side expectations are joined by the need for expectations about input costs and realized production conditions. On both counts, room for errors of judgement exist and the entrepreneur's profit expectations can be less readily calculated with any confidence. It seems that product innovators need to be made of sterner entrepreneurial stuff than their process-innovating counterparts. For the analyst, the supply side considerations *per se* make the product innovation case similar to that of the process innovation as far as the traverse consequences are concerned. And, as for that case, the nature of the traverse will depend upon whether the new production process is associated with producing a means of production or a consumer commodity.

The last case of new combinations considered by Schumpeter was his '(3) The opening of a new market . . .', probably in a foreign country, in which an existing commodity can be sold (ibid., p. 135). This is most immediately a demand-side innovation type and access to entrepreneurial profit will be conditional upon applying price discrimination in the new market. The established markets and the new one must be sufficiently 'separated' so that the latter can carry a sustainable higher commodity price. Schumpeter's treatment of this case was quite brief and his tenor suggests that he did not consider it to be of great importance outside of some particular historical episodes. There remain, however, aspects of the case that should be recognized if its implications for development are to be properly understood. First, the new market must be capable of delivering its effective demand in a hard-currency form if it happens to be in a soft-currency country. In modern-day cases of exploiting potential consumers in the ever more open Eastern bloc and Chinese markets, this contingency is of great concern to entrepreneurs. Perhaps effective penetration will be easier with means of production than with consumer commodities because the former may be supported by government development programmes. Secondly, once the effective demand is assured, the place to look for the traverse effects is back in the domestic economy. The implications there are on the supply side. Given that the quality of the commodity to be sent to the new market is identical to that sold at home, all that is required is for the productive capacity to be expanded by means of a new plant set up by the entrepreneur. But, in a full-employment situation, this new capacity will only be able to be found by means of some resoure reallocation with all the ramifications akin to a process innovation. In particular, the entrepreneur must be prepared for higher production costs when entering the new market. The traverse that follows from the innovation must show how the *diversion* of part of the total available commodity-producing capacity from the domestic to the foreign market will be absorbed by domestic consuming agents. And again, the particular way that this works out will be affected by whether the commodity is a means of production or a consumer item. A simpler alternative available to the entrepreneur who already produces the commodity to be exported is to direct part of existing capacity to serving the new market with its higher price. In this case, too, the reverberations in the domestic market will depend on whether a consumer item or a means of production needed for replacement and/or net investment is involved.

Enough has now been said on this theme to make the point that Schumpeter's five types of new combinations cannot legitimately be treated as homogeneous generators of economic development and business cycles. Each one has something in common with one or more of the others, but there are always additional and/or different implications for the traverses induced that need to be followed up and explicated. Schumpeter did not face up to the considerable demands of dealing with each type fully in his main analysis of motion and confined his attention largely to process and product innovations. But, as we have seen, these two have sufficiently different implications, too, to warrant quite separate treatment in any explanation of the business cycle. My critical exposition to follow will reveal that Schumpeter was often rather too casual about how these two categories were included in his arguments.

6.5 Financing new combinations

There are two aspects of the financing processes in economic development that require attention. The first, considered in this section, concerns the means by which potential entrepreneurs obtain the funds they need to facilitate innovations. Here, then, the focus is on the more or less microeconomic and operational facets of financing development. The activities dealt with have broader ramifications as well in that they take place in and through a particular monetary system. Schumpeter's analysis of this second, more macroeconomic aspect of development financing is taken up in the next chapter.

When it came to analysing how entrepreneurs finance their innovation endeavours, Schumpeter continued to treat them as isolated agents and sought an independent source of funding that is not linked to any existing economic activity. To a large extent this had to be the case because his methodology required that innovations be introduced into a steady circular-flow state where all production and consumption is funded by current revenue flows and no stocks or flow-sources of savings are available by definition. He was called upon, therefore, to show that there exists an institutional source of *ad hoc* created credit to which nascent entrepreneurs who have no financial resources can turn for their funding needs.

Schumpeter summarized his opening gambit in the analysis of innovation financing in the form of 'three propositions, which sound strange but are tautologically true for an economic world embodying our assumptions' (*Cycles*, p. 110). The first of these was that entrepreneurs 'borrow all the "funds" they need both for creating and for operating their plants – *i.e.*, for acquiring both their fixed and their working capital' (ibid.). Notice again here, in passing, that if working capital includes the funding of all intermediate goods in production, then Schumpeter's common sense has led him outside of the circular-flow model to take account of the need for entrepreneurs to purchase durable produced means of production. The availability of such means requires explicit explanation, as has already been suggested. Secondly, he posited that 'nobody else borrows' (ibid.). His intention here was to emphasize that his concern was with productive credit rather than consumer credit, for only the entrepreneur 'is a debtor by the nature of his economic function' (*Development*, p. 103; cf. pp. 70, 104–5). Thirdly, he made explicit his intention to have entrepreneurial funds 'consist in means of payment created *ad hoc*' (*Cycles*, pp. 110–11). To these 'three propositions' he hastened to add that they 'are nothing but pieces of analytic scaffolding to be removed when they have served their purpose . . .', a promise never really honoured except in a most desultory manner (e.g. ibid., pp. 114–15). However, the point of the 'three propositions' was still well made in that they opened up the 'logical relation . . . between what is called "credit creation by banks" and innovation', with the credit creation '*considered as the monetary complement of innovation*' and its relation to innovation considered as 'fundamental to the understanding of the capitalist engine' (ibid., p. 111, original emphasis).

As a practical matter, the banks in Schumpeter's theory are expected to provide what amounts to 'venture' capital under quite risky and unsecured conditions if the terms of the theory are taken at face value – the budding entrepreneurs need have no experience, no equity finance capital and no collateral. If we allow for the embodiment of innovations in some durable means of production, then at least the banks can take a mortgage charge over the new firm's assets as security. But they cannot do so immediately because the required means must first be produced. Or, as Schumpeter put it, 'the entrepreneur may mortgage goods, which he acquires with the borrowed purchasing power' but the 'granting of credit comes first and collateral must be dispensed with, at least in principle, for however short an interval' (*Development*, p. 101). This leaves the bank with some degree of 'venture' in its lending. Of course, Schumpeter recognized that agents would meet with a better reception at the bank if they set out with some real or financial asset backing of their own. The situation remains, though, that in his theory the 'entrepreneurial function is not, in principle, connected with the possession of wealth, as analysis and experience equally teach . . .' (ibid.), for it is 'leadership rather than ownership that matters' (*Cycles*, p. 103). Schumpeter's approach to financing the entrepreneurial activities of individuals served to emphasize this 'principle'.

Schumpeter's thesis concerning the generation of economic development depends on there being a logical link between *ad hoc* bank credit and innovation. Strictly speaking, this calls for banker agents to act passively in their responses to the demand for credit. To the extent that they cannot always be expected to do so, the behaviour of the bankers becomes another variable in the development processes affecting the initiation and diffusion of innovations. They may impede or facilitate these processes as they see fit in accordance with their own motives and criteria for doing business. As Schumpeter astutely noticed, while bankers are in the business of lending – their 'product' is credit or purchasing power – their 'sales' are not merely geared to the demand they face because they must be as sure as possible that they will get their 'product' back. For them, the character of the customer matters and 'every transaction with every customer . . . [is] an individual case, which cannot be dealt with in the same way as the sale of a pair of boots' (ibid., p. 640). It is against this background of the need for caution in lending that banks exercise often conservative controls over their 'trading' positions: 'while most shopkeepers will normally congratulate themselves whenever they are "sold out", the banker does not typically aim at being, and does not congratulate himself if he is "loaned up". On the contrary, this means for him an exceptional and undesirable situation of embarrassment and of danger . . .' (ibid., p. 641). Crucial in this caution is the appropriate assessment of customers and their purposes for borrowing. 'Judging the chances of success of each purpose', Schumpeter argued, 'and, as a means to this end, the kind of man the borrower is, watching him as he proceeds and granting or withholding

urther support accordingly – these are the fundamental functions of
. . [a bank's directing] committee . . .' (ibid.). A banker must,
:herefore, 'know the customer, his business, and even his private habits,
and get, by frequently "talking things over with him", a clear picture of
his situation' (ibid., p. 116).

It is evident from these arguments that Schumpeter's understanding
of the realities of banking practice should have led him to conceive of
bankers as very active agents in the development and business-cycle
processes. At one point, he did note in passing that regarding the merits
and viability of an innovation project, 'the only man . . . [the entrepre-
neur] has to convince or impress is the banker who is to finance him . . .'
(*Development*, p. 89). That is, bankers may be very active in the sense
of mediating in the logical connection between planned innovations and
their realization. What needs to be noted, though, is that Schumpeter
wanted to avoid giving this idea of bankers being active too broad a
range. He went to some lengths to explain that with some exceptions,
banks are not the *initiators* of any real economic phenomena (*Cycles*,
pp. 641ff., 115–16) and remain 'passive' in the particular sense of
responding to economic conditions rather than being their cause (ibid.,
p. 643n). His idea in all this was to distance himself from monetary
theories of the business cycle in which banks are given such an 'active'
role that the explanation of fluctuations centres almost exclusively on
their operations (e.g. *Development*, p. 230n; cf. *History*, pp. 1117ff.).
However, whatever his objections to monetary theories as such, it is not
unreasonable to suggest, I think, that the variable nature of the relations
between bankers and potential entrepreneurs could have been made a
more explicit part of the initiation and diffusion of innovations and the
traverses that result. The banker's mediation in this is vital to Schumpeter's theory and how he responds affects the form of the business
cycle, especially in the initial stages of the upswing from a 'neighborhood of equilibrium'.

6.6 Entrepreneurial profit

I noted in section 6.2 above that Schumpeter was rather coy about
ascribing a purely profit-seeking motivation to his entrepreneurs. But it
seems clear that he thought of some expectation of a profit return as a
precondition for decisions to innovate and that he saw the key source of
profit in a capitalist economy as the innovation process itself. In this
section, the motivation question is not at issue. Rather, what is in focus
is the nature of and explanation for the profit that accrues to entrepreneurs as a consequence of their successful activities.

Most baldly stated, entrepreneurial profit comprises 'a surplus over costs' or 'the difference between receipts and outlay in a business' (*Development*, p. 128). In order to help this idea along, Schumpeter added an attempt to define 'costs' or 'outlay' as 'all the disbursements which the entrepreneur *must* make directly or indirectly in production' (ibid., emphasis added). These phrases are question-begging at best and demand, in particular, a more precise specification of *which* 'disbursements . . . in production' *must* be made. He did not address this issue directly but simply went on to compound the puzzle by asserting that the following items 'must be added' to the disbursements, whatever the latter are: 'an appropriate wage for labor performed by the entrepreneur, an appropriate rent for any land which may chance to belong to him, and finally a premium for risk' (ibid.). Schumpeter's point here was to try to ensure that the profit component of the entrepreneurs' income is focused upon in isolation by distinguishing it from the wage he or she could claim under market conditions for doing the work involved in setting up the innovation and from the market rent of any 'land' he or she happens to own. And, as was emphasized in section 6.2 above, the 'risk premium' cannot accrue to the entrepreneur *as such* for in *this* role the agent bears no risk. Any such compensation here can only be claimed by the entrepreneur to the extent that he or she is also a capitalist, having personally provided some or all of the finance needed to establish the new firm and plant. Otherwise, the risk premium should accrue to the credit provider as an element in the interest obligations of the entrepreneur. Whether or not these latter income items should be considered as 'outlays' is a matter of definition. But, what we do have so far is that the after-innovation revenue flows of an entrepreneur must cover at least the undefined 'costs' of production, the wage and rent claims of the entrepreneur together with, presumably, the interest obligations (and principal repayments if applicable) on any credit borrowed, including the risk premium, and/or an 'internal' charge for such interest on finance capital provided by the entrepreneur himself or herself. The profit is then the residual that Schumpeter referred to as a 'surplus', although as I will detail further below, he rejected the residual idea in this context (*Development*, p. 153).

Leaving aside any concern with the nature of the 'costs' in the equation, Schumpeter introduced his explanation of the *origin* of the surplus as follows:

> Our solution may be expressed briefly: in the circular flow the total receipts of a business – abstracting from monopoly – are just big enough to cover outlays. In it there are only producers who neither make profits nor suffer losses and whose income is sufficiently characterised by the phrase 'wages of management'. And since the new combinations which are carried out if there

is 'development' are necessarily *more advantageous* than the old, total receipts must in this case be greater than total costs. (ibid., p. 129, emphasis added)

The *items* comprising the 'costs' are now common to both the circular flow and development processes of production, so our attention is shifted to the 'more advantageous' phrase elicited here to help account for the surplus. It was at this point in *Development* that he went on to discuss at length the cases of new combinations dealt with in section 6.4 above (ibid., pp. 129ff.). The important general result to emerge from these cases was that each in its own way, because of the economic advantages' it brings, gives rise to a surplus that accrues to the entrepreneur as profit. Where a process innovation is concerned, the advantage is one of a reduced cost of production of the output commodity. Thus in the power-looms case used by Schumpeter to illustrate such innovations, 'the [new] looms produce a greater physical product than the services of labor and land contained in them could produce by the previous method . . .' (ibid., p. 131). The appearance of a surplus would then be assured provided the cloth can be sold at such a price and the inputs required by the entrepreneur can be had at such costs that the effects of the productivity improvement are not cancelled out. His usual assumption was that the commodity price remains constant, at least for some time, after the initial innovation, but the innovator must expect some rise in input costs over present levels because of demand effects.

In the case of a product innovation, the source of the surplus is not quite so clear cut (ibid., pp. 134–5, 135–6). Where the new product is different but serves an existing purpose, e.g. Schumpeter referred to the partial replacement of wool by cotton textiles in the last quarter of the eighteenth century, the surplus is dependent upon the new product being cheaper to produce per unit of the service it provides to consumers. A higher quality replacement commodity, by contrast, will usually be expected to command a greater price than established for the original version, while a completely new commodity that serves a newly-emergent or created need must be expected to command a price that exceeds the 'costs' and other 'outlays' necessary for its production. Innovations that involve establishing new markets also depend upon it being possible to realize a higher price for the commodity to be exported (ibid., p. 135). Assuming no quality change in the commodity, its production cost in the domestic market will remain unchanged unless any expansion of capacity undertaken to provide for the new market bids up unit input costs to an extent not compensated for by any economies of scale. The entrepreneur's decision to move into the new market will then be based solely on the expectation that a higher price can be charged for the same commodity, *cet. par*. By contrast, the availability of a new source of supply for one or more inputs will provide a surplus only if the *inputs* now cost less (ibid., pp. 133–4). The output commodity price is not at issue in this purely supply-side case. Finally, the case of an organizational change in an industry, 'the introduction of large-scale manufacturing businesses . . . previously unknown' was Schumpeter's example (ibid., p. 133), where it can be carried through by a single entrepreneur acting unilaterally, will facilitate lower cost production and the realization of a surplus as a consequence. He did not mention that the large scale has a potential demand side advantage as well in that the new firm may take on a price-leader role and increase its surplus by raising the commodity price.

Now in all these cases, the more precise origin of the surplus is to be found in the nature of capitalist property rights, an issue not considered by Schumpeter in direct terms. The entrepreneur, even if he or she borrows all the finance that he or she needs, becomes the *de jure* owner of the means of production stock used to produce the commodity sold, whatever the form of innovation involved. By virtue of that ownership status, the entrepreneur is the immediate owner of the commodities produced with the means of production and the sole claimant of the sales revenue generated by their sale, net of any legally binding 'external' cost obligations. The residual (see below) net revenue becomes his or her income and may cover any or all of the range of 'claims' cited by Schumpeter: a wage, some rent, some interest on personal finance capital, as well as the surplus that becomes entrepreneurial profit. A further requirement must be added here, though, in order that the income include the profit component, namely that the entrepreneur must hold some degree of monopoly power over his or her market or markets by virtue of the innovation undertaken. That is, he or she holds some discriminatory pecuniary advantage *vis-à-vis* supply and/or demand conditions relative to those other producers who are 'competitors' in one sense or another. By being able to charge a higher commodity price and/or by producing at lower cost, the entrepreneur can raise revenues above costs by more than is possible under existing conditions – in the purely competitive circular-flow case, revenues must equal costs in the senses used by Schumpeter. He was well aware of this monopoly power condition, writing in *Development*, for example, that 'since the entrepreneur has no competitors when the new products first appear, the determination of their price proceeds wholly, or within certain limits, according to the principles of monopoly price' (p. 152). In *Cycles* he thought of the new firm's position as similar to monopolistic competition with its emphasis on product differentiation, arguing that 'an enterprise in our sense almost necessarily finds itself in an "imperfect" situation, even if the system be otherwise a perfectly competitive one'. Under these conditions, entrepreneurial profits 'might . . . be also included in the category of monopoloid gains' (p. 107).

There are several implications of this theory of entrepreneurial profit for the place of profit generally in any explanation of income distribution. First, for Schumpeter, profit was only an income derived from monopoly power positions. In the case of entrepreneurs, the position and the profit are usually temporary, a point to which I will return later in this section, but in other cases they may be more permanently established. One thing that Schumpeter wanted to do was to keep the latter cases separate from that which arises through innovation: in this regard he even expressed misgivings about using the same term 'monopoloid gains', quoted above, to refer to entrepreneurial profits in case it should 'blur the specific character of our case . . .' (*Cycles*, p. 107; cf. *Development*, p. 153).

Secondly, the category of profit income must be isolated from the tenets of the marginal-productivity theory of distribution to which Schumpeter otherwise adhered (e.g. *Development*, p. 25; cf. above Chapter 4, section 4.4.3). Thus, 'while wages are determined according to the marginal productivity of labor, profit is a striking exception to this law: the problem of profit lies precisely in the fact that the laws of cost and of marginal productivity seem to exclude it' (*Development*, p. 153). And, 'profit is a net gain' in the sense that 'it is not absorbed by the value of any cost factor through a process of Imputation' (*Cycles*, p. 105; cf. p. 127n). In particular, Schumpeter wanted to deny that profit could be attributed to any factor of production called 'capital': 'Entrepreneurial profit is not . . . a return to capital, however one may define capital' (*Development*, p. 153). Capital as finance capital is not a factor of production and commands an *interest* income yield which he emphasized as very distinct from profit (e.g. *Cycles*, pp. 126, 129). Interest is a purely monetary phenomenon, a thesis that will be taken up in the next chapter. Also, while they are no doubt physically productive, produced means of production are neither capital nor a factor of production for the purposes of Schumpeter's analysis (e.g. *Development*, pp. 161–2) and no profit can be attributed to their existence. It also followed, thirdly, from Schumpeter's arguments that there can be 'no reasons for speaking about a tendency towards equalisation of [rates of] profits which does not exist at all in reality: for only the jumbling together of interest and profit explains why many authors contend for such a tendency, although we can observe such extraordinarily different [rates of] profits in one and the same place, at the same time and in th same industry.' (ibid., p. 153; cf. *Cycles*, pp. 105, 127n).

Although Schumpeter did not notice it, this non-uniform realizatio of profits is partially a result of their *residual* nature, a fact that h rejected as a consequence of the fourth implication to be referred t here. 'We want finally to emphasise', he wrote, 'that profit is also no wages, although the analogy is tempting. It is certainly not a simp residuum; it is the expression of the value of what the entrepreneu contributes to production in exactly the same sense that wages are th value expression of what the worker "produces".' (*Developmen* p. 153). He reiterated this cryptic assertion in *Cycles* when, again so a not to 'blur the specific character of our case', he wrote: 'we do no include profits among wages, although the former are returns t personal exertions and although we do define the latter as returns t personal services' (p. 107 and n). It is difficult to be sure exactly wha Schumpeter intended to convey in these passages. In his isolationis approach to the entrepreneur, there can be no *market* for the services c such agents, so even if their profit is viewed as a reward for thes services it remains a residual of highly variable value. He argued mor or less these points himself, albeit without reference to the idea of residual, when he wrote that 'it cannot be said of . . . [the size of th profit] that it just suffices to call forth precisely the "quantity c entrepreneurial services required". Such a quantity, theoretically deter minable, does not exist. And the total amount of profit actuall obtained in a given time, as well as the profit realised by an individua entrepreneur, may be much greater than that necessary to call forth th entrepreneurial services which were actually operative.' (*Developmen* pp. 154–5). Here it is clearly the profit, or an expectation of it a least that 'calls forth' the actions of entrepreneurs independently of all of th other motivations previously outlined (section 6.2 above).

Moreover, for Schumpeter, the monopoly-power origins of the prof did not impede its wage-like status: 'the fact that a return has somethin to do with monopoly does not affect its *economic* nature' (ibid, p. 107n emphasis added). Here the rationale for distinction drawn betwee 'monopoly' and 'economic' is unclear. He went on to try som analogies: 'There is probably a large monopoloid element in the incom of a leading tenor, yet this income is nevertheless a wage. Any stron labor union secures monopoly gains. Its members earn efficiency wage all the same.' These analogies led him to conclude that the 'nature of "service" is one thing' while the 'method of pricing which is bein applied to that service is another thing' (ibid.). The analogies were however, poorly chosen: the tenor's wage includes a market-determine quasi-rent with its origin in a scarcity of such talent, and the workers' monopoly gains' are delimited by their employers' 'calculated' capacity to pay, whether that capacity be real or imagined. By contrast, while entrepreneurial talents are scarce, as already indicated, their value is not market-determined here. And, entrepreneurial profit is not the outcome of anything like the bargaining cum institutional processes that are involved in settling a 'monopoly' wage, although in cases where innovations have a relevant demand side, some implicit consumer-producer 'bargain' could be imagined. All that can be said by way of a conclusion about this part of Schumpeter's argument is that beyond some 'puritanical' notion that it is the *labours* of the entrepreneur that should be amply rewarded, his attempt to draw any link between profit and wages for services rendered is a pointless digression.

There was one thing concerning entrepreneurial profit about which Schumpeter had no doubts, however. That is its strictly temporary status (e.g., *Cycles*. pp. 106–7, *Development*, pp. 131–2), a characteristic of the results of entrepreneurial activity that was to play a central role in the explanation of the instability of capitalist motion. As the profit is dependent upon the entrepreneur's monopoly power position in each case of innovation, anything that erodes the strength of that position lessens his or her ability to maintain more than the 'normal' differential between revenues and costs, where that 'normal' differential may be zero. The key force of erosion here is imitation. Faced with rising input costs, in order to compete with their new entrants to the market, existing producers will endeavour to apply the same innovation. And, attracted by the profit, other new entrants will emerge as well. For a time, the entrepreneur may be able to implement measures of protection that prevent or impede imitation, for example, secrecy or patents, but Schumpeter's belief was that in the majority of cases, the innovations of any period would ultimately be diffused throughout the industry involved (e.g., *Cycles*, pp. 130ff.). His claim was then that entrepreneurial profit . . . and also the entrepreneurial function as such, perish in the vortex of competition that streams after them' *Development*, p. 134).

Schumpeter offered very little by way of explanation of this claimed erosion of profits by imitation and diffusion. In the power-looms case of process innovation, he was content to assert that 'the final result must be a new equilibrium position, in which, with new data, the law of cost again rules . . .' (ibid., p. 131). This so-called 'law of cost' was invoked to the effect that commodity prices, in this case cloth, would be reduced to an alignment with costs at the post-innovation level by competition from the *additional* production by imitating new entrants. It is self-evident that this mechanism has very limited applicability beyond the situation of perfect competition and that a return to a profitless steady circular-flow state is an *analytical* aberration with little relevance to the reality of motion. The innovative activities of the entrepreneurs make them into capitalist owners of means of production. As such, whatever the new state that emerges from the post-innovation traverse, they will not operate without some rate of profit on the funds they have invested in their firms. So, beyond the *ab ovo* generation of motion out of the circular-flow model, the 'neighborhoods of equilibrium' must represent capitalist economies in which some vector of rates of profit is established. With finance capital mobility, there will probably be some equilibrium relativity of the rates that reflects differential risk and other particulars of conditions in the various industries. In subsequent bouts of innovation, then, it is a rate of profit above the industry 'norm' that an entrepreneur would expect and may ultimately lose through competition. But it should be added that in imperfectly competitive industries the effect of an innovation may well be to generate a higher rate of profit that is protected by barriers to entry that have nothing to do with the innovation itself. However, whatever the elicited qualifications, the fact remains that in any exposition of Schumpeter's analysis of motion we can do little else but proceed on the assumption that imitation and diffusion of innovations reduces or eliminates the profit prospects for further innovation and that, as a consequence, the impetus for motion from that source subsides. The place of this mechanism in the business cycle will be explored in Chapters 8 and 9 below.

6.7 Summary

Various facets of the economic development process have been explored in this chapter.

1. Three issues were posed by the idea that economic development is to be explained by the introduction of new combinations into a steady circular-flow state: first, which agents are to organize the application of the new combinations; secondly, what resources are to be used by those agents; and thirdly, how do the agents obtain command over the required resources?

2. Agents with particular entrepreneurial talents, motivated ultimately by the prospect of entrepreneurial profit, were argued by Schumpeter to be those responsible for initiating development. Entrepreneurs are new men (and women) who set up new firms with new plant and equipment and thereby add a new dimension to the existing productive capacity.

3. The resources required by entrepreneurs were to be drawn from existing resources by a market-induced reallocation in response to their added demand. By this means, Schumpeter kept economic development isolated from any growth of the resource base.

4. Newly-created bank credit was to provide the entrepreneurs' command over the required resources in the absence of any capacity for prior saving in the steady circular-flow state.

5. Entrepreneurial profit is generated by the ability of entrepreneurs to lift resource productivity or product quality above established norms and thereby gain a cost and/or price advantage over existing producers. Such profit was argued by Schumpeter to have a finite life. This life is determined by the rate of diffusion of the innovations to other producers that erodes the entrepreneurs' economic advantage.

7 Interest, money and credit in economic development

7.1 Interest and the money market

Schumpeter's original presentation of his theory that interest is a monetary phenomenon, causally linked to the processes of innovation and economic development, is to be found in the first edition of *Development*, although the rudiments of a 'dynamic' theory had been outlined in *Das Wesen* (pp. 384ff.). The theory attracted some critical responses and brought him into controversy with his contemporaries most especially Böhm-Bawerk (see Haberler, 1951b). However Schumpeter's response to the criticism was to stand firm on his ideas – e.g., in his reply to Böhm-Bawerk published in 1913 (*Aufsätze* pp. 411ff., cf. *Development*, pp. x, 157–9; *Cycles*, p. 123n) – and except for a shortening of the presentation, the theory remained intact through all subsequent editions of *Development* (see especially pp. 157ff.). It was applied in his other writings on motion as required including brief restatements in *Cycles* (pp. 123ff., 602ff.). In this chapter, I will not be concerned with the controversial aspects of pure theory broached by Schumpeter's thesis – especially not with that curiosum, the so-called zero rate of interest in the steady circular-flow state – nor with the details of why he rejected other theories (see, e.g. *History*, pp. 924ff.). My focus is only upon the involvement of interest in his theory of motion, although it should be noted at the outset that he denied that the latter theory depended in any way upon his special explanation of the former. His argument was, rather, that he had worked out his theses on development and business cycles in a way that made them independent of any particular theory of interest (*Cycles* p. 123n).

It does not follow from the above point that interest had no role in Schumpeter's analyses. He summarized his general position in the following passage from *Development*:

> Our argument should also explain the movement in time in the rate of interest. It is from this class of facts that verification of the fundamental idea might primarily be expected. If the interest of business life – what it is usual to call 'productive interest' – has its roots in entrepreneurial profit, both should move closely together. As a matter of fact, this is true of short period fluctuations. In longer periods we may still observe some relation between the prevalence of new combinations and interest, but there are so many elements to be taken account of, and 'other things' remain so imperfectly

equal as soon as we go beyond the span of say a decade, that verification becomes extremely complicated. (p. 210)

It is apparent from this piece that he believed his explanation of interest to be consistent with the temporal patterns of interest rates during business cycles. And, importantly, from this perspective, interest rates are treated as *consequences* rather than as independent causal elements in the traverses of fluctuations (cf. *Cycles*, pp. 602ff., especially 626ff.), a point of view that was a further reflection of his desire to keep his distance from any links with monetary theories of cycles.

For Schumpeter, interest was a permanent income flow that accrues to lenders of finance capital of whatever institutional status, be they individual savers, banks or any other financial intermediary. It is paid as a result of loans which draw on savings stocks and on credit created *ad hoc*. Consumers and governments may borrow, but he was not directly concerned with these sorts of financing and they remained in the background as quantitatively significant, but unexplained elements in the totality of lending. His analytical focus was on 'the great social phenomenon that needs explaining' which he saw in the existence of *interest on productive loans (Produktivzins)*' (*Development*, p. 157).

The essential principle on which any payment of interest is based was perceived by Schumpeter as the 'premium on present over future purchasing power' (ibid.). Such a premium could not simply be attributed to the inherent preferences of individual agents, but rather it called for some explicit economic explanation (ibid., p. 158). Schumpeter grounded his explanation on the fact that under some conditions, 'the possession of a sum of money is the means of obtaining a bigger sum'. He went on: 'On this account, and to this extent, a present sum will be normally valued more highly than a future sum. Therefore present sums of money – so to speak as potentially bigger sums – will have a value premium. . . . *And in this lies the explanation of interest.*' (ibid., p. 190, original emphasis; cf. *Cycles*, pp. 123, 125, 126). The reason for the premium is more specifically that currently-held finance capital can give command over means of production and other resources that an agent does not already own and which he or she expects can be applied to production such as to generate a net revenue over costs. The premium itself will be manifested in the price of present purchasing power over and above its nominal value, leaving aside inflationary expectations for which Schumpeter made explicit allowance by referring to the real value of the premium (ibid., p. 127). 'Interest', he wrote, '– more correctly the capital sum plus interest – is . . . the price paid by borrowers for a social permit to acquire commodities and services

without having previously fulfilled the condition which in the institu
tional pattern of capitalism is normally set on the issue of such a socia
permit, i.e. without having previously contributed other commoditie
and services to the social stream.' (ibid., p. 123). In Schumpeter
analysis, it was the innovating entrepreneur upon whom he focused i
this respect.

Schumpeter's argument was that '[u]nder our present assumptions
the only people who have a higher estimation for present as agains
future purchasing power are the entrepreneurs. Only they are th
bearers of that market movement in favor of present money, of tha
demand which raises the price of money above par as we define it
(*Development*, p. 191). In effect, then, 'the prospect of business profit i
the pivot on which the valuation of sums of present purchasing powe
actually turns . . .' (ibid., p. 189) and 'although it is possible to den
that innovation is the only "cause" of interest within the realm c
production and commerce, it is not possible to deny that this "cause" i
sufficient to produce it in the absence of any other' (*Cycles*, p. 125)
Now while this argument links interest to profit generated by rea
commodity-producing economic activity, Schumpeter expressly denie
that the interest premium could be explained by real forces *per se*. H
granted that 'in every case, corresponding to money interest, that is t
the premium on purchasing power, there is a premium on goods of som
kind. It is true that goods and not "money" are needed to produce in th
technical sense.' But, when *explaining* interest, 'it is impossible to pierc
the money veil in order to get to the premiums on concrete goods. If on
penetrates through it one penetrates into a void.' (*Developmen
p. 184). He therefore denied the existence of any 'natural' rate c
interest that arises from physical productivity alone (*Cycles*, pp. 126–7
and gave great emphasis to his belief that interest is a purely monetar
phenomenon.

For Schumpeter, then, 'interest actually is, not only on the surface bu
essentially, a monetary phenomenon' (ibid., p. 125). Interest exist
because entrepreneurs must demand money balances *before* they ca
engage in production and 'the money required for innovations const
tutes the chief factor in the industrial demand on the money marke
(*Development*, p. 158). So we may say that interest *must* be pai
because entrepreneurs are required to borrow finance capital and it *ca*
be paid because of their ability to innovate and produce a surplus c
revenues over prime costs by using that capital.

An intermediate problem posed by linking interest payments directl
to entrepreneurial profit is that while interest is a *permanent* source c
income to the owners of finance capital, its source is said to be

emporary income flow that only exists for one phase of the business
ycle. Schumpeter treated this apparent dilemma very seriously and
devoted considerable effort to resolving it within the logic of his
theoretical analysis. Three questions are pertinent, he thought, to
providing a resolution (ibid., p. 159). First, where does the flow of
commodities whose value constitutes the surplus out of which interest
can be paid as a net income come from? Secondly, why does this
permanent net income accrue to the finance capitalists in particular?
And thirdly, 'by far the most difficult question, which may be described
as the central problem of interest on capital: how does it happen that
this stream of goods flows permanently, [so] that interest is a net income
which one may consume without impairing one's economic position?'
ibid.). His elaboration of the answers to these three questions took the
form of six 'propositions' which effectively comprise his theory of
productive interest (ibid., pp. 173ff.).

The first three of Schumpeter's 'propositions' have already been
effectively worked through above and they are restated now more or
ess as a summary of the ideas involved. First, interest flows from the
surplus value generated by entrepreneurs through their innovative
activities, for it can 'flow from nothing else since there are no other
surpluses in the normal course of economic life' (ibid., p. 173). Then the
second proposition extends this idea to take account of the fact that the
surplus must actually accrue to entrepreneurs as their profit since the
money revenues in which it is included immediately flow into their
possession. But, it is in the nature of the process that development 'in
ome way . . . sweeps part of the profit to the [finance] capitalist.
nterest acts as a tax upon profit.' (ibid., p. 175; cf. p. 210). Thirdly, he
added the qualification that 'neither the whole profit nor even a part of it
can be directly and immediately interest, because it is only temporary'
ibid., p. 175). This led him to re-pose his most basic question: '*how is
his permanent stream of interest, flowing always from the same capital,
extracted from the transitory, ever-changing profits?*' (ibid., pp. 175–6,
original emphasis).

In order to elicit his fourth proposition, Schumpeter shifted his
attention to a centrally-planned economic system with no market
exchange. There can be '*no interest as an independent value phenomenon*' in such a system because the 'agent for which [*sic*] interest is paid
imply would not exist . . .' (ibid., p. 176, original emphasis). The
proposition is, then, that there is something about the way that the
allocation of resources in a market-capitalist economy is carried out that
causes interest to be paid. In particular, it seems to be the mediating
agent' finance capital that attracts interest as a consequence of its

allocation function. Here Schumpeter's argument shaded off into t
fifth proposition. He observed that 'technically, production is always t
same process under whatever organisation it may occur' (ibid.). B
access to production depends upon command over resources and in t
two systems here considered, the modes of exercising such comman
are quite different. The point that Schumpeter wanted to make was th
if the entrepreneurs could simply command by physical appropriatio
the input resources that they need, they could still enjoy an entrepr
neurial profit from innovation without the obligation to pay interes
That is, they could act as central planners may do in the planne
economy and shift resources from one site to another *ad hoc*. Th
approach to resource command is denied to them because of t
existence of property laws and freedom of occupational choice under
capitalist regime. Schumpeter concluded, then, that it 'is only becaus
other people have command of the necessary producers' goods that t
entrepreneurs must call in the [finance] capitalist to help them
remove the obstacle which private property in means of production
the right to dispose freely of one's personal services puts in their wa
(ibid., p. 177). It is this necessary mediation of the finance capitalists
the innovation process that gives them the claim to some share of t
profit generated. As an aside on this point, it is perhaps interesting
note that Schumpeter's attitude towards these capitalists and the
interest charge was sometimes rather hostile. He argued that unli
profit, interest is not 'a direct fruit of development in the sense of a pri
for its achievements'. Rather, it is 'a brake . . . on development, a kir
of "tax on entrepreneurial profit" ' and 'a parasite in the body of wag
and rent . . .' (ibid., pp. 210, 173; cf. p. 175). On this basis, he ev
hinted that the demise of the finance capitalist could well be engineer
without damage to the virtues of the capitalist system! (ibid., p. 211;
Keynes's much-neglected Chapter 24 of the *General Theory*, 1936).

Returning to Schumpeter's propositions, we find that after five
them he had established why and from where interest is paid. Th
challenge still remained to answer the key question about how t
variable flow of entrepreneurial profits can be converted into a perm
nent and uniform flow of interest on finance capital. His sixth propo
tion was that '*interest is an element in the price of purchasing pow
regarded as a means of control over production goods*' (ibid., p. 18
original emphasis). At face value, this observation does not seem
take us very much further, but it is the idea that purchasing power has
'price' that is of importance here. What Schumpeter did in order final
to answer his question was to invoke the money market as t
institutional mediation through which interest acquires its permane

atus. In that market, purchasing power is traded at a 'price' which in
ɔtal comprises the repayment of principal plus a further 'element' of
ɪterest (cf. ibid., pp. 192, 198; *Cycles*, p. 123). The point is, then, that
ɔ this market itself is asserted to have a permanent status, the 'pool' of
nance capital can be turned over in the sense that it is on permanent
ɔan but to an ever-changing group of entrepreneurs: 'the lender may
. . secure a permanent income by shifting his money from opportunity
ɔ opportunity as each of them arises' (ibid., p. 125). It is possible for
ɪis to occur because the interest is not the immediate product of any
articular real production and does not follow its fortunes. Through the
ɪediation of the money market, its 'source' is a separate legal claim to a
ɪare in profit and this claim is mobile in that once principal and interest
re repaid, the lender may move on to fund other real means of
ɔroduction without any further concern for the economic fate of past
ɪeans that have been funded. Now while this argument may be correct
ɪ principle and as far as it goes, it does not fully answer Schumpeter's
uestion. What has been overlooked is that the fortunes of the
ntrepreneurial group come and go more rapidly than the period of the
usiness cycle. The finance capitalists who lend to successful entrepre-
eurs in the upswing phase of the cycle may well accrue interest and a
ɛpayment of their principal sums. But, after the wave of innovation
ɛases, as it must in the logic of Schumpeter's model, there will be a
ɛriod of time before the next wave during which the demand for
nance will be close to zero. If entrepreneurial profit is to be the
ɔminant source of interest payments, then its *continuity* is certainly not
ɔsured even though it may be considered 'permanent' in a cyclical sort
f way.

Independently of the above argument, it is a fact that interest is paid
ɪ finance capital and Schumpeter correctly located its determination in
money or capital market. He was clear about the market's mediating
nd necessary, but not driving, role in the capitalist process, for he saw
ɪat it 'becomes the heart, although it never becomes the brain, of the
apitalist organism' (ibid., p. 127). The dominant demand in the market
, overwhelmingly the funding needs of entrepreneurs, indeed the
ɪarket is only a phenomenon of development (*Development*, p. 124; cf.
. 158), even though it must continue to maintain 'the pulse of the
ɪrcular flow' (ibid., p. 125). In effect, then, 'only one fundamental
ɪing happens on the money market, to which everything else is
ccessory: on the demand side appear entrepreneurs and on the supply
de producers of and dealers in purchasing power . . .'. The activities
re centred upon 'the exchange of present against future purchasing
ower . . . [and in] the daily price struggle between the two parties the

fate of new combinations is decided' (ibid.). Here Schumpeter expressed the view that 'the price of short-term credits' that is decided in the market is instrumental in the potential entrepreneurs' decisions to innovate or not. It is in this sense that the supply responses of bankers hold the key to the economic impact of a wave of innovation ideas. As Schumpeter put it, the 'money market is always, as it were, the headquarters of the capitalist system, from which orders go out to its individual divisions, and that which is debated and decided there is always in essence the settlement of plans for further development' (ibid., p. 126). Even in the light of his own earlier metaphor, he somewhat exaggerated the role of the market in this piece – it becomes more a 'brain' than a 'heart' here. Its short-term interest rate orders are only one influence on the entrepreneurial 'divisions' and, possibly, not even the most effective one where the rate is high and yet the entrepreneurs are full of 'animal spirits', to use Keynes's felicitous term, or where the rate is lower and 'animal spirits' are depressed.

Schumpeter correctly emphasized the sensitivity of the market to economic and other events: 'There is scarcely a piece of news that does not necessarily influence the decisions relative to the carrying out of new combinations or the money market position and the opinions and intentions of entrepreneurs. The system of future values must be adapted to every new situation.' (ibid.). However, in spite of this volatility, he had to provide some analytical explanation for the establishment of a market-clearing rate of interest. In order to do so, he modelled the market as comprising demand and supply functions in a Marshallian partial-equilibrium context, even though, as I will point out later in this section and in the next, he had grave doubts about the viability of any *function* on the supply side (ibid., pp. 191ff.). The market's operations were dealt with in two stages: in the first, the supply of finance capital to the market comprises only the reallocation of the existing funds of economic agents, while in the second, the additional facility of credit creation is introduced. The first situation corresponds to the attempt by entrepreneurs to innovate by means of borrowed funds that are already in use in the steady circular-flow state, but which are free to be diverted to this alternative use. So it is that here, a 'capitalist would . . . be one who is ready under certain conditions to transfer a definite sum to the entrepreneur by withdrawing it from its customary uses, that is by restricting his expenditure either in production or consumption' (ibid., p. 191). It should be noted that there is no nascent 'liquidity preference' argument here because in the circular flow there is no uncertainty and there are no *idle* money balances. All balances are active in that they are dedicated to intended expenditures. The change hat the financing of innovations brings is merely that who does the pending shifts from some existing agents to the entrepreneurs. This will hift the pattern of existing resource use, even though in this case the otal demand for resources is not increased. As far as Schumpeter was oncerned, the existence of the possibility of diverting the flow of funds ives rise to a 'definite' supply function of entrepreneurial finance vhich, presumably, is upward sloping in response to rising interest ates.

On the demand side, a similarly 'definite' demand function can be stablished. At the level of the individual entrepreneur, the function 1ay comprise only a short segment with discontinuities at the minimum ow of funds the agent requires and at the maximum flow he or she can ossibly use given the innovation in hand. Schumpeter assumed, hough, that in aggregate, a continuous demand function can be stablished with the total demand for finance declining as the interest ate to be met increases, given a certain profile of profit expectations hat is attached to the current wave of innovation prospects. He argued he point most clearly in *Cycles*: 'any amount of dollars plus the profit an ntrepreneur hopes to realize by means of it . . . [may be called] his demand price" for that amount . . .'. On this basis, he continued, 'we eem to be able to build a curve or schedule of entrepreneurial demand or present dollars, the ordinates of which are expressed in terms of uture dollars, and to conclude in the familiar way that interest will qual marginal profit . . .' (pp. 602–3). And, as far as Schumpeter was oncerned, the possible extent of any innovation wave, and hence the emand for finance, have no particular limits, as a matter of physical- echnical principle, and, because of this, 'the possibilities of profit are ractically unlimited, [although] they differ in size and most of them are . . only small' (*Development*, p. 198). The point of this dubious ssertion seems to have been to emphasize the roles that the limited vailability of entrepreneurial talent and that supply conditions will ave in ultimately determining the flow of innovations actually realized ibid., p. 197).

The operation of the market was analysed by Schumpeter in a way hat would apply to a stock exchange (ibid., pp. 192–3). The offers to ɔuy' purchasing power, reflecting the 'demand prices' of entrepreneurs, re considered by existing agents who hold access to flows of it. Whether nd to what extent the latter choose to give up control over their funds ⱱill depend upon the interest on offer as compensation for the listurbance of their established positions in the circular flow. For every :entative' price offered, there will be an 'unequivocally determined' mount of supply and demand. Where these amounts do not coincide,

the entrepreneurs will bid up the price in the face of an excess demand
at the offer price and vice versa in the face of an excess supply. The
ultimate outcome was cogently summarized in the following passage.

> Thus in the exchange struggle on the money market a definite price for
> purchasing power will be established just as on any other market. And since
> as a rule, both parties value present more highly than future money – the
> entrepreneur because present money signifies more future money for him
> the lender because under our assumptions present money makes possible the
> orderly course of his economic activity while future money is merely added to
> his income – the price will practically always be above par. (ibid., p. 193)

The re-expression of this argument along marginalist lines added no
further insight into the market mechanism (ibid., pp. 193–4).

In the second stage of his money market analysis, Schumpeter
introduced the *ad hoc* creation of credit as a source of entrepreneurial
finance (ibid., pp. 195ff.). This, as I indicated earlier (Chapter 6,
section 6.5), was his standard situation. The effect of the new source in
the present context is to alter the supply side of the money market while
leaving the demand side largely untouched. 'Supply', he noted, 'is now
put on another basis; a new source of purchasing power, of a different
nature, appears, which does not exist in the circular flow. The supply
also comes from different people now, from differently defined "capitalists", whom we call "bankers" . . .' (ibid., p. 195). There are two
potential limits to this source of finance, both associated with the
caution of bankers' behaviour, that Schumpeter mentioned at this point:
one is the risk of failure by entrepreneurial borrowers and the other is
the risk of fuelling an inflationary depreciation of the value of the credit
outstanding (ibid.). The former limitation can be ignored, he reasoned,
because its implications can be covered by bankers adding a risk
premium to all loans in recognition of the expected bad-debt burden.
The latter is more significant and experience will have taught the
bankers that they must keep an eye to the *collective* effects of their
lending decisions on the *real* demand and supply relativities in the
economy (cf. ibid., p. 114; *Cycles*, p. 121). In practice, bankers will also
operate within some framework of reserve and other legal requirements
that may limit the amount of credit individual banks can provide
(*Development*, pp. 112–14; *Cycles*, pp.120–21). The overall limit,
though, is an 'elastic . . . nevertheless . . . definite, magnitude' (*Development*, p. 114; cf. *Cycles*, pp. 121–2). The conclusion that Schumpeter
came to in *Cycles* on this matter is indicative of his position: 'Nothing
. . . is so likely to give a wrong impression of the operation of credit as
taking a mechanistic and static view of it and neglecting the fact that our
process, by virtue of its own working, widens the limits which, *ex visu* of

a given point of time, seem to be rigid fetters.' (ibid., p. 122). That is to say, the presence of potential entrepreneurial borrowers who are prepared to pay the asking rate of interest can render most limits on lending 'flexible' somehow, whatever their source. The banker is here reinforced as the crucial mediator in the innovation process. Indeed, such is the range of their discretion that Schumpeter was led to doubt the relevance of a supply function of credit at all. So, as 'there is never any such thing as a definite quantity of bank accommodation available . . . it is necessary to recognize an element of indeterminateness in the problem of interest . . .' (ibid., p. 606). The matter of the indefinite nature of the money supply is taken up again in the next section of this chapter.

There was a further complication that Schumpeter recognized in connection with this problem of a determinate outcome from the credit supply and demand relation. In a 1927 paper, he made reference to the 'Marshall-Pigou-Keynes' idea of 'k' in the 'Cambridge' version of the quantity theory as a theory of the demand for money (*Essays*, p. 40 and n). His view was that any instability in this behaviourally-based proportionality between money demand and income could compound the problems of assessing the role that any limits on the supply of credit may have in the innovation process. The consequences were summarized in outline only and never followed up, even when ample opportunity presented itself in *Cycles*: '(1) that movements of "k" can, and often do, accentuate or mitigate the effects of credit creation; (2) that movements of "k' may, and often do, effect what otherwise would have to be effected by credit-creation; (3) that movements of "k" may sometimes technically enforce and so *cause* credit creation, whence a very complex tissue of mutual interaction.' (*Essays*, p. 40n, original emphasis).

Now while the idea of credit creation may have dominated Schumpeter's analysis of the supply of finance capital for innovation purposes, he was aware that a much broader picture of such supply would be required if the analysis was to claim any degree of comprehensiveness. In particular, once development-induced motion is actually underway and profit is being generated, the issue of savings as a source of finance had to be considered within the analysis. He referred to this source as 'the great reservoirs of money which actually exist [and] arise as a consequence of development . . .' (*Development*, p. 195; cf. p. 199). The effect of extending the money market to include these 'dynamic' sources of finance was not great and the nature of the analysis was altered little except for a shift of emphasis away from credit creation and

a lowering of the interest rate profile below what it otherwise might hav
been (ibid., p. 201).

In *Cycles*, he elaborated extensively on the broader pattern (
financial sources that are potentially available to borrowers in
developed capitalist economy, although not all of them are relevant t
entrepreneurial activities (pp. 578ff.). The sources listed were: (;
previous receipts; (b) overspending; (c) selling assets; (d) temporar
investment; (e) issuing promises to pay; (f) mining and importing th
monetary metal; (g) borrowing from a bank; (h) using one's own, (
borrowing savings of others; (i) taxation and the issue of governmer
fiat money; (j) buying on credit; and (k) borrowing from abroad. Som
of these are self-explanatory and require no further comment. Previor
receipts may be devoted to three different sorts of transactions, namel
exact repetitions as involved in the steady circular-flow, adaptiv
variations in economic activity, and new transactions involving inno
vations. Each can be drawn from revenue flows provided they includ
some surplus over 'necessary' outlays, however defined, with th
possibility of diverting existing expenditures being an option as wel
There is a considerable overlap here with the item, borrowing one's ow
savings. Overspending implies running down money balances helc
Selling assets involves the take up by banks or non-banks of financi;
assets issued by firms. The taxation and fiat money item was included t
cover historical situations where governments were directly involved i
business projects. Temporary investment is *defined* as borrowing i
advance of an intended, more far-off investment project and investin
the funds in an interim project that will return them before ther
ultimate use is due. It is to be noticed that borrowing from a bank an
selling financial assets to a bank were still given more emphasis than an
of the other sources here. They were first of all included in the mo:
essential group of sources that were discussed by Schumpeter at greate
length in the context of his analysis of financial aspects of business cycl
events (ibid., pp. 584ff.). This group comprised items (a), (b), (c), (g
and (h) from the above list and probably included those most significar
empirically. He then singled bank lending out as being the mo:
pertinent to innovative activity such that a rough empirical 'correspor
dence between innovation and loans, still more between innovation an
deposits' is to be expected (ibid., p. 601).

In the context of this discussion, Schumpeter also recognized th
distinction between short-term financing of innovations and the long
term funding of the firms established to implement them. While in th
early stages of its 'life-cycle' a firm may depend solely on bank credit fc
its finance, its short-term loans will probably be switched to longer-terr

ontracts or paid out from accumulated internal savings once its
perations are successfully established. Thus, firms 'go ahead on bank
redit and then . . . "fund" the debt by the issue of stocks and bonds'.
Tore generally stated: 'Savings . . . step in to relieve bank credit, and in
his sense the old theory that it is savings that finance the expansion of
he industrial apparatus comes partly true after all, even in the presence
f credit creation. But, they do so with a lag, which is responsible for a
equence of phenomena that would be absent if . . . savings financed
nterprise from the start . . .' (ibid., p. 588). Readers familiar with
Leynes's work will recognize this general thesis, but he was not
cknowledged as an antecedent here.

.2 Money and credit in the development process[1]

The particular questions about money in Schumpeter's analysis that I
vill address in this section are first, what did he understand by 'money'
n the development context, and secondly, how and to what extent did
e consider that money 'matters' in the development processes? The
eneral tenor of his stance on money is summarized in his statement
hat: 'Economic action cannot, at least in capitalist society, be explained
vithout taking account of money, and practically all economic proposi-
ions are relative to the modus operandi of a given monetary system.'
Cycles, p. 548). In the light of this assertion, the questions just posed
ppear to be important ones.

On the question of what Schumpeter meant by 'money', it is first of all
ignificant to distinguish between the steady circular-flow and the develop-
nent states of the system. In the former state, money provides only the
ervices of a 'neutral' means of exchange. No scope exists for it to do
therwise, as he made clear in *Development* (pp. 47ff.) and in much
reater detail in the first seven chapters of *Wesen des Geldes*. Under the
trict conditions of the operations of the circular flow, Schumpeter was
uite comfortable about restricting money to its metal-commodity form –
old coins in particular. Clearly, other forms of circulating medium could
e included in the facilitation of the unchanging round of exchanges,
ncluding credit-based instruments. But, provided that the total nominal
alue of money flows per period does not change, it is not necessary to take
ther money forms into account as they change nothing essential about the
ubstance of the circular-flow processes (*Development*, pp. 53, 105).
Money has a certain established purchasing power in terms of resources
nd commodities to be traded and its status is confined to that of a counter-
low that mirrors the real flows that it facilitates.

Once economic development is to be initiated by some agents
ecoming innovating entrepreneurs, the meaning of the money category

must be broadened. While the money of the circular-flow state must continue to circulate as before, development requires that the flow of purchasing power be increased, with the proviso that the velocity of circulation of existing money remains the same for the sake of emphasizing the monetary needs of the additional processes (ibid., p. 105). As we have seen already (Chapter 6, section 6.5), the new combinations are assumed to be funded entirely by bank credit created *ad hoc* for the purpose. Thus: 'Only the entrepreneur . . ., in principle, needs credit; only for industrial development does it play a fundamental part, that is a part the consideration of which is essential to an understanding of the whole process.' (ibid.). A money market is now needed, too, in order to 'price' and allocate the credit money whereas in the circular flow no such facility is required. Nonetheless, the money flows of the circular-flow dimensions of economic activity must be integrated into the new totality of money flows: 'with development . . . bank credit penetrates into the transactions of the circular flow . . . [and] these things become, in practice, elements in the function of the money market. They become a part of the organism of the money market . . . [and] we feel in every money-market article the pulse of the circular flow.' (ibid., pp. 124–5). The money flows of the two processes are blended as 'the requirements of the circular flow are added to the entrepreneur's demand in the money market on the one hand, and money from the circular flow increases the supply of money in the money market on the other'. Schumpeter maintained, though, that 'this must not prevent us from distinguishing the transactions in the money market which belong to the circular flow from the others. Only the latter are fundamental; the former are added onto them, and the fact that they appear in the money market at all is merely a consequence of development.' (ibid., p. 125). What is emerging here is clearly a shift of emphasis in what is to be considered as money. The development process brings a situation where the nature and role of money is dominated by its bank-credit form, as the 'kernel of the matter lies in the credit requirements of new enterprises' (ibid.). Schumpeter's 'dynamic' treatment of money is, then, most aptly considered to involve a 'credit theory of money' (cf. *History*, p. 717).

A more comprehensive perspective on money in such a theory would have to include all forms of credit-based means of exchange, a fact which Schumpeter acknowledged and to which he gave some explicit attention. His view at one point was that 'all forms of credit, from the bank note to the book-credits, are essentially the same thing, and that in all these forms credit increases the means of payment . . .' – an argument that he felt was 'uncontroversial' (*Development*, p. 99). A subtle qualification was added to this when, on reiterating that the external form of the credit instruments is quite irrelevant', he went on to require that *relevant* credit instruments must 'circulate' (ibid., p. 109). That is, not only should they provide the means by which new entrepreneurs can command resources, but they must also enter the flow of circulating means of exchange that will be available to facilitate the increase in aggregate expenditures and incomes that the innovations will bring. In this sense, credit increments are always effectively money increments and the money supply remains strictly as measured by the volume of the *circulating* medium. Thus, Schumpeter argued, while in 'various ways, firms may create means of payment themselves', some of their credit instruments may not be means *per se*: 'A bill of exchange or a note is not, in itself, such a means. On the contrary, it generally requires financing and thus figures on the demand rather than the supply side of the money market.' Only if 'it circulates in such a way as to effect (economically, though not in the legal sense) payments, . . . [does it become] an addition to the circulating medium' (*Cycles*, p. 113, cf. pp. 580, 581). It was Schumpeter's argument, then, that 'certain claims to "money" serve, within wide limits, the same purposes as legal tender itself . . .' (ibid., p. 546; cf. 1956, p. 167). He was very keen on the following analogy as a means of explaining the peculiarity of money in this respect: 'While I cannot ride on a claim to a horse, I can, under certain conditions, do exactly the same with claims to money as with money itself, namely buy.' (*Development*, p. 97n; cf. *Essays*, p. 37; 1956, p. 167).

One serious analytical consequence to which this aspect of credit money contributes was alluded to by Schumpeter when he noted that 'it is not only necessary to include the existing amount of such claims [to money] in the total quantity of money (typical cases: bank notes, deposits subject to check), but also evident that the very concept of [a] quantity of money becomes doubtful'. Indeed, he went on, it *'is, in fact, impossible to speak of the quantity of "money" in the sense in which we speak of the quantity of a commodity'* (*Cycles*, p. 546, original emphasis; cf. *Essays*, p. 37). Apropos this difficulty, it is to be understood first of all that the 'impulse to changes in the quantity of bank money comes from the *demand* for credit. No more bank money can be created than is demanded by the business world, it is not possible for the banks to force arbitrary amounts of money upon the market.' (1956, p. 201, emphasis added). Furthermore, credit instruments can be created without resource restrictions or production functions in the usual sense. They are, therefore, largely able to be made available *ad hoc* with quite different sorts of quantitative restrictions applying to decisions about their 'production'. And, as we have seen above in the previous section whatever the credit demand position, bankers may exercise various constraints on their credit creation. There is, then, a significant discretionary and 'endogenous' element in the determination of the flow of credit that appears in any one period that is difficult to represent within a normal supply and demand framework.

The situation is further complicated by the fact that credit lending may well take place independently of any commodity-money (gold base or any collateral or 'asset backing' requirements. Where credit is based upon some mortgage over an existing asset, Schumpeter used the term 'normal' credit and the 'creation' of it amounts to but a 'mobilisation of existing assets' (*Development*, p. 100). Where credit is granted without collateral being secured, and with or without a mortgage over *subsequently-produced* assets, he used the term 'abnormal'. The former comprises 'claims to the social dividend, which represent and may be thought of as certifying services rendered and previous delivery of existing goods', while the latter involves creating 'claims to the social product . . . as certificates of future services or of goods yet to be produced' (ibid., p. 101). So it is that uncovered bank credit money is a 'claim ticket' to the flow of real resources and commodities without being a 'receipt voucher' for any income created by such flows. The result is that the 'credit structure projects not only beyond the existing gold basis, but also beyond the existing commodity basis' (1956, p. 203 *Development*, p. 101). Overall, then, the existence of a range of media that act as purchasing power, combined with the flexibility in their periodic additions to the supply of circulating purchasing power, leaves the money supply largely determined by *ad hoc* requirements.

But, whatever its supply conditions, Schumpeter was very clear in asserting his belief that in the steady circular-flow state, money 'matters very little while in the processes of development and the business cycle i 'matters' in a different way and to a greater degree. To repeat an important passage quoted before, with respect to the steady state he wrote that 'it is clear that the essential lines of our picture are not altered by the insertion of intermediate links, that money only performs the function of a technical instrument, but *adds nothing new to the phenomena* . . . [so that it] represents only the cloak of economic things and *nothing essential is overlooked in abstracting from it*' (ibid., p. 57 emphasis added). The implication here is that the working of the real processes of the circular flow can be understood quite independently of their monetary reflection. But, this observation cannot be sustained in the opposite direction, for as Schumpeter recognized, the monetary phenomena of a capitalist economy, in its steady or developing state re a *product* of the real processes with which they are connected. He argued that 'monetary magnitudes and monetary processes are meaningful only because of the magnitude and processes inherent in the corresponding commodities; hence, understanding of the monetary processes presupposes understanding of the processes in the commodity world and the former cannot be communicated independently from the latter' (*Wesen des Geldes*, p. 119). This reasoning was a little more elaborately and considerably more graphically put in the following piece.

> It is clear that the function of money in the economy is in principle of a merely technical nature, i.e. money is essentially a device for carrying on business transactions, a mere satellite of commodities, a servant of the processes in the world of goods. The monetary expressions and the monetary movements which make up the epidermis of economic life in the market economy, can be explained only by observations of the body which they cover and to which they adjust themselves – hence, by observation of the world of goods, where the really significant events take place. (1956, p. 150)

Now whatever may appear to be Schumpeter's convictions in these passages about the deterministic dominance of real over monetary phenomena, there remained in the explanation of motion some degree of mutuality between the two spheres of action. In *Development*, he argued that money 'matters' in a causal sense by positing what he felt were 'two heresies' against the thesis that money is 'neutral' and merely a 'veil'; 'first . . . the heresy that money, and then . . . the second heresy that also other means of payment, perform an essential function, hence that processes in terms of means of payment are not merely reflexes of processes in terms of goods' (p. 95). The latter 'heresy' concerning credit means of payment is of special significance in Schumpeter's theory because it provides the means whereby development in his sense is able to proceed at all. He reasoned that it is the relation between innovation and credit creation 'which is fundamental to the understanding of the capitalist engine . . . [and] is at the bottom of all the problems of money and credit, at least as far as they are not simply problems of public finance' (*Cycles*, p. 111; cf. *History*, p. 318). At the same time, though, he still wanted to keep his distance from any notion that endogenous monetary changes could have an independent causal role in the pattern of motion (cf. *Cycles*, p. 73). Money has a necessary part to play in any explanation of motion in that its creation is integral to the development process and the form of its interventions affects the traverses that appear. But, the *ultimate origin* of motion itself is to be found in the *real* actions of agents. Schumpeter was emphatic that his theory does not belong to those which seek the cause of the cycle in the

money and credit system, however important the element of th
creation of purchasing power is in our interpretation. Nevertheless, w
do not deny that cyclical movements could be influenced and eve
prevented by credit policy.' (*Development*, p. 230n). The mutuality c
the real and the monetary dimensions of 'business phenomena' wa
reinforced when in his 1930 paper, 'Mitchell's Business Cycles', h
described the following assertions as '*erroneous*': 'that economic life i
changed to its very core by the intervening of money, that a mone
economy must be explained on principles differing *toto caelo* from thos
applicable to a non-monetary life, or that, finally, . . . pointing to th
difference between making goods and making money . . . is pointing t
a fundamental cleavage . . .' (*Essays*, pp. 82–3).'

It is worth recording here, finally, that Schumpeter's ideas on mone
led him to reject the Quantity Theory as the basis for understanding th
role of money in the economy, although he maintained that it had som
heuristic value as a guide to money and price relations (e.g. 195€
p. 177; *History*, pp. 313–14). One of the reasons for this position was hi
belief that the money supply has a significant endogenous componer
that is responsive to demand. His point was, as we have seen, that th
volume of money in circulation 'is altogether variable and tends t
adjust itself to every situation in economic life'. And, on this basis, h
concluded that as far as the fundamentals of the theory are concerned, i
'one were to say that our discussion implied a refutation of the quantit
theory, I should not myself object' provided 'the content of truth an
practical value' of the theory is also emphasized (1956, p. 177; c
pp. 182ff.). When he reflected on the Quantity Theory in the *Histor*
manuscript, he chose to define it as comprising four conditions (p. 703)
First, 'the quantity of money is an independent variable – in particular
. . . it varies independently of prices and of [the] physical volume o
transactions', a condition that is negated by the existence of credi
money and endogenous pressures for its increase that originate in rea
economic activity. Secondly, velocity of circulation is an institutiona
datum that varies slowly or not at all, but in any case is independent o
prices and [the] volume of transactions', a condition that is inconsisten
with the variations in the demand for money that are part of th
observed business-cycle traverses (e.g. *Cycles*, p. 546). Thirdly, 'trans
actions – or let us say, output – are unrelated to [the] quantity of money
and it is only owing to chance that the two may move together'. Thi
condition is directly linked to the fourth one: 'variations in the quantit
of money, unless they be absorbed by variations in output in the sam
direction, act mechanically on all prices, irrespective of how an increas
in the quantity of money is used and on what sector of th

:onomy it first impinges (who gets it) . . .'. Schumpeter's explication of ιe increase in the money supply as a direct consequence of innovation rocesses in particular industries that induce a sequence of subsequent ≀al and price responses that are diffused unevenly through the :onomy, provides a direct negation of these two conditions. This was a ɔint that he evidently had recognized some 40 years earlier in *Das 'esen* (see Reclam, 1984, pp. 20ff.).

.3 **Summary**

ι this chapter, we have identified the role of money and credit in :humpeter's theory of economic development and considered the ∍termination of the rate of interest as the cost of credit.

For Schumpeter, interest was a monetary and 'dynamic' phenomenon linked to the demand for credit by entrepreneurs. They are prepared to pay interest because of their expectation of entrepreneurial profits from innovation, although their capacity to pay would come and go with those profits. Schumpeter did not successfully explain interest as a permanent payment on this basis.

Money was perceived by Schumpeter as playing an essential and integral role in the economic phenomena of capitalism. His focus was on endogenously created credit money, which he saw as having its origins in the requirements of real economic activity. He accepted that money is neutral in the steady circular-flow state, but argued that it has a vital facilitating role in the economic development and business-cycle processes. However, he maintained that it could not have the causal role attributed to it by some business-cycle theorists.

ote

Schumpeter's work on money dates from *Das Wesen* in 1908 (pp. 276ff.) with two major pieces on the subject following, one in 1917, 'Das Sozialprodukt und die Rechenpfennige: Glossen und Beiträge zur Geldtheorie von heute' (*Aufsätze*, pp. 29ff.; translated as Schumpeter, 1956), and the other during the 1920s, the manuscript given the title *Das Wesen des Geldes* by its editor when the work was finally published in 1970. Other than various pieces on money in *Development, Cycles* and *History* to be referred to in the text,there were three other papers from 1913, 1925 and 1927 that dealt with themes about money and credit (*Aufsätze*, pp. 1ff., 118ff. and 158ff.).

In the secondary literature, the most comprehensive coverage of Schumpeter's 'credit theory of money' is to be found in Reclam, 1984 and in a series of papers by James Earley (1981, 1983 and 1987). Earlier views may be found in Stolper, 1943; Marget, 1951; and Warburton, 1953. Other recent contributions include Tichy, 1984b; Bellofiore, 1985a, 1985b; Vercelli, 1985; and Minsky, 1986, 1988.

8 The primary business cycle

8.1 Business-cycle methodology

For Schumpeter, the business cycle was the temporal *form* taken by the traverse processes that comprise and are induced by an expansion in economic activity that is initiated as economic development. He distinguished this instability of capitalist motion from what he saw as the secular stability of the system that is associated with continuous economic growth with its origins in 'pure' capital accumulation and population increases. Causally, the business cycle was linked directly to the innovations that Schumpeter argued would come in discontinuous 'waves' or 'clusters' and provide the impetus for economic development. The logic of the system then ensured that the subsequent sequence of events would result in economic activity following out a wave-like temporal pattern.

In this section, I begin my critical exposition and reassessment of the business cycle as the centrepiece of Schumpeter's theory of motion with a brief discussion of some particular methodological aspects of the analyses that follow. These comprise, so to say, the 'stylized' issues that are pertinent to any business-cycle theory and they indicate some of the particular challenges that would be faced by any analyst setting out to explain the phenomenon.

A definitional framework for the business cycle was formulated by Schumpeter in an endeavour 'to make our meaning perfectly precise to the specialist' (*Essays*, p. 135). As a statistically presented object of study, he saw two aspects of a 'cycle' upon which analysis should focus. First, it should be recognized that 'sequences of values of economic quantities in historic time (as distinguished from theoretic time) do not display monotonic increase or decrease, but (irregular) recurrence of either these values themselves or their first or their second time-derivatives'. And secondly, it should further be recognized that 'these "fluctuations" do not occur independently in every such time series, but always display either instantaneous or lagged association with each other' (ibid., cf. *Cycles*, p. 200). These two aspects of the cycle make it clear that its substance is a set of relations between economic variables set in *historical* time. The 'variables' will have both quantitative as well as qualitative dimensions for the analyst to contend with. As directly observed and measured, the cycle is a purely quantitative phenomenon. Its various characteristics, such as its 'unit' duration, amplitude and phases of events, all require quantitative data for their expression and hence quantitative variables receive priority in any theoretical represen-tation. In a truly comprehensive theory, however, the qualitative 'dynamics' that lie 'behind' the quantitative appearances will not be omitted and the human and institutional substance of the phenomenon will be given due attention.

With respect to the quantitative variables most immediately in focus, the first question to be raised is: Which variables should be selected for primary emphasis in any explication of the cycle? Sometimes the matter is not given much direct consideration by analysts, but it is necessary for clear argument at least to distinguish which *indicator* variables most appropriately trace out the time-series manifestation of the cycle, i.e. 'those of our series which are most symptomatic of the pulse of economic life as a whole' (*Essays*, pp. 140–1). Mostly, these 'systematic' variables will be aggregate ones when macroeconomic cycles are the object of analysis, but Schumpeter drew some distinctions between different classes of such variables and a number of them turned out to be sub-aggregate in their scope. He chose to divide the 'systematic' variables into those that he considered to be 'synthetic', such as price levels and the physical volume of production, where some composite index measurement is required, and those he saw as 'natural', such as interest rates and unemployment, where the relevant symptomatic inferences are drawn by direct observation of the immediate data (ibid., p. 141; cf. *Cycles*, p. 18). In addition to this distinction, Schumpeter introduced a class of variables called 'individual' which are symptomatic of 'special cycles' in particular industries or markets (*Essays*, p. 141). He stressed the complementary significance of these latter variables and cycles for extending our understanding of 'systematic' business-cycle fluctuations: 'There is hardly any event, or peculiarity of structural pattern, *in any industry* which would be irrelevant to the question[of] why the business cycle is what it is.' (ibid., p. 142, emphasis added).

A further classification of the indicators used to measure business cycles distinguishes between their variations in *absolute* terms and their variations as *rates of change*. This is an important distinction in that it vitally affects the interpretation of the cycle path: for example, a fall in the *level* of real GDP in a downswing may have a quite different explanation and quite different implications from a fall in the rate of growth of real GDP. It is appropriate here to distinguish between 'classical' business cycles couched in terms of absolute fluctuations and 'growth' cycles that are argued in terms of rates of change (cf. Zarnowitz, 1985, pp. 530, 532–3). The key difference between the two forms in an analytical sense concerns the way in which the phases of each particular observed cycle unit may be presented. In a 'classical' cycle presentation, high *growth* rates of economic activity will be associated with the middle stages of expansion and, perhaps, during a rapid recovery phase. Towards the end of a 'classical' expansion, growth rates will slow and low, zero and then negative rates will persist during the upper turning-point crisis, recession and depression stages. By contrast, in the 'growth' cycle presentation, the phases themselves trace out changes in the growth rate with rates continuously accelerating to higher levels during the upswing phases and continuously decelerating to lower, *possibly* negative, levels during the downswing phases. With 'classical' cycles, the growth rates are zero at the turning points whereas in the 'growth' cycle, the rates are at their maximum or minimum (maximum negative). Now while Schumpeter was aware of this distinction, at least as a statistical matter, his theoretical analyses were presented only in the 'classical' terms that dominated the cycles literature of the era.

He also had little to say at the theoretical level about the problematical relationship between monotonic trend values of variables and their cyclical fluctuations in value. His approach to the analysis of economic growth *per se* suggests that he believed that trends could be isolated and set aside to be reintegrated into an analysis of motion after fluctuations have been explained in their absence. At the statistical level, he did discuss the nature of trends in time-series, at least at a superficial level (*Cycles*, pp. 200ff.). I will not pursue his discussions here as they provide no additional insight into his theoretical treatment of motion.

Yet a further consideration concerning the classification of cyclical variables is the relative time phasing of fluctuations in their values. The 'natural' categorization here at an heuristic level is to follow accumulated empirical evidence and designate particular variables as leading or lagging some core set. No such classification can be unique or unchanging over historical time, but observations suggest that such variables as gross domestic product, industrial production and unemployment rate are usually at the core of any cyclical pattern. Leading these are often new business formations, new finance appropriations for manufacturing, contracts and orders for produced means of production, rate of capacity utilization, ratio of price to unit labour cost and profit margins. The lagging variables include unit labour costs, interest rates and bond yields, and expenditures on produced means of production (Zarnowitz, 1985, p. 531). If such a categorization is taken seriously as a part of the theoretical object to be explained, then the analytical ramifications are quite profound. Even allowing for a degree of abstraction in order to make the object analytically tractable, it is clear that the business-cycle traverses are required to explain the paths of the core variables selected and then to link these through various causal relations involving some patterns of lead or lag in time to other selected variables. Any comprehensive theory of business cycle should include an explication in these terms.

Schumpeter's own list of 41 empirical 'symptoms' at the beginning of *Cycles* (pp. 15–17) went some way towards recognizing the desirable multi-variable representation of business cycles and he pointed to the need for a proper semeiology involving the 'interpretation and coordination of such symptoms' (ibid., p. 15). His treatment of the relative phasing issue was, however, desultory and haphazard at best. He hinted at the *problem* as follows: 'Also each symptom must be judged in the light of the corresponding (*not necessarily exactly contemporaneous*) states of some of the others, which precisely means judging it in the light of the whole business situation.' (ibid., emphasis added). The nature and implications of this parenthetical remark were never given the precise and detailed treatment that they warranted. Indeed, in his theoretical analysis, Schumpeter was not even very precise about which particular economic variables he included in his analytical framework let alone what relative time phasing they could be expected to follow.

In the empirical section of *Cycles*, where he was concerned with the observed form of business fluctuations, Schumpeter did home in on certain key variables in the form of what he called 'Pulse Charts' (pp. 463ff.). These comprise time-series of four variables measuring (according to the data available and most relevant for each country concerned) an index of wholesale prices, an index of output, the stock of the circulating medium and a selected rate of interest. On the status of these charts it is appropriate to let Schumpeter speak for himself.

> In the workshop of the writer a habit has grown up of referring to these charts as Pulse Charts. The reason for this is obvious. Little though the writer thinks of the explanatory value of aggregative theory, and far though he is from claiming barometric value for the four constituents of these charts, they nevertheless give a rough picture of the economic process in time and, in a sense, *sum up what we have to account for by our analysis*. (ibid., p. 463, emphasis added)

Unfortunately here the horse is following the cart. Well may the charts sum up what is to be explained, but they appear only after the *theory* upon which the explanation is to depend has been completely formulated. That, in itself, is not a major problem. Rather, it is that the correspondence between this precise framework of variables and the theoretical argument intended to deal with it was very loose indeed.

Schumpeter's theoretical analyses lacked any such consistent framework and variables seemed to be simply called up as they came to mind.

To some extent, this shortcoming can be explained by the open-ended way that he treated his theoretical endeavours (see Chapter 1, section 1.1). In his 1927 review article on Pigou's *Industrial Fluctuations* for *Economica*, he explained that in his own theory, what he sought to do was to identify the 'fundamental cause' of business cycles. He was not concerned to formulate 'a general theory, as exhaustive as may be, of all the elements contributing, or likely to contribute, to the phenomena we observe and of their interaction' (*Essays*, p. 23). This meant emphasizing what he thought to be *the* causal factor in waves of innovation, a factor '*adequate* to produce the phenomenon [of the business cycle] without extraneous influences'. This gave him 'an explanation of what we may call the "essence" or "nature" of the phenomenon' (ibid. p. 22n, original emphasis). Perhaps with such a limited immediate objective in mind, Schumpeter considered any preconceived and definite framework of variables to be manipulated within some self-contained model as unnecessary and/or undesirable for his purposes. We should recall his dictum: 'I never wish to say anything definitive; if I have a function it is to open doors not to close them.' (quoted by Haberler, 1951a, p. 46).

It would be incorrect to assume from the particular specificity of Schumpeter's analytical focus that he pursued a monocausal theory of the cycle. While he found in waves of innovations *the* necessary cause of economic development and its business-cycle form, he did not consider this cause to be sufficient, in itself, to explain the *manifestation* of business-cycle phenomena, even at an abstract level. The latter explanation requires, first of all, that the innovation process be situated in a minimum analytical context of associated structures and operations – as posited in the circular-flow model – and secondly, that due attention be paid to at least the more significant 'external' effects that modify the sequence of events generated by the former, primary impact and diffusion of innovations. Therein lies the essence of the methodological separation between the present chapter on the primary model of the cycle and the extensive analysis of secondary effects considered in the next.

Open-ended or not, the theoretical analysis of the business cycle that Schumpeter endeavoured to formulate was to be, in its essentials, an *endogenous* one. He defined such a theory retrospectively in the *History* manuscript as one which shows 'how each phase of the cyclical process is induced by the conditions prevailing in the preceding one' (p. 745). Thus, for him, a meaningful theory of the cycle could not ultimately depend on external factors as sufficient explanation. These factors must be used to broaden a theory and enable it to explain particular historical episodes of fluctuations, but they cannot comprise the essence of the cycle's generation. Schumpeter's standard of theoretical explanation was one of strict logical necessity and he identified waves of innovations as the only internal source of recurring fluctuations that is inherent in the nature of the capitalist system as he defined it. Fluctuations caused by any other source, including external factors and internal structural and/or operational malfunctions of the system were not business cycles in his essential sense. They could only be complementary phenomena or empirical aberrations requiring separate *ad hoc* explanations. 'I always thought, and I still think', he wrote in 1927, 'that in order to find out whether or not cycles are a phenomenon *sui generis*, clearly standing out as such from *the rest of industrial fluctuations* [emphasis added] and arising from *within* the economic system, we ought, in the first instance, to assume the absence of outside disturbances . . . acting on the system.' (*Essays*, p. 25, original emphasis except as stated; cf. *History*, p. 1133).

The claimed endogenous nature of Schumpeter's theory requires the driving force of innovation waves be explained as an integral part of the sequential behaviours, conditions and operations that comprise the business-cycle traverses. According to his own definition of endogeneity, because the wave appears in the prosperity phase that follows a pass through a 'neighborhood of equilibrium', its origins must lie in the 'equilibrium' state itself and, perhaps, in the phase that precedes it. Schumpeter never stated this requirement very precisely, but consistency demands it. However, he provided no *explanation* of why waves of innovation appear periodically, if irregularly, to restart each business-cycle unit. It was more an act of faith than anything else to believe that each 'neighborhood of equilibrium' will induce nascent entrepreneurs to act *en masse* to generate a renewed expansion of economic activity. This belief can only be based upon the assumptions that the conditions in the equilibrium *are* those which will bring such a result and that enough new and otherwise uncommitted agents with the appropriate talents and access to the required knowledge and inventions always exist to participate in it. There is little point in pushing this issue any further. The belief is crucial to Schumpeter's whole theory and we can only proceed here with it as an accepted element of the lore upon which he constructed the theory. Innovation waves can simply be treated instead as an external *impulse*, i.e. as an externally imposed change in the data that appears and gets the cycle underway each time, but this would not comply with Schumpeter's ideas of endogeneity.[1]

8.2   Essentials of the business-cycle theory

Schumpeter centred his business-cycle theory around the steady circu
lar-flow state, or more generally, around a 'neighborhood of equili
brium' as an empirically-modified representation of the 'pure' version
for convenience, I will refer to this state below as simply *'equilibrium'*
Each cycle unit is initiated by a wave of innovations that disturb the
'equilibrium' state and generate the processes of development that tak
on the form of fluctuations in economic activity and other associate
events. That is, each cyclical expansion 'begins' from an 'equilibrium'. I
is readily appreciated, of course, that the whole idea of definite cycl
units that 'begin' from somewhere is an artificial imposition upon what i
in reality a continuous and interdependent complex of causes, event
and consequences. The imposition is made necessary by the demands o
analytical tractability, but as there is no unique way of handling th
theoretical 'reconstruction' of the cycle format, I will return below i
this section to consider further the choices that Schumpeter made in thi
respect.

It is worth emphasizing right from the start that the phase o
expansion and prosperity that follows immediately after the 'equili
brium' is disturbed is the *only* phase in the cycle, as Schumpete
formulated it, in which innovations take a *direct* role in determining th
traverse. The remaining phases comprise events that are the results o
responses and adjustments induced by the initiating wave, probabl
complicated by a myriad of other internal and external factors tha
ultimately determine the substantive and temporal form of the cycle. I
may be said, then, that the expansion into prosperity and boom is th
action phase of the cycle while the others all comprise sequences o
reaction.

Initially, the cycle takes the form of a phase of economic developmen
as argued out in detail in an earlier chapter (Chapter 6 above). The firs
analytical challenge that must be met in order to turn the theory o
development into a theory of the cycle is to show, by means of a
appropriate traverse sequence, how the forces of development and th
prosperity conditions they engender are brought to an end. Only if thi
can be shown to occur by virtue of internally-generated countervailin
forces can the theory comply with Schumpeter's definition of endoge
neity. Part of this challenge must be to say something, at least implicitly
about the way in which the duration of the prosperity and its 'amplitude
are determined. At the end of the prosperity phase, or at the end of th
boom period that may be part of it, a crisis of some sort and degree mus
set in. Expansion slows and comes to a halt and the subsequen

:actions and adjustments lead the economy into a contractionary phase
a a traverse usually referred to as the upper turning point.
Some care is needed in interpreting the nature of the contractionary
hase in Schumpeter's theory. In particular, there was an important
ift in terminology between the *Development* and *Cycles* versions
hich reflected an extension of the formal argument in the latter work.
he contraction phase in the seminal model of the cycle was explained
lly in terms of the 'normal' forces of reaction and adjustment inherent
the structural and operational logic of the developing circular-flow
ate. That is, the contraction was treated as a *logically entailed*
onsequence of the prosperity-boom phase. Now at first, this primary
orm of the contraction was called a *depression*. Later the term used was
cession, although some carelessness of expression led Schumpeter to
ontinue to use the former term in this role when he had explicitly given
another meaning. This point is much more than a semantic one, for
riefly in *Development* (e.g. p. 226) and then in later versions of the
ycle theory, beginning with the 1935 paper on 'The Analysis of
conomic Change' written for the *Review of Economic Statistics*
Essays, pp. 134ff.), the contraction phase was 'extended' to include
hat he called 'secondary-wave' effects which were superimposed upon
e primary recession (*Cycles*, pp. 145ff.). The result was what he
eferred to after *Development* as a *depression form* of the contraction.
ot only does this extension comprise the onset of a deeper contraction,
ut also the forces involved in bringing it about are quite different from
ose operating in a recession. The depression is not logically entailed
y the expansion phase that precedes it and requires certain additional
xternal and internal factors to be present before it will appear. These
tter forces are highly contingent in their nature, strength and scope
nd little by way of theoretical generalization can be applied to their
nalytical representation. And, what is more, the matter is rather more
roblematical than it may appear at first sight. The reason is that the
epression forces cannot legitimately be simply 'added' into the traverse
f the recession because some of them will have their origins back in the
xpansion phase and in the crisis that brought it to an end. There is a
ense, then, in which the recession as such 'disappears' within the
epression phenomena. Enough has been said on this for the present to
einforce the need for two distinct terms in order to deal effectively with
chumpeter's analysis of the contraction phase. More on this anon.
  The next challenge to be faced in cycle analysis is to formulate a
ontraction traverse that includes the forces that bring it to an end, too.
n Schumpeter's case, the challenge is doubly complicated by the fact
nat he had to provide two lots of reasoning here: one that used only the

primary logic of the recession and another that took account of some *particular* additional forces that comprise a case of depression. Both sorts of contraction must be shown to end in a lower turning point traverse and while the former case can be secure in its logic, the latter cannot be so decisively dealt with. Schumpeter, therefore, left some understandable lacunae in his analyses of depressions. The primary recession was always argued to end in a new 'equilibrium' state. This is assured because the crisis of the upper turning point leads agents into a definite sequence of reactions and adjustments. These constitute adaptations designed to mitigate the adverse effects of the collapse and to reap many of the as yet unrealized economic benefits of the wave of innovations that generated the prosperity in the first place. For Schumpeter, somewhat paradoxically, the 'pure' recession phase was designated as a period of continuing economic *prosperity* in its literal sense. Indeed, the whole idea of formulating the 'pure' form of the primary cycle, including its prosperity, boom, upper turning point 'crisis' and recession components was to emphasize the *essentially non-pathological and beneficent* nature of some fluctuations in the capitalist economy. They comprise periods of 'disturbance' between two 'equilibria' that are logically necessary in order that the human benefits of innovations may be fully realized and diffused. However, Schumpeter was well aware that this abstracted primary core of fluctuations could only be considered to be a 'first approximation', a 'pure model' or a mere 'skeleton' of or 'chassis' for any cyclical reality (ibid., p. 130).

The extension of the primary wave analysis to include the causes and consequences of depression had the effect of requiring two additional traverse phases to be explicated within each business-cycle unit, although, as I noted above, there are some potential analytical difficulties in arguing the recession and depression as separable, temporally sequential phases of a secondary contraction. But, however this is to be handled, once the lower turning point is rationalized, the next phase that begins the upswing is to be considered as a recovery or revival period. The resulting four-phase cycle unit, consisting of prosperity, recession, depression and recovery, Schumpeter referred to as his 'second approximation' (ibid., pp. 145ff.). Again here, care in interpreting the nature of the phases is required. The recovery phase, and the lower turning point that precedes and initiates it, must be kept analytically separate from the prosperity phase that forms the other 'half' of the total upswing period from the end of the depression to the next boom. As already indicated, *the recovery phase cannot be attributed to innovations* and some other rationale must be sought for its origins in the lower turning point traverse. Then, the recovery traverse must be shown to lead to a restoration of the circular-flow 'equilibrium' which marks the completion of the business-cycle unit. It is only in the restored state of 'equilibrium', as was the case with the primary two-phase model, that a new wave of innovations can occur and generate the phase of prosperity that 'begins' the *next* cycle unit. So, not only is the upswing period as a whole divided into two phases separated by an 'equilibrium' state of some unspecified duration, but also the two phases are in different cycle units.

Figures 8.1 and 8.2, respectively, show the primary and secondary

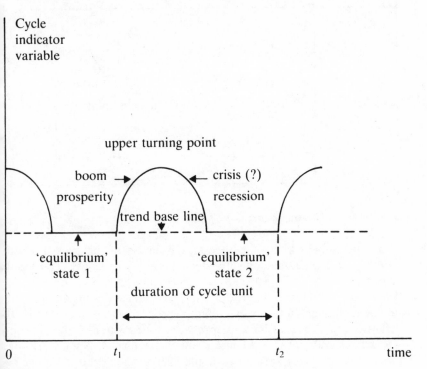

Figure 8.1   The primary two-phase cycle

cycle paths in outline. Each is self-explanatory in the lights of the above discussion except for three points that call for some clarification. First, there is a question-mark appended to the crisis 'position' on the two-phase cycle in Figure 8.1 because, as I will argue in section 8.4 below, it is doubtful if the concept is applicable in the context of such a core model of the cycle. Secondly, the trend base line shown in each of the figures is drawn horizontal for convenience as well as to reflect what

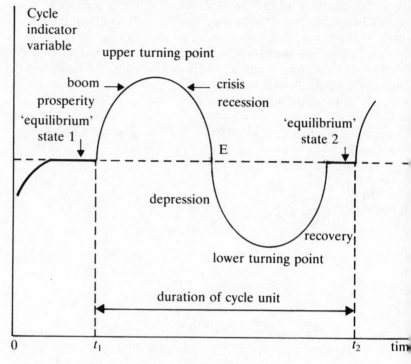

Figure 8.2   The secondary four-phase cycle

Schumpeter held to be the necessary isolation of the cycle from th
'pure' growth phenomenon with which it is mixed in reality. Thirdly, th
status of the point E 'between' the recession and depression phases i
Figure 8.2 is not immediately evident. I will discuss this matter further i
the next chapter, but already enough has been said to indicate that th
'transition' from recession to depression, if 'transition' is the appropri
ate term at all, presents considerable analytical difficulty. At som
points, Schumpeter seemed to argue that E should be designated a
some sort of 'interim equilibrium' state. This would follow from th
logic of the recession that precedes it if the 'pure' form is retained 'prio
to' the depression forces being added in. He was never too definit
about this view, though, because he knew that the roots of th
depression reach back well before E.

This latter characteristic is featured in Figure 8.3 where the two cycl
paths are brought together in a single diagram (cf. Marschak, 1940
p. 890). Here the 'secondary wave' effects which serve to accentuate th
amplitude of the primary cycle are shown as coming into effect from th

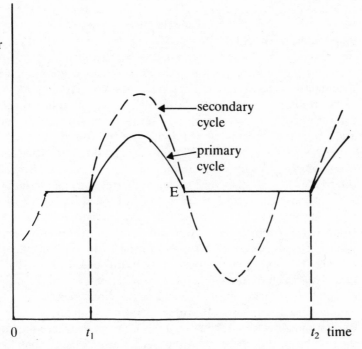

Figure 8.3 The primary and secondary cycle mix

beginning of the latter's expansion phase at time t_1. The diagram also shows the two cycle paths as having the same period from time t_1 to time t_2. While common sense would suggest that one probable 'distorting' effect of secondary dimensions that appear during the cycle would be to alter the period, the common point E must be preserved. This is necessary in order to ensure preservation of some theoretical and empirical relationship between the two-cycle formats as demanded by Schumpeter's fundamental tenet that the primary wave is the core around which the secondary one is constructed. A more complete discussion of the key status of the point E must wait until the next chapter. By contrast, the coincidences of the paths at time t_1 and t_2 are not necessary, for there is no logical reason why the secondary factors would not begin to take effect before or after each of these points in time.

The next stage in the elaboration of Schumpeter's original primary-cycle model also appeared first in the 1935 *Review of Economic Statistics* paper cited above (*Essays*, pp. 134ff:), although the idea was referred to in passing in 1931 (ibid., pp. 96–7). It was the 'three-cycle schema' that was amplified in *Cycles* (pp. 161ff.) as the 'third approximation' in the totality of his cycle theory. The schema was intended to represent, in an empirically meaningful and analytically tractable way, the real-world interaction of multiple simultaneous cyclical fluctuations. As with the secondary dimensions of the cycle in the 'second approximation', the schema has its roots in empirical manifestations of the cycle rather than in the primary theory itself. In the schema, cycle units in each of the three categories were classified in terms of their *duration* and named after the analyst most well-known for his 'discovery' of empirical examples of each: Joseph *Kitchin* for the shortest, 40-month cycle; Clément *Juglar* for the nine- to ten-year cycle; and N. D. *Kondratieff* for the 54- to 60-year long-wave cycle. The categories had immediate links back to various complications in their causal origins *vis-à-vis* Schumpeter's primary focus on innovation waves and once again he ended up with a heap of complex analytical puzzles to address if the schema was to be fully explained. In this case, the consensus amongst most contemporary and later commentators on this 'third' extension to the primary model has been that it would have been better left aside. I will critically examine the schema in more detail in the next chapter.

One particular analytical problem raised by the above business-cycle outline concerns where the cycle units are most appropriately deigned to 'begin', given that the empirical object is actually a complex continuity of events. For Schumpeter, the point at which to 'break into' this continuity was implied in the way his theory was constructed. In defining the boundaries of the cycle unit, he asserted, 'we are not at liberty to count cycles from any phase we please. The phenomenon becomes understandable only if we start with the neighborhood of equilibrium preceding prosperity and end up with the neighborhood of equilibrium following revival.' (ibid., p. 156). The recovery phase must be the last in each four-phase unit because it essentially 'belongs to' the lower turning point and the depression that precedes it. 'Revival', he wrote, 'is the last and not the first phase of the cycle. If we count from troughs we cut off this phase from the cycle to which it belongs and add it on to a cycle to which it does not belong. Counting in this way, we lose the fundamental distinction between revival and prosperity.' (ibid.). As recovery is to end in a newly-established 'equilibrium' in which a new wave of innovations will ultimately appear, the cycle unit must 'begin' from this position as all of the prosperity and recession events are the logical 'products' of the wave. Schumpeter saw the failure to keep the two phases of the upswing separate and thus to 'begin' a new cycle unit after recovery has been traversed as 'one of the main sources of faulty analysis' in business-cycle studies (*Essays*, p. 138). This latter claim was rather an exaggeration, for we should recall that the need to divide the upswing into two phases was a direct consequence of the construction of his analysis and not due to some logic that he had shown to be inherent in the nature of the system.

8.3 The primary expansion into prosperity

The most fundamental point of Schumpeter's primary theory of the business cycle was his belief that the innovations are most appropriately modelled as coming in discontinuous waves. Their immediate consequences, that make up the traverse of the ensuing expansion into prosperity can, therefore, be represented as finite so that the initial impetus given to economic activity will peter out over time. He posed the issues involved in the questions: 'why is it that economic development in our sense does not proceed evenly as a tree grows, but as it were jerkily; why does it display those characteristic ups and downs?' To these he provided the 'short and precise' answer that it is 'exclusively *because the new combinations are not, as one would expect according to general principles of probability, evenly distributed through time . . .* but *appear, if at all, discontinuously in groups or swarms*' (*Development*, p. 223, original emphasis). This answer, he felt, contained an unambiguous statement of '*the only "cause" of cycles*' (*Essays*, p. 32, original emphasis). The waves of innovation bring a strictly limited period of expansion because entrepreneurial activity 'slackens and stops at a point which can be theoretically determined', an outcome which will result for reasons inherent in [the development mechanism] . . . and by virtue of its own effects and of the business situations it creates' (*Cycles*, p. 135).

By applying his 'isolation' methodology, Schumpeter endeavoured to formulate a 'pure model', a 'sort of chassis' or 'skeleton' for his whole theoretical analysis of the business cycle on the basis of the premises just outlined (ibid., pp. 130, 138). The procedure was initially to restate the theory of economic development, but with more decisive emphasis on the 'dynamics' of the entrepreneurial agents' activities over time; the seeking out and taking up of innovation opportunities by progressively greater numbers of entrepreneurs, together with the subsequent progressive decline in this activity and its consequences. In this 'dynamics', the key issue is to identify the reasons for this latter decline. Here Schumpeter gave great weight to the most evident of the results of innovative activity, entrepreneurial profit. Specifically, he argued that the profit is eroded over time by a process of 'competition' and that it is an uncertain form of income in the first place. His view was that entrepreneurs make decisions to innovate knowing that their immediate profit gains will be eroded by imitators (*Development*, p. 231). Not only will their initiative be copied by followers in the same market, but there will also be growing pressure on resource input prices as innovators begin to appear in greater numbers in other markets.

This prospect of profit erosion is compounded by the fact that profit expectations must be formed by agents in the face of some degree of uncertainty that will depend largely upon the degree of 'novelty' that their innovations involve. That is, the cumulative profit results that a particular entrepreneur can expect from his or her innovation can only be calculated *ex ante* with a significant margin for error. The extent of market success of the innovation and the impact and duration of competition just cannot be known in advance. Inevitably, some entrepreneurs will have overestimated their prospects and their business demise will come sooner rather than later in the traverse of expansion. We should recall Schumpeter's opinion that *nine out of every ten* entrepreneurs who actually get their projects underway fail in some way (*Cycles*, p. 117). But, as he gave no details of the time profile of such failures nor of their precise nature, it is difficult to know the extent to which he saw this uncertainty aspect as contributing to the decline in the effect of innovative activity during the expansion phase. What is clear is that in spite of its claimed quantitative significance in *Cycles*, he had maintained in *Development* that uncertainty and miscalculation by entrepreneurs are generally not crucial as impediments to the continuation of their activities. In the latter work, he wrote that 'the essence of the disturbance caused by the boom does not lie in the fact that it often upsets entrepreneurs' calculations', even in cases where 'the consequent general extension of production proves to be wrong' (*Development*, p. 231 and n). And, by more direct contrast with his later belief about their likely failure rate, he seemed to base his argument on the sanguine suggestion that 'production is entered upon by sane men only on the basis of more or less careful investigation of the facts' (ibid., p. 227). What he failed to give due weight to here is that so much of what the entrepreneur, sane or not, must decide upon cannot be based upon 'facts' because the uncertain, incalculable and unknowable future is involved.

Thus, it remained Schumpeter's view that unrealized expectations about entrepreneurial profits may be 'a supporting and *accentuating* circumstance, but not a primary cause necessary to the understanding of the principle. There would still be cyclical movements – *though in a milder form* – even if no one ever did anything that could be described as "false" from his point of view; even if there were no technical or commercial "error", or "speculative fever", or groundless optimism and pessimism; and even if everyone was gifted with wide foresight.' (ibid., pp. 227–8, emphasis added). There is some concession here, indicated by the emphases, to the aggravating effect that any sort of entrepreneurial failure may have on their role in the cycle, but it is a secondary effect that does not belong in the core primary analysis. On this basis, in both *Development* and *Cycles*, Schumpeter chose, as a matter of principle, to abstract from uncertainty and disappointed expectations in the 'pure model' of the cycle (see pp. 227 and 54 respectively). For this purpose, these things were said to be of 'a consequential or incidental character', whatever their empirical significance may be (*Cycles*, p. 135). His 'heroic assumption' was to be, effectively, that 'not only the full increase in the new product, which will be brought about by more and more firms taking up production, and the incident fall in its price have been perfectly correctly foreseen by the first [entrepreneur] in the field, but also that those who came later also foresaw correctly what possibilities were left to them.' (ibid.). In spite of this resolve, though, there are still occasions in his discussions where the common-sense implications of uncertainty intrude.

In order to explain the curtailment of the prosperity and boom phase, even with perfect foresight by initiating innovators and their imitators, Schumpeter introduced several other 'circumstances' that he considered to be pertinent to such an outcome (*Development*, pp. 231ff.; *Cycles*, pp. 135ff.). Here it is appropriate to distinguish between what happens over time to the new firms that appear with the implementation of new combinations and what happens to existing or 'old' firms whose otherwise established and stable place in the circular flow of economic life is disturbed by the emergence of these new firms. It is worth noting that, probably in deference to the realities of capitalism, even in the context of the 'pure model' analysis, existing firms in 'equilibrium' have some quasi-rent based profit incomes, although the precise source of them was not discussed. The effect, though, is to give those firms a 'cushion' of economic viability which must be removed by innovation-induced input price increases and/or later competitive commodity price reductions before they can fail during the upswing and thereby contribute to the slowing of the rise in economic activity (*Development*, p. 232).

Consider first the fate of new firms whose expenditures associated with their input needs to activate new combinations and whose production at lower cost comprises the mobilizing force of the expansion phase. An analysis of the price and quantity effects of the new products that flow from them, where such products must be interpreted broadly to include all those for which production is affected by any innovation, independently of its form (cf. *Cycles*, p. 135), must recognize that they arrive on their markets in a wave. While they may enter the market at the established price, there will be some degree of downward pressure on that price due to excess supply, depending upon the nature of the market involved. The subsequent price-decline profile will then be the result of the rate at which the new products appear on the market, a rate that is technically determined initially, but is later affected by 'the tempo in which the multitude follow the leaders' (*Development* p. 233n). It is this rate that Schumpeter thought 'fundamentally explains the length of the boom' (ibid., p. 233), for in any market, the new firms must ultimately face a limit to their viable production levels at the initial price and hence profit level. He argued that 'since entrepreneurial activity characteristically starts off in a definite direction and does not distribute itself equally all over the industrial field – since it aims typically at production of a given commodity or group of commodities – its possibilities are, in every instance and in every given state of the economic body, definitely limited' (*Cycles*, p. 135). And, while the 'fall in prices is in practice generally postponed through many circumstances . . . [,] the underlying state of affairs is only accentuated, not eliminated by the postponement' and the fate of the entrepreneurs is generally sealed, a fate which, we recall, they fully expect (*Development* p. 233n). 'It is easy to see', Schumpeter wrote, 'that a point will be reached at which our new commodity will be produced at minimum unit cost equal to the price at which it will sell. Profits will be eliminated, the impulse of innovation will, for the time being, have spent itself. (*Cycles*, p. 135). The ultimate effect as far as the business cycle is concerned, then, is that 'the fall in prices, which on its part terminates the boom, *may* lead to a crisis, *must* lead to a depression [read recession], and starts all the rest' (*Development*, p. 233, original emphasis).

Implicit in Schumpeter's analysis of the expansion phase was distinction between two groups of existing firms according to the nature and extent of their involvement with the innovation wave. First there are those firms whose output is immediately innovation-competing They face initially increased input costs as the entrepreneurial demand have their effects in the resource markets and, ultimately, their realized output price may begin to decline due to the excess supply effect alluded to above. Any quasi-rent income they enjoy will be eroded by both supply and demand side pressures and with their economic future appearing less and less viable, a decision to cease production by their managing agents becomes probable. Where such firms have the prospect of holding out until they take up the new combination as an

mitator, it is possible that they may arrange credit to support them
through the lossmaking period. This may act to mitigate the overall
ffect of competition from new firms during the expansion phase
Development, p. 233).

A second group of existing firms comprises those whose products are
not directly affected by demand side competition from the new firms
because they sell in different markets from those in which the new
product waves appear. That is, the overall pattern of the breakdown of
existing firm viability 'is moderated by the fact . . . that the boom is
never general at first, but centres in one branch or a few branches of
industry, leaving other areas undisturbed, and subsequently only affects
the latter in a different, and secondary, manner' (ibid.). As a 'secondary' matter, then, these firms may be affected on their input side in the
same manner as the other group above. Their quasi-rent 'cushion' is
threatened by increasing input costs, as far as these increases actually
affect the particular inputs that they use. However, why this should be
referred to as only a 'secondary' effect is not clear, for such a threat,
where relevant, may have a very rapid and significant impact according
to the basic tenets of Schumpeter's argument.

Overall, as far as existing firms are concerned, 'the boom means
distress for many producers' (ibid., p. 232). There is, though, the
prospect that some innovative activity can be carried out by these firms
rather than by new competitors (ibid.). To the extent that this occurs,
the traverse of the expansion phase will be considerably modified in
terms of the competitive pressures that contribute to the end of the
boom. This possibility received little attention in Schumpeter's theory
even though it has the potential significantly to affect the form of the
cycle.

Another element in the dynamics of the prosperity and boom phase
that Schumpeter felt would affect the flow of innovations supporting it
was the changing economic context in which especially the imitating
entrepreneurs must operate. The phase must be characterized by
widespread economic flux and disequilibrium. It is a time when the
relative prices of inputs and of outputs are constantly changing, with
the characteristic uncertainty which results from the new creations of
the boom . . . always immediately observable. The result is that in such
a situation, 'accurate calculation [is] impossible in general, but
especially for the planning of new enterprises' (ibid., pp. 235–6; cf.
Essays, p. 29). Or, as Schumpeter reiterated the thesis in *Cycles*,
innovators face an 'impossibility of calculating costs and receipts in a
satisfactory way', with 'the difficulty of planning new things and the risk
of failure . . . greatly increased' (p. 135). Here he went on to cite Fritz

Machlup's argument, expressed in a lecture to Schumpeter's business cycle class at Harvard, that 'entrepreneurial risk of failure is at minimum in equilibrium and slowly rises as prosperity develops. Entrepreneurial activity stops at a point at which that risk is maximum.' (ibid., p. 136n). Schumpeter hastened to add, though, that this dictum was quite compatible with his idea that the entrepreneur is not a risk bearer in the sense of facing possible personal financial loss from innovation failure. The point that is at issue is rather that for entrepreneurs, it is the prospect of pecuniary and non-pecuniary success itself that acts as a strong motivating force. With the rising riskiness of innovative ventures as the expansion phase proceeds, this prospect weakens and with it the incentive to innovate. The effect is aggravated by the fact that as innovative activity spreads, the agents who become involved are less and less bold, confident and able.

Notice here how Schumpeter has maintained the relevance of uncertainty as a decision variable in spite of his expressed view elsewhere that it should be eliminated from the primary cycle. As was often the case, his desire to keep his 'pure' theory in touch with the realities of capitalism is evident. Notice also that in arguing the disturbing effect on potential entrepreneurs of the disequilibrium conditions of the boom, he gave little attention to the countervailing atmosphere of optimism that may pervade such a period. It may well be that during such times it is the 'animal spirits' of innovators, rather than their ability to calculate costs and returns, that dominate decision making. He did at one point, though, note the ease with which any degree of optimism can be turned into pessimism. There is then the prospect that this will bring more negative attitudes towards profit prospects and perhaps even cause a panic flight from investment (*Development*, p. 236).

Schumpeter also nominated 'credit deflation' as a cause of the slowdown in expansion during the later stages of the prosperity-boom phase. This phenomenon has its beginnings in the present phase, but its effects continue to develop through the crisis and recession periods to follow. He saw the 'deflation' as arising from two sources: one is the repayment of credit loans used by entrepreneurs to establish their operations and the other comprises the decisions by bankers and/or the central bank to restrict the growth or reduce the outstanding volume of credit. While Schumpeter recognized the potential significance of the second source, he was not immediately concerned with it. The banker' reactions to the boom may be 'practically very important and frequently starts a real crisis; but it is accessory and not inherent in the process. That is, it has no '*primary* causal role' (ibid., p. 234, emphasis added). Such credit restrictions involve a further active role for bankers in the cyclical process and may also reflect a certain monetary policy stance by government, but both factors are secondary to the core of events (*Cycles*, pp. 136–7).

By contrast, the former sort of 'credit deflation' was perceived by Schumpeter as an immediate consequence of the logic of the system in that 'money and credit do react in a definite way, that their behavior is nothing but adaptation to an underlying economic process . . .' (ibid., p. 137; cf. *Development*, pp. 234–5). He explained that the rationale for this 'behavior' is to be found in the reaction of entrepreneurs to their economic success: 'the appearance of the results of the new enterprises leads to a credit deflation, because entrepreneurs are now in the position – and have every incentive – to pay off their debts . . .'. Such action results in the 'disappearance of the recently created purchasing power just when its complement in goods emerges . . .' (*Development*, p. 233; cf. *Essays*, p. 137). Schumpeter referred to this as an 'Autodeflation' as it 'occurs without any initiative on the part of the banks and would occur even if nobody ever went bankrupt or restricted operations, and if no bank ever called [in] or refused a loan' (*Cycles*, p. 136).

Having made the point, though, Schumpeter went on to add that the 'thesis requires careful safeguarding' in the sense that it must be quite heavily qualified when assessing its actual significance in the slowdown. First, the rate of debt repayment by entrepreneurs may be rather slow in cases where the innovation investment in durable means of production is considerable and the flow of revenue in any period that is dedicated to amortization is a relatively small proportion of the original outlay. Schumpeter claimed that only this part of revenue is available to repay the entrepreneur's debt and then compounded the peculiarity of such a claim by adding that 'resorption of the new purchasing power by savings alters nothing in this deflationary process . . .' (*Development*, p. 234). No reason was given for rejecting the possibility that an 'autodeflation' could be accelerated by the use of saving out of profits to repay debt. A second qualification posited by Schumpeter here was that entrepreneurs may not feel the need to repay their debts in an economy where operating on a credit basis is widely accepted (ibid.). He did not go on to make it clear that under such circumstances, the entrepreneurs now as *capitalists* have an incentive to maintain their credit base and apply their savings to the expansion and further improvement of their productive capacity in the pursuit of added profitability.

Thirdly, a necessary part of the 'autodeflation' mechanism that requires particular explanation is why additional entrepreneurial borrowers do not continue to appear and take up the credit that is repaid by their predecessors in the wave (ibid., pp. 233, 235–6). The numbers of these additional borrowers is limited for several reasons, two of which Schumpeter designated as fundamental. Both have been canvassed above as they have their origins in what are effectively more direct factors in the slow down. One consists of the limits imposed by market demand patterns and the need for new producers to continue to cover costs in the face of downward pressure on commodity prices and of upward pressure on input prices. That is, there is a limit beyond which even production at lower costs after innovation cannot be pushed and once this limit is approached and entrepreneurial profit expectation begin to waver, the number of imitators demanding credit will begin to fall off. The other main limitation on the flow of new borrowers comprises the ever-increasing difficulty that agents have in calculating *ex ante* their cost and profit prospects in the disturbed economic atmosphere of the boom phase. Finally, Schumpeter noted that certain external effects may modify the effects of these limitations on the appearance of new entrepreneurs (ibid., p. 236). For some unexplained reason, he cited one of these as the onset of a *pessimistic* attitude amongst existing producers, potential entrepreneurs and bankers that may lead to panic reactions and their negative consequences for innovation and expansion generally. Secondly, there could emerge a flow of what he called 'fortuitous events'. These, such as 'unfavorable political rumours', 'always occur but . . . acquire an importance from the uncertainty created by the boom such as they did not have before' (ibid.). The third external factor is intervention in innovative activity by virtue of institutional fiat. He mentioned 'a conscious pull on the reins by the central bank . . . [as] usually the most important' (ibid.), but the intervention could as well be positive as negative and could involve other institutions, especially government agencies.

What emerges from the above discussions is that for various reasons, with certain qualifying features, the expansion phase of prosperity and boom must come to an end. The impetus coming from the wave of innovations peters out over a traverse path and time period that Schumpeter left largely unspecified. During the upper turning point stage, the economic conditions move from slowed expansion to a zero (or minimum trend) growth rate and then into contraction. This upper turning point was also dealt with by Schumpeter with little concern for the precision that might be expected in the construction of a 'pure' core model. In spite of his ever-present desire to keep his reasoning in touch with the real world, there remained an analytical void where the upper turning point traverse should be. His readers were expected to move from a cessation of entrepreneurial-induced expansion into an actual phase of contraction with little guidance as to the logical necessity for uch a turn of events. The rather vague implication in his argument was hat within the collapse of the boom there lurk forces whose effects are ret to be fully realized. The end of the boom is a state of disequilibrium and the logic of the circular-flow model dictates that further adaptations and adjustments must ensue in order to return agents to some state of table satisfaction. What needs to be shown, at least, is that subsequently these disequilibrium pressures lead agents to the contractionary lecisions and behaviours that must constitute the recession traverse. Moreover, this traverse must be shown to lead to a restoration of teady-state 'equilibrium' at the end of the contraction. I turn to Schumpeter's endeavours to formalize these matters in the next section.

8.4 The primary crisis and recession

n the context of the movement of the economy into a contraction, chumpeter often referred to the idea of a 'crisis' as distinct from the ecession proper. Both terms usually have negative connotations in ousiness-cycle literature. But, while the recession phase comprises a ogically-entailed sequence of traverse events that Schumpeter treated as having positive consequences, the status of the crisis remained unclear. One possible reading is that it has no place in the *primary* cycle at all. For instance, in *Development*, he drew very sharply the distinction between recession as a ' "normal" process of resorption and iquidation' and 'the "abnormal process of liquidation" ' which he eferred to as 'the course of events characterised by the outbreak of a rrisis – panic, breakdown of the credit system, epidemics of bankruptcies, and its further consequences' (p. 236; cf pp. 217–18, 242, 251). Such crisis events have a touch of *secondary* complications about them and the use of the term 'abnormal' does not fit with the tenor of the primary cycle as it can be said to originate in the necessary logic of capitalism. In *Cycles*, Schumpeter was reluctant to use the term at all because of the lack of consistency and precision in its common usage. He resolved not to give 'any technical meaning to the term *crisis* but only to prosperity and depression' (p. 5, original emphasis). Here we must allow for the slip of the pen in the use of 'depression' rather than ecession, for later it will become clear that he never intended to give any *precise* 'technical' meaning to the former phase either (see Chapter below). Indeed, he added in the same work that the crisis has 'no title o be considered as a phase' of the cycle in the usual sense (p. 156n). Especially, he thought, the category does not belong in the primary heory because of its association with all sorts of particular 'pathological' episodes in economic history. Overemphasis on such episodes in a

formal analysis of fluctuations can only serve to obscure the essenti[
nature of the cycle (*Cycles*, p. 162). Where he continued to use the ter[
was generally in the context of describing particular historical dow[
turns, as a glance at the *Cycles* index reveals (pp. 1082–3).

Schumpeter also made reference to the usually negative connotatio[
associated with the term recession. By contrast, his view was that th[
process involved in the 'pure' sense of the term comprises both thos[
that have adverse effects as well as those that finally realize the totali[
of benefits that flow from the prosperity-boom phase (*Developmen[
pp. 241–2; *Cycles*, p. 142). In this sense, he followed Clément Juglar[
dictum that the only cause of recession is prosperity (ibid., p. 139 an[
n). Most importantly, 'recession is a process that fills a function and [i[
not simply a misfortune'. Even the 'recessive symptoms which peop[
dislike are part of the mechanism of that process and not accidental to
. . .' (ibid., p. 143n). Recession is thus 'a time of harvesting the resul[
of preceding innovation . . . [and] its indirect effects' (ibid., p. 143). I
ultimate outcome is the restoration of a steady-state 'equilibrium' an[
as far as Schumpeter seemed to be concerned, the traverse that is [
ensure such a consequence is 'readily seen' and 'perfectly clear' (ibid[
p. 137). A sympathetic interpretation here would suggest that suc[
hyperbole, not uncommon in his cycle analyses, was merely designed [
encourage his readers rather than to set out to deceive them! I turn no[
to an exposition of those elements of the traverse that he did endeavo[
to make clear.

The situations faced by surviving 'old' firms from the origin[
'equilibrium' on moving into the recession state of the economy are f[
many of them considerably altered when compared to their form[
tranquil existence. Some will be running at a loss as a consequence [
high input costs and/or the fall off in commodity prices. To varyi[
degrees, they must compete with the now firmly established ne[
enterprises and their survival may depend upon them having been ab[
to hold on to 'peculiar advantages' or 'lastingly superior techniqu[
(*Development*, p. 242). Those with no such compensating advantag[
now face three possible fates in Schumpeter's reasoning: 'to decay [
they are unadaptable for objective or personal reasons; to take in sa[
and try to survive in a more modest position; finally, with their ow[
resources or with outside help either to change to another industry or [
adopt other technical or commercial methods which amount to exten[
ing production at lower cost per unit' (ibid.). Each of these possib[
outcomes, but especially the last one, would contribute to a compl[
traverse of consequent adjustments elsewhere in the economy th[

demand detailed explication if they are to be shown necessarily to contribute to a restoration of 'equilibrium'.

At the same time, and adding to the complications of the recession traverse, the new firms and the new entrepreneurs now functioning as managerial capitalists are beginning to 'undergo their first test' (ibid.). Their correct position in the emergent steady circular flow must be established while they continue to face a state of disruption and flux all around them. And, 'even if no mistake was made when they were founded, there must in many respects be much to revise' (ibid.). Some of the problems of adaptation to recession that they must handle will be similar to those faced by the 'old' firms, but, with less experience, they will be more vulnerable to lingering maladjustments. The return to 'equilibrium' requires that such conditions be largely overcome during the traverse period.

The fact is that for many managing agents in 'old' and new firms, their conduct 'is clearly ruled by the element of actual or impending loss', at least in those parts of the system where they are 'exposed to danger' through a lack of capacity to protect their market positions. These losses occur or are imminent . . . as long as all businesses, and hence the system as a whole, are not in stable equilibrium . . .' (ibid., p. 243). The implication of this, according to Schumpeter, is that the disequilibrium can only be removed by adjustments at the individual firm level that enable them to 'produce at prices approximately covering costs' (ibid.). But, the details of the equilibrating mechanism were left implicit. It apparently revolves around the idea that loss-making agents, or those so threatened, will take continuing steps to remedy the situation until they establish a circular-flow position that ensures them of at least a sustainable cost-covering revenue flow (ibid., pp. 252–3). The recession traverse must continue until virtually all such positions are secured by 'old' and new firms (ibid., p. 243). Schumpeter's position on this matter warrants quotation in full:

> . . . the struggle towards a new equilibrium position, which will embody the innovations and give expression to their effects upon the old firms, is the real meaning of a period of depression [read: recession] as we know it from experience, so it may likewise be shown that this struggle must actually lead to a close approach to an equilibrium position: on the one hand, the driving impulse of the process of depression [read: recession] cannot theoretically stop until it has done its work, has really brought about the equilibrium position; on the other hand, no new disturbance in the form of a new boom can arise out of the economic system itself until then. (ibid.)

Part of the adjustment traverse towards the new 'equilibrium' depends upon lossmaking firms being liquidated. Some of these may be

'old' firms unable to recover their former market positions or appropri
ately to adapt to their new situations, and some may be new firm;
unable to make the transition to operating without entrepreneuria!
profit. The expectation that a subsequent expansion may return them to
a position where quasi-rents can be appropriated may forestall liquidations as managerial agents, supported by the firms' creditors, endeavou
to produce and trade their way through the recession. In Schumpeter';
view, this means the survival of 'many firms really not fit to live as wel!
as many that are . . .' (ibid., pp. 243–4). The effect of the maintenanc
of lossmaking operations is clearly that it 'retards or prevents th
attainment of a settled equilibrium position' (ibid., p. 244). Thus, h
argued, in its traverse towards anything like a complete 'equilibrium'
the 'economic system cannot do without the *ultima ratio* of the complet
destruction of these existences which are irretrievably associated wit!
the hopelessly unadapted' (ibid., p. 253). In these arguments, Schum
peter foreshadowed his well-known thesis of 'Creative Destruction' tha
appeared in *Capitalism* many years later. There he emphasized the nee
for analysts of motion to switch their attention from 'how capitalisn
administers existing structures . . . [to] the relevant problem . . . [of
how it creates and destroys them' (p. 84). The process of motion, and it;
development and business-cycle dimensions in particular, is, in thi;
view, one of 'industrial mutation . . . that incessantly revolutionizes th
economic structure *from within*, incessantly destroying the old one
incessantly creating a new one. This process of Creative Destruction i;
the essential fact about capitalism. It is what capitalism consists in an
what every capitalist concern has got to live in.' (p. 83, origina!
emphasis; cf. n).

There may also be some non-competitive aspects of markets tha
impede the necessary adjustment processes towards an 'equilibrium'. I
particular, Schumpeter referred here to the resilience of large-scal
enterprises that may survive and resist pressures to change through th
recession with low or negative returns. They are able to do so by virtu
of their accumulated reserves and/or of imperfections in the financ
capital markets that give them access to credit on special terms. Thus
'in consequence of the financial strength of some firms, especially th
older ones, the adjustment is not always very urgent, not an immediat
question of life or death' (*Development*, p. 244; cf. p. 252n). It may wel
be, also, that well-meaning governments may engineer subsidies an
other modes of protection for large firms in difficulties on economic cum
political and social grounds. These arrangements are often made 'upor
the *bona* or *mala fide* assumption that the difficulty is only a temporar
one, created by extraneous circumstances' (ibid., p. 244). All thi;

reflects Schumpeter's growing awareness of the 'progressive trustification of economic life' that 'facilitates the permanent continuance of
maladjustments in the great combines themselves and hence outside of
them . . .' (ibid.).

There was also the continuation from the boom phase of 'uncertainty
and irregularity' in the economy for managerial agents to contend with
in their decision making during the recession. In this regard, Schumpeter wrote that the 'course of events in periods of depression [read:
recession] presents a picture of uncertainty and irregularity which we
interpret from the point of view of a search for a new equilibrium, or of
adaptation to a general situation which has been changed relatively
quickly and considerably' (ibid., p. 238). More particularly, because the
customary data are altered for every business', together with the
'incalculable events' and 'speculation' that are characteristic of such
times, the situation becomes one in which the ' "mere businessman"
faces problems which lie outside his routine, problems to which he is not
accustomed and in the face of which he makes mistakes which then
become an important secondary cause of further trouble'. It is, then, the
uncertainty of the data and values involved in the new adjustment, the
losses which apparently occur irregularly and incalculably, [that] create
the characteristic atmosphere of periods of depression [read: recession]'
ibid., pp. 238, 239). The effect of these complications is, at least, to
delay the adjustments demanded by the traverse to the new 'equilibrium' because the 'extent and nature of the change [in data] . . . can
only be learned from experience . . . [and] the right attitude towards
new economic facts has to be found . . .' (ibid.).

I mentioned earlier on in this section that Schumpeter identified the
normal' processes of recession as largely positive and beneficial to the
ongoing progress of capitalism. Thus he argued that 'the economic
picture of a *normal* period of depression [read: recession] is throughout
not so black as the mood pervading it would lead one to suspect. Apart
from the fact that a great part of economic life remains almost
untouched as a rule, the physical volume of total transactions in most
cases falls only insignificantly.' He believed, too, that 'any official
investigation of crises' is bound to reveal how 'exaggerated the popular
conceptions of the ravages caused by a depression [read: *normal
recession*] are . . .' (*Development*, pp. 245–6, original emphasis). From
his perspective, Schumpeter was intent on showing that a recession
fulfils what the boom promised' by means of 'the diffusion of the
achievements of the boom over the whole economic system through the
mechanism of the struggle for equilibrium . . .' (ibid., pp. 245, 251).
And, consequent upon the 'digestion of the innovations', the positive

effects that emerge are 'lasting, while the phenomena felt to be unpleasant are temporary'. Specifically, he went on, the 'stream of goods is enriched, production is partly reorganised, [*real*] costs of production are diminished, and what at first appears as entrepreneurial profit finally increases the permanent real incomes of other classes (ibid., p. 245; cf. n).

Schumpeter went on to discuss the last of the assertions in this passage concerning the income redistribution consequences of a recession in more detail. Unfortunately, most of his ideas and conclusions were presented without adequate analytical substantiation (ibid., pp. 246ff.) This is evident, to begin with, in his treatment of the non-labour income aspects of the issue where his argument was exceptionally vague and inconclusive. The most significant matter here is that of clarifying the fate of entrepreneurial agents once their profits have fallen away. Schumpeter seemed reluctant to give profit any status as a permanent component of income or to state categorically that entrepreneurs must turn into means of production owning capitalists, probably because the latter agent transmutation would complicate his inclinations to ignore the former phenomenon. And yet, he referred at one point to 'produced means of production already in existence', albeit without any indication of their origins or ownership (ibid., p. 251). Other complicating passing references were made to 'other entrepreneurial income' (ibid., p. 247) and to a 'part of entrepreneurial profit which is not annihilated' (ibid. p. 251), with the overall result that it remained totally unclear what happens to entrepreneurs and their income during the recession. A little more certain was the assertion that finance capitalists continue to receive interest income, although at a lower rate. 'Land' owners incomes may be contractually fixed and they, along with other fixed income receivers, namely 'pensioners, rentiers, [and] officials', will all be better off in real terms as the general price level falls (ibid., p. 247) - it was not made clear what a 'rentier' agent does as distinct from a finance capitalist or 'land' owner. Some 'land' owners, though, are not in this position and their rents will, according to Schumpeter's reasoning, move in conjunction with the wages of labour power because both are demanded in combination as the only ultimate inputs to production (ibid., p. 248; cf. p. 251).

The treatment of the income fate of wage workers in the recession was much more detailed, but equally unsatisfactory in its presentation (ibid., pp. 248ff.). Schumpeter recognized, sometimes only in passing that the totality of the problem would have to include movements in individual wage rates, the total wage bill and the share of wages in national income, all in both nominal and real terms, along with the

ssociated movements in employment. He began his argument by
ecalling that in the boom phase 'wages must rise' both in terms of their
ndividual rates and as a total payment in nominal values. But, as this is
ccompanied by a 'rise in the general price level', what happens to real
ages in each sense requires explication (ibid., p. 248). Schumpeter
oncluded in this respect that real wages must normally increase. This is
ecause nominal wage rises in the expansion phase will always run
head of the price rises where the additional purchasing power impinges
nitially on the price of labour power. Whether real wages will fall
owards the end of the boom where demand for labour power stabilizes
nd commodity prices continue to rise we were not told (ibid.,
p. 248–9).

However, whatever happens to real wage variables in the upper
eaches of the boom, Schumpeter began his analysis of the recession
ith the claim that at least 'the purchasing power of the unit of wages
ises' consequent upon the price deflation that occurs (*Development*,
. 249). And, at the same time, while 'the money expression of the
ffective demand for labor falls in consequence of the automatic
eflation which the boom starts', he asserted that 'the effective real
emand for labor *could* remain undisturbed . . . [and] the real income
f labor would then still be higher, not only than in the previous
pproximate equilibrium position, but also than in the boom' (ibid.,
mphasis added). The significance of the '*could*' in the passage is that
hat is argued therein must be arraigned against *observations* that
uggest that 'real wages regularly fall in depression [read: recession], yet
nly by a part of the amount which they had gained in the boom' (ibid.,
. 248n). Schumpeter's response to this inconsistency was to elicit
ertain 'circumstances' that act to impede employment maintenance and
eal wage rises in recessions.

He pointed first to the possibility of a temporary decrease in
mployment due to the low economic activity levels of 'old' firms. Next
e referred to the potential for gains in employment through the new
rms that were established in prosperity and are consolidated in
ecession to be offset by some 'mechanising [of] the productive process'
hat comes with innovations (ibid., p. 250). It is evident that with
abour-productivity improving technological change, there will be
ecessarily a diminution of the labor required per unit of product; and
ften, though not necessarily, . . . a diminution of the quantity of labor
emanded in the industry in question in spite of the extension of
roduction which occurs' (ibid.). As far as Schumpeter was concerned,
hough, this sort of reduction in real labour power demand can be only a
ransitory' difficulty that is soon overcome by compensatory employ-

ment that has its source in consumption and investment expenditure that flow from entrepreneurial profit. The wholly unsatisfactory asser tion here was that 'the total real demand for labor cannot in genera permanently fall, because, neglecting all compensating and all second ary elements, the expenditure of that part of entrepreneurial profi which is not annihilated by the fall in prices necessarily more tha prevents any lasting shrinkage' (ibid., pp. 250–1). The deployment o entrepreneurial profit that is under such great pressure of elimination a a *certain* basis for the re-employment of labour power displaced b technological change is a dubious *deus ex machina* at best. We are no told what the other 'compensating' and 'secondary' elements are, so it i impossible to judge their significance. It is clear, though, that Schum peter wanted to believe that unemployment could find no permanen source in technological change, or anywhere else for that matter because the recession had to be shown to restore 'equilibrium' in whic near full employment is a necessary characteristic.

But even this conclusion needs to be tempered by the final 'circum stance' that Schumpeter cited where a new combination 'shifts the relative marginal significance of labor and land . . . to the disadvantage of labor' (*Development*, p. 251). This harks back to the most abstrac and least meaningful notion of the 'pure' circular-flow model according to which production may be adequately represented as requiring only inputs of labour-power and 'land' services from 'outside' the firm (se above, Chapter 4, sub-section 4.4.2). And yet Schumpeter proceeded to use this unrealistic analytical framework as the basis for his conclusion that only the shifts cited above can explain a 'permanently lower . . real demand for labor', with the added claim that it means that 'not only the share of labor in the social product but also the absolute amount o its real income may permanently fall' (ibid.). However, as an after thought, probably in deference to common sense, he added the following qualifying remark: 'Practically more important than this case - but again not necessarily of a permanent nature – is a shift in the demand in favor of produced means of production already in existence. (ibid.). Here he came close to contradicting his earlier conclusion regarding the effects of 'mechanising the productive process', although it is difficult to see how such a process can depend upon means o production 'already in existence'. The only type of technological change that makes sense here is that which involves labour-power employmen reductions that come from some reorganization that improves efficiency and productivity using the same means of production stock. If it wa such 'disembodied' change that he had in mind on this occasion, it wa not made clear.

About all that can be said about Schumpeter's handling of the problem of income redistribution and employment effects of a recession is that it was left in a largely untenable and inconclusive state. Most particularly, none of the results alluded to is traced sequentially to its ultimate destination in the 'equilibrium' position. According to my reading, the standard of analytical acumen that he exhibited in this piece is amongst the lowest in all of his writings.

The recession phase that I have just considered in this section was claimed by Schumpeter to conclude in a restoration of an 'equilibrium' state. The potentially strict requirements of a 'pure' equilibrium were, as always, softened by his recognition that 'the position reached in the end never completely corresponds to the theoretical picture of the system without development . . .' (ibid., p. 244). However, he maintained his belief that there exists an actual operational tendency to realize 'equilibrium' by arguing that the 'relatively short duration of depressions [read: recessions] alone prevents this' and that 'an approximation to a position without development *always occurs* . . .' (ibid., emphasis added). What is more, his theory of the cycle depended very heavily upon this tendency having a real-world manifestation, as he quite frankly admitted: 'This is important for us, not only because such an intermediate position [between recession and the next expansion] actually exists and the explanation of it is incumbent upon every theory of the cycle, but also because only the proof of the necessity of such a periodic quasi-equilibrium position completes our argument.' (ibid., p. 245).

The traverse to 'equilibrium' 'completes' his argument in two related senses. One is that the primary cycle unit is defined to include the two phases of prosperity and recession followed by a period of 'equilibrium'. The other is that this period is necessary because it provides the conditions in which the most talented potential entrepreneurial agents search out and make plans for the implementation of the opportunities to innovate that will, when realized, induce the next expansion into prosperity and begin a new cycle unit. In Schumpeter's words, 'there is, theoretically, depression [read: recession] as long as no . . . equilibrium is approximately attained. Nor will this process [of movement towards 'equilibrium'] be interrupted by a new [prosperity and] boom before it has done its work in this sense.' For, 'until then, there is necessarily uncertainty about what the new data will be, which makes the calculation of new combinations impossible and makes it difficult to obtain the cooperation of the requisite factors' (ibid., p. 243).

The lower turning point of the two-phase, primary business cycle is, effectively, the 'equilibrium' period and its recovery phase is then constituted by the expansion into prosperity that follows. The situation with the four-phase cycle that includes secondary effects is very different and I consider it in detail in the next chapter.

8.5 Summary
The focus of this chapter has been the core theory of the primary business cycle formulated by Schumpeter.

1. After outlining some general methodological issues raised by business cycle analysis, the essential nature of Schumpeter's presentation was set out. It was noted that the primary cycle, induced by waves of innovations, comprises an expansionary or prosperity phase and a contractionary or recession phase between two 'neighborhoods' of equilibrium. Such a 'pure' cycle form is usually complicated in reality by the presence of secondary factors which affect its traverse path and may turn the delimited recession into a deeper depression. The secondary cycle unit, superimposed, in effect, on the primary core, must be completed by the addition of a recovery phase of expansion back to a 'neighborhood' of equilibrium from whence the next cycle can begin.

2. The first stage of analysing the primary cycle required that Schumpeter explain how the expansion into prosperity and boom, induced by the wave of innovations, is brought to an end at the upper turning point. New, innovating firms and existing firms are involved in the traverse in different ways. For the former, the diffusion of innovations and downward pressure on prices due to oversupply erode initial profitability and production is cut back. Existing firms that are innovation-competing face both input cost increases and ultimate downward pressure on output prices that reduce their profitability. Those firms not directly affected by the innovation wave are still involved in the increased competition for inputs and face a cost-induced squeeze on profitability. All firms must endure, as well, what Schumpeter called an 'autodeflation' brought about by a shrinkage of the volume of credit outstanding.

3. The nature of the upper turning point transition from boom to recession was not argued at all precisely by Schumpeter. However, it is appropriate to recognize that because of the nature of the recession to follow, the term crisis should not be applied to the downturn in this context.

4. For Schumpeter, the recession phase of the primary cycle was presented as a period of positive and 'normal' events that serve to realize the full economic potential of the previous boom. He eschewed the usual negative connotations of the phase in favour of

emphasizing the benefits of a period of 'shake out' and reorganization. The recession ends in a new 'neighborhood' of equilibrium that effectively becomes the lower turning point of the cycle. In the tranquility of the renewed steady-state conditions, the next wave of innovations will be stimulated and the cycle will begin anew.

Note

1. Cf. here the views of Hansen, 1951 and Tinbergen, 1951. Of related interest is the mechanical analogy of an *immanently-generated* impulse sequence developed by Ragnar Frisch in 1933 as a representation of Schumpeter's waves of innovations thesis (1966, pp. 183ff.). According to Frisch, this analogy had Schumpeter's approval (ibid., p. 184), a claim that the latter never denied in any of his references to Frisch's writings (e.g. in *Cycles* – see the index, p. 1085).

9 Secondary dimensions of the business cycle

9.1 The idea of the secondary wave

Schumpeter claimed that his primary, two-phase business-cycle model captured that mechanism of the capitalist economy's fluctuations that could be considered as essential or 'normal'. That is, the model was said to replicate the core characteristics of every cycle unit, even though the observed historical manifestations of them vary widely due to the superimposition of external and 'abnormal' internal distortions on the primary features. These latter distortions were referred to by Schumpeter as the secondary-wave effects and, as was outlined in the previous chapter (section 8.2), they generate the usually-observed secondary, four-phase cycle format (*Cycles*, pp. 145ff.).

The secondary-wave effects constitute the empirical overburden that often obscures the essential nature of business cycles. Thus, it is 'a long way from this schema [of the primary cycle] to the point of junction with historical fact. Innumerable layers of secondary, incidental, accidental and "external" fact and reactions among all of them and reactions to reactions cover that [primary] skeleton of economic life, sometimes so as to hide it entirely.' (ibid., p. 137). The challenge was, then, Schumpeter argued, most immediately to deal with 'primary causes and the characteristic feature of the explanation, not with the question of when causes become visible'. And, while this 'creates an apparent discrepancy between our theory and observation', it should be recognized that 'every such discrepancy can only become an objection if it is shown that it is not satisfactorily explained' (*Development*, p. 252n). This latter part of the theoretical challenge was met by identifying and taking into account the secondary-wave phenomena and their effects.

For Schumpeter, the primary-secondary force distinction in his theory of the cycle set it apart from many other analyses of the phenomenon that had not penetrated beyond the cycle's appearances. The analysts concerned take the immediate empirical form of the cycle as their theoretical object. This 'much wider surface' with its 'great mass of fact' is 'much easier to observe' and 'strikes the eye first' (ibid., p. 146). His opinion was that this concentration on the 'surface' of cycles explains the frequent neglect by analysts of the core causal status of innovation waves in their studies. The process of innovation 'hides behind, and is sometimes entirely overlaid by, the phenomena of what appears at first glance to be simply a general prosperity, which is conspicuous in many branches and strata' (ibid.). Such concentration, therefore, 'helps to explain and partly to justify a large group of "theories" which, though missing the essential phenomenon, are yet perfectly satisfactory when viewed as descriptions of part of the mechanism of the secondary waves superimposed on the primary ones' (*Essays*, pp. 137–8). In contrast to all this, Schumpeter's approach was to begin his analysis 'from within', so to say, by constructing the primary logic of the cycle first. Only then did he feel it appropriate to put some 'flesh' on the 'skeleton' in order to give it some closer approximation to the phenomenon as it is observed.

Handling the secondary-wave effects at the theoretical level presented a problem for Schumpeter because of their highly contingent and variable nature. His cavalier claim in *Development* that in formulating a cycle theory 'the abnormal presents no fundamental problems (p. 236) proved to be unfounded when he came to try to work out some general theses about such dimensions, most especially later in *Cycles*. It was not simply a matter of adding another layer of more complex 'pure' theory, for the secondary wave has no identifiable necessary or sufficient elements that can be isolated. He distinguished 'the problem of a theory of the concrete factors of individual cycles' from 'the problem of explaining the [primary] nature and mechanism of the cycle' (*Development*, p. 227n). The latter was taken care of in the primary model while the former required that he attempt some formalization of the four-phase cycle framework within which each phase is presented as 'a distinct composite phenomenon, not only distinguishable by a characteristic set of features, but also explainable in terms of the different "forces" which dominate it and produce those features' and where 'these "forces" consist in . . . concretely observable phenomena . . .' (*Cycles*, p. 156; cf. *Essays*, p. 138). In the next section, I set out those elements that Schumpeter elicited as constituting the substance of the 'composite phenomenon' of each secondary phase, along with the relevant 'forces' that he claimed give rise to each phase.

9.2 The substance of the secondary wave

Considered from a general perspective, one of the central secondary elements upon which Schumpeter focused his attention was the 'psychology' of economic agents caught up in the fluctuations. Crucial in this respect were 'cyclical clusters of errors, excesses of optimism and pessimism and the like [which] are . . . not necessarily inherent in the primary process . . . although they can be adequately motivated by it' (*Cycles*, p. 146). He rejected any notion that the essence of the cycle is to be found in psychological sources such as 'anticipations' or 'errors of judgement, excesses (overdoing), and misconduct'. Any theory based on such sources 'must assume that people err periodically in a way most convenient to the economist' (ibid., p. 140). For this reason he concluded in *Cycles*, while it is 'of some importance that the reader should satisfy himself that the analytic schema here presented is not a psychological theory . . ., [it remains the case that] the behavior of the entrepreneur is amenable to description in psychological terms' (p. 140n). At one point, in a 1935 paper, Schumpeter linked the secondary wave more or less directly to the consequences of agent 'psychology': 'The sum total of these induced [secondary] phenomena which are at the center of the mass psychology of cycles and greatly intensify their amplitudes, we call "secondary waves".' (*Essays*, p. 137). Notice that in this passage, the secondary effects are 'induced' and thus can be taken to be endogenous to the analytical framework under consideration. Clearly, the secondary wave did not rely only on external factors for its explanation in Schumpeter's theory. It would be going too far, though, I think, to attribute to him the idea that the relevant psychology is part of the *logic* of capitalism. The system gives agents the scope to exercise many of their reactive psychological traits, especially optimism, pessimism and speculation, but the resulting behaviours are just too varied and unreliable to be generalized at the theoretical level.

Schumpeter gave speculation a somewhat more explicit role to play in the secondary responses of agents as they affect the working of the credit system. The facility of credit plays a vital positive part in the primary cycle as we have seen. Now, with the added complication of agent speculation, it can take on less economically attractive characteristics. Two particular consequences are of significance here: first, an 'abnormal' increase in the demand for credit as the boom intensifies and secondly, an 'abnormal' number of liquidations of firms as over-optimistic expectations fail to be realized (*Development*, p. 236). At this secondary level, too, it is clear that the banker agents have an active role to play: in the former, excessive growth of credit case, they must be able and willing to acquiesce (*Essays*, pp. 41–2, 41n) and in the latter collapse of credit case, they can either force the pace of or slow down the liquidation rate by virtue of their legal positions as creditors (*Cycles*, p. 150n). In regard to this collapse, Schumpeter argued at several points that there is potential in the banks' actions, perhaps with the aid or push of government policy, to mitigate the depth of a depression by allowing firms in difficulties the time and additional credit support needed to trade out of their predicament (*Development*, pp. 252n, 254–5; *Cycles*, pp. 147–8; *Essays*, pp. 41n, 42–3).

In the case of the prosperity phase, Schumpeter carefully specified the secondary effects of credit creation in order to keep them separate from the necessary and beneficial means of expansion that it provides in the primary cycle (*Cycles*, pp. 146–8). The primary origin of debt growth lies in the new demand for credit that flows from innovating entrepreneurs. No 'dire consequences' can follow from this even though entrepreneurial miscalculations' can and do occur – remember that nine out of ten failure rate of new enterprises (ibid., p. 117)! The same reasoning applies to existing agents and firms who borrow to fund imitative innovations or the expenditures needed to adapt to the state of flux in which they find themselves in an expansion. One way or another, credit advanced for all these purposes serves to boost or maintain productivity. There is also the fact that such 'normal' debt is self-extinguishing, a process Schumpeter referred to as 'self-deflation' (*Essays*, pp. 37–8). The profitability ensured by productivity-raising economic activity will give agents the potential to repay their supporting creditors as an integral part of the prosperity and subsequent phases of the cycle. A part of this repayment pattern may involve the trans-mutation of short-term into long-term debt (ibid., p. 38n).

By contrast, the secondary, problematical aspects of credit arise because of '*over*indebtedness induced, primarily, by easy money' (*Cycles*, p. 147, original emphasis) that can emerge as part of the optimism of the prosperity-boom period. Under these circumstances, Schumpeter wrote, '[n]ew borrowings will no longer be confined to entrepreneurs, and "deposits" will be created to finance general expansion, each loan tending to induce another loan . . .' (ibid., p. 145). He also referred to 'unproductive loans' that have their origins in demand for credit by households who 'will borrow for purposes of consumption, in the expectation that actual incomes will permanently be what they are or that they will still increase . . .'. As well, 'old' firms 'will borrow merely to expand old lines' and 'farms will be bought at prices at which they could pay only if the prices of agricultural products kept their level or increased' (ibid., p. 147). In the atmosphere of optimistic prosperity, the problems of calculation in the face of rapid change and gross uncertainty are overriden and 'present earnings which are ephemeral and future earnings which are imaginary, are capitalised' (ibid., p. 147n). Schumpeter's perception was that all this build up of debt, on the speculative basis that the prosperous conditions would continue for sufficient time for the obligations to realize their fruits and to be repaid, made the economy vulnerable to a secondary crisis. His dictum was that 'the credit machine is so designed as to serve the improvement of the productive apparatus and to punish any other use' (ibid., p. 147).

The booming capitalist economy with its excessive debt burden is not brought to account by any secondary mechanism *per se*. Schumpeter argued, rather, that the aggravated crisis that leads the system into depression is initiated by the otherwise benign end to the primary boom. The 'break in secondary prosperity is . . . induced by the turn of the underlying process [of the primary cycle]', with the latter providing the 'only adequate explanation of the former' (ibid., p. 148). More specifically, the secondary wave brings with it a booming economic situation in which 'there is much more to liquidate and adjust', with the accompanying fact that in 'the atmosphere of secondary prosperity there will . . . develop reckless, fraudulent, or otherwise unsuccessful enterprise, which cannot stand the tests administered by [primary] recession' (ibid.). The situation is one in which the high degree of 'exposure' of many firms is made evident even by the 'normal' downward adjustment of many commodity prices as the success of new combinations comes to fruition *en masse*. While there is no logic inherent in the system that entails any particular agent reactions to this emergent situation, it could well be one of panic which then 'feeds on itself' to form what Schumpeter called a 'Vicious Spiral' that involves a process of 'Abnormal Liquidation' (ibid., pp. 148–9).

There are two aspects to these phenomena to notice. One is that 'any fall in values which enforces liquidation, induces quite mechanically another fall in values' as agents endeavour to maintain some cash flows by selling at ever-lower prices. In such deflationary circumstances, it is likely that a collapse will be aggravated by 'frightened banks' (*Essays*, p. 41) calling in loans in order to maintain their liquidity at a 'safe' level. Such events as these 'drive debtors in the well-known way toward the very rocks which those measures were taken to avoid'. Unfortunately, as the 'well-known' allusion here signals, Schumpeter was not prepared to provide any traverse details of this spiral. Indeed, his general stance regarding the secondary dimensions of the downturn was summarized in the assertion that 'we will not stay to describe the details of a pattern that is familiar to everyone' (*Cycles*, p. 148; cf. p. 150 and n). The only suitable response to this hyperbole is: *hardly*! The second aspect of the spiral to which he referred was the probability that panic would bring a shift from the dominance of optimism to an emerging pessimism, a 'bearish anticipation' (ibid., p. 149), which 'may for a time acquire a causal role' (ibid., p. 148). Again, though, Schumpeter emphasized that this panic and switch of attitudes is exclusively a secondary phenomenon that distorts the otherwise 'objective facts' of the primary recession.

Without the latter to work through, the secondary forces can have little significant effect (ibid., p. 149).

It is important here to remind ourselves of the status of secondary effects in Schumpeter's overall image of cyclical fluctuations, for it was instrumental in leading him into an analytical bind from which he never effectively extracted himself. He always stressed that 'while recession and – if depression occurs – revival are necessary parts of the cyclical process of economic evolution, depression itself is not. We are able to make it understandable or plausible that from the business situations which necessarily obtain in recession, depression may easily develop, but in all its essential aspects the cyclical process would be logically complete without it' (ibid., p. 150). 'Understandable' the secondary contraction may be, but only in a sense that lacks analytical precision to any general degree, for 'no *theoretical* expectation can be formed about the occurrence and severity of depressions' (ibid., original emphasis). The analytical difficulty into which this lack of logical necessity and theoretical imprecision concerning the depression phase led Schumpeter is to be found in his endeavours to settle on a relation between it and the primary recession that it modifies.

The recession *per se* is to end in a restored 'equilibrium' position. As we have seen, for the purposes of the four-phase cycle, the impression given by Schumpeter was that this primary phase can readily be included in the argument by considering the depression as some sort of 'exten-sion' of the recession conditions (see Figure 8.2 and the associated discussion in Chapter 8, section 8.2 above). The secondary forces were said to cause the disruption of the equilibrating tendency of the primary wave such that the economy 'overshoots' the 'equilibrium' and moves into a further state of disequilibrium that is the basis for its depression traverse. In terms of my earlier outline of the cycle paths (especially as portrayed in Figures 8.2 and 8.3 above), the problem raised concerns the precise analytical status to be given to point E that appears to lie 'between' the recession and depression phases. What is to be empha-sized now is that Schumpeter seems to have been unable to decide on such a status and this left him without a clear exposition of the traverse in which the recesson 'becomes' a depression. He used such expressions as the secondary wave 'superimposes' its effects on the primary cycle (*Cycles*, p. 145). And he gave some clue as to the form of this superimposition in the following definition of depression: 'our process [of recession] will generally, although not necessarily, outrun (as a rule, also miss) the neighborhood of equilibrium toward which it was heading and enter upon a new phase, absent in our first approximation. . . . For this phase we shall reserve the term Depression.' This form was then immediately enlarged upon a little further: in recession, 'a mechanism is at work to draw the system toward equilibrium' but now a 'new disequilibrium develops' and 'the system again draws away from a neighborhood of equilibrium' (ibid., p. 149).

Now it is not clear from this argument just 'when' the recession turns into a depression; that is, when the so-called 'new phase' begins. However, as I suggested in the previous chapter in connection with Figures 8.2 and 8.3, it is inappropriate to argue such an implied 'sequence' at all because the stage has already been set for the depression during the aggravated secondary boom conditions that preceded it. The depression need not happen, of course, as Schumpeter was well aware, and in theory such a hyper-boom could turn into something akin to a 'normal' recession. But, whichever way things go, it is probably best to see either the recession or the depression traverse as originating in the upper turning point or before. The effect of this is to render the recession and depression forms of contraction as mutually exclusive paths. Unfortunately, this does away with the idea of a four-phase cycle: either there are two or three phases once the contraction traverse is dealt with in this way.

It is still the case, though, that the primary contraction remains embedded in the secondary depression, and this seems to be what Schumpeter wanted to keep before his readers. But it is in this regard that the problem of point E becomes apparent. Wherever it is located along the secondary downswing path, the idea that it represents a dividing point 'between' recession and depression does not appear to be a helpful description of its status. It is evident that, at times, Schumpeter thought of it as a sort of 'interim equilibrium' position (e.g. *Cycles*, pp. 207–8). He referred to the depression as 'a movement away from equilibrium' and drew a parallel between prosperity and depression in the sense that 'in each case the system draws away from equilibrium and into disequilibrium' (ibid., pp. 153, 156). However, it is clear that such assertions are just excessively loose modes of expressing the idea that the primary cycle remains at the core of whatever form the secondary traverse takes. The point E could, therefore, well be erased from my Figures 8.2 and 8.3.

Once a depression traverse is underway, with its characteristic wave of 'Abnormal Liquidations', the challenge for the business-cycle analyst is to identify some reason or reasons why it might come to an end. Schumpeter called this the 'Problem of the Recovery Point' (ibid., p. 151) and he realized that there emerged here an analytical intractability that did not apply to the arguments required to bring the recession traverse to an end. As already indicated, because of its very nature, the forces of depression are not readily amenable to theoretical generalizations. To reiterate, the depression 'has not simply a definite amount of work to do. On the contrary, it has a way of feeding upon itself and of setting into motion a mechanism which, considered in isolation, could in fact run on indefinitely under its own steam.' (ibid.). So it was, then, that in order to rationalize the empirical existence of recovery points, Schumpeter had to suggest some generalized factors that would bring an end to the contractionary spiral with its tendency to be self-sustaining.

One idea that he applied in this respect took account of the fact that the spiral traverse may begin with 'a number of unfavourable individual events, such as bankruptcies, breaks in individual markets, shutdowns' (ibid., p. 153). But, built into the inevitable diffusion of the effects of such 'individual events', Schumpeter identified a general self-activating mitigating tendency. These events

> . . . induce similar events, but it is readily seen that each of them taken by itself loses momentum as its effects spread. The failure of a concern may cause the failures of other concerns, but part of its liabilities will be to firms which can stand the loss and which therefore act as buffers. Each addition to unemployment will cause further and further unemployment but, *taken individually*, at a decreasing rate. Individual contractions of output breed contraction all round, but the impact of each of them slackens and stops after having gone a certain way. (ibid., original emphasis)

Such processes as these, and their interactions, demand more elaboration if the depression traverse and its ultimate cessation are to be fully explained. However, unlike the case of the recession, where Schumpeter had a definite logical sequence to work out as a traverse, the case of the depression required rather more specification of the *particular conditions* involved than he was prepared to provide if any coherent sequence was to be formalized.

Another means by which the spiral may be broken comes in the form of what Schumpeter called 'depression business' (ibid., pp. 153–5). The point to be made here is that while the depression has widespread negative economic and social effects, there are also particular agents and firms for whom it brings the opportunity to realize economic gains. The liquidation of one producer may enable another to expand into any remaining market gap, especially where input prices are falling relatively faster than the concurrent decrease in effective commodity demand and prices. As Schumpeter saw things, the relative quantitative and temporal profiles of costs, prices and demand cannot be worked out a priori. 'But', he went on, 'what can be said is that since demand and cost curves do not shift uniformly, opportunities arise for transactions which would not be possible otherwise and which will do something to counteract the ravages of the spiral.' (ibid., p. 154). The economic relevance of any such opportunities will depend very much upon the attitudes and responses of the agents that confront them. In a depression, pessimistic expectations may well predominate in an overall sense, but there could remain some exceptional individuals with an optimistic outlook prepared to take on new or extended economic activities. Moreover, there will be cases where 'whatever the business-man's state of mind, he will take current business that offers itself', where such behaviour may be more significant in 'industrial' markets than in those where speculation normally dominates decision making (ibid.). We should remind ourselves here, though, that Schumpeter made no allowance for opportunities to innovate as a force that may emerge in a depression, although this was an oversight that is probably understandable given the construction of his core thesis (see, e.g., ibid., pp. 157, 501).

Having argued out these potential means by which the depression can be brought to an end, Schumpeter remained sceptical, to some degree, about their effectiveness. So, 'though it may . . . be shown that a restorative tendency will develop to work against the spiral, there is nothing to prove that it will prevail against it'. There remains 'the possibility of a system so conditioned and of a spiral so violent that the tendency may fight a losing battle at any given moment and . . . the system may never conquer the breathing space in which it could recover of itself' (ibid., p. 154). He granted that his scepticism here can be largely attributed to his endeavour to provide some theoretical reasoning about depressions that is as general as possible, given their varied causation and form. There are, he added, certain 'restrictive assumptions amply verified by common sense and historical fact' that could be included in the reasoning with the result that the automatic correction processes would be more obviously effective (ibid., p. 155). His view was, though, that by reaching too far into empirical conditions that have no necessary basis in the logic of capitalism at all in order to provide an explanation would be contrary to his search for *theory*, at least as far as it is possible.

Furthermore, there was a sense in which Schumpeter wanted to emphasize his scepticism by means of the 'inconclusiveness' of his theory. He reiterated that 'depression, unlike recession, is a pathological process to which no organic functions can be attributed' beyond some 'work of reorganisation and adaptation' (ibid.; cf. *Development*, pp. 253, 254). From this perspective, the phenomenon is not one to be endured if it is avoidable in any way: 'It follows that proof, even if it were more satisfactory than it is, that depressions will find a "natural" end, does not in itself constitute an argument for letting things take their course or trusting to "the restorative forces of nature".' (*Cycles*, p. 155). This conclusion led him to support some government corrective policy action in the depression situation even though it would never be appropriate in the case of recession (ibid.). His belief was that the 'phenomena of the normal and of the abnormal course of events are not merely distinguishable conceptually. They are in reality different things; and with a sufficiently deep insight, concrete cases even today may generally be recognized immediately as belonging to one or the other.' (*Development*, p. 254). In the context of this particular passage, he was arguing for a credit-support policy for selected firms in 'abnormal' contractions. Thus: 'Such a policy would have to distinguish, within the mass of businesses threatened by disaster in any given depression [read: '*abnormal*' recession], those made technically or commercially obsolete by the boom from those which appeared to be endangered by secondary circumstances, reactions and actions; it would leave the former alone, and support the latter by granting credit.' (ibid., p. 255). Theory has a central role to play in the design of any policy to manage depressions once the *political* decision has been taken to apply it. On this matter, too, Schumpeter was sceptical in that he doubted whether the available theory and factual knowledge of capitalism was adequate for the task: 'The technical prerequisites for such a policy, a comprehensive insight into the facts and possibilities of economic and cultural life, although theoretically obtainable in time, are at present undoubtedly not available.' (ibid., p. 254). This was his position in *Development*. Whether or not he considered the subsequent advances in theoretical and empirical knowledge, including his own, to have improved the situation he never said in any extant writings.

However it is realized, the end of the depression brings the analyst face to face with the need to explain the lower turning point traverse and the subsequent recovery phase. What is it, then, that will actually bring about recovery? Schumpeter's reply to this question was a curt: 'This is easy.' (*Cycles*, p. 152). He based this sanguine reply on his trust in the operational rationality of economic agents that makes the effectuation of the turn into recovery more or less a matter of course: 'For saying that firms will not act in the way which will lead to recovery and eventually to a neighborhood of equilibrium woud be synonymous with saying that they will deliberately forego gains and incur losses which it is in their individual power to make or to avoid, and scrap plant and equipment which could be profitably used.' (ibid.). That is, the disequilibrium state at the bottom of a depression somehow offers opportunities for adaptations and adjustments – *not* innovations – which can generate profit increases for some surviving firms. Such an assertion could not amount to an explanation and the occurrence of the lower turning point was effectively posited as an act of faith in Schumpeter's analysis. No attempt was made to formulate the relevant traverse from the end of depression into recovery.

As far as the recovery traverse itself was concerned, Schumpeter had very little to say, either, beyond asserting that it will ensue as an equilibration process analogous to that of a normal recession: 'recession and revival . . . differ in the nature of the deviations they liquidate or absorb and in the signs of the latter . . . [but] they are alike in the nature of the mechanism at work which in both cases consists of equilibrium relations between the elements of the economic system asserting themselves' (ibid., p. 156). On the nature of the mechanism in the particular case of recovery he wrote simply that 'when depression has run its course . . . the system starts to feel its way back to a new neighborhood of equilibrium . . . Expansion up to equilibrium amounts then sets in and yields temporary surplus gains or eliminates the losses incident to operation at the trough amounts.' (ibid., p. 149). There would be, he added, a 'gradual elimination of the abnormalities . . . existing [at the end of the depression] – low stocks, unused plant, unemployed labor, idle credit facilities . . .' (ibid., p. 157). But, while these 'abnormalities' may give ready *scope* for recovery, their mere existence cannot explain their 'elimination' or provide any indication of the nature of the traverse that would restore 'equilibrium'.

The one thing that Schumpeter did make clear in this context was that the new 'equilibrium' reached at the end of the recovery 'will not be the same as that which would have been reached without abnormal liquidation' (ibid., p. 149). 'Recovery' from a *recession* comprises merely the recession itself as an equilibration process and the new 'equilibrium' is approached from 'above' where, to draw parallels with the depression conditions specified above, the state of stocks cannot be specified, plant is overused, labour overemployed and credit overextended. So, even though both recession and recovery lead to 'equilibrium', they start out from very different initial disequilibrium conditions and, as well as reaching different 'equilibria', the form of the traverse path taken to reach them must be quite different. Once again, though, Schumpeter's awareness of the analytical problem did not lead him to attempt any formal solution and his readers were left with an imprecise idea of what the recovery process involves. Perhaps it is possible to put this further lacuna down to the indefinite secondary nature of the whole depression-recovery phenomenon and his consequent perceived inability and unwillingness to be too specific about any theoretical representation of it.

One other aspect of Schumpeter's theoretical treatment of the four-, or more aptly, three-phase cycle calls for some comment. The expansion period portrayed comprises three stages: a recovery phase, an 'equilibrium' period and a prosperity-boom phase. What this means is that (near) full-employment of labour power, other resources and existing capacity is realized as a result of the *recovery* phase alone. The traverse to prosperity and boom takes place in an already (near) full-employment economy. This was a quite unusual feature, for most cycle theories of the time involved an expansion path that begins with extreme unemployment in recession and runs *progressively* to an over-full employment situation in the boom. For example, Gottfried Haberler put the generally-accepted position this way in 1937: 'an expansion could not go on very long if it started from a state of full employment or after it has reached such a state in the course of its progress' (1964, p. 365; cf. pp. 283-4, 284n, 287–9). Full-employment is an end state rather than an interim state in the usual representation of the expansion phase. But, what must be kept in mind in making comparisons with Schumpeter's argument here is that, for him, there is capacity growth beyond the (near) full-employment state at 'equilibrium' because of innovations that lift resource productivity. If innovations appeared anywhere in the other cycle theories, it was as a stimulus for recovery from depression so that their separate consequences were obscured by the general expansion that ensued. Schumpeter saw innovations as a much more essential force in motion and the *construction* of his cycle model was designed to emphasize that perception.

9.3 Extensions and complications

As a further step in formulating his 'second approximation' version of the business-cycle theory, Schumpeter introduced 'a few other facts' into his argument (*Cycles*, pp. 157ff.). He saw this step as extending and complicating his analyses without affecting their essential veracity. In this section, I examine these 'facts' and consider the extent to which their inclusion can affect what Schumpeter had argued in their absence. His own treatment of the implications will again be found to be too brief and indecisive to be accepted as a complete recognition of the analytical issues raised.

Two of the 'facts' introduced do turn out to have relatively insignificant effects on the nature of the cycle analysis even though they may complicate it to a greater degree than he seemed to envisage. One concerns allowing for the spread of credit creation throughout the economy in response to demand from non-innovating firms (ibid., p. 159). This brings about a more extensive involvement of banks in all phases of the cycle, but especially in those other than prosperity where entrepreneurs are their main customers. Credit creation may now appear during recovery to fund the expansions of surviving firms and may be maintained at higher levels during recessions or early in depressions as existing firms adapt and take up any expansion opportunities that flow on from innovations in prosperity. The other 'fact' that is to be mentioned here concerns a more definite recognition of the extensive indirect effects that innovations have on a range of industries (ibid.). In particular, Schumpeter wanted to include industries more remote from the innovating ones as part of the prosperity traverse and of its reflection in the subsequent recession or early depression. Similarly, he wanted to consider more fully the spread of effects from expanding industries during the recovery phase. This second 'fact' has somewhat more effect on his theory than the first one because it requires an explicit sectional disaggregation to be introduced. Such disaggregation is necessary if there is to be any formal analysis of the more complex traverses that the diffusion processes would bring. However, as he devoted only one paragraph to the inclusion of this 'fact', little more can be said about what its implications meant to him.

The third of the 'facts' to be dealt with here involves the lifting of a crucial assumption. As Schumpeter put it, 'we must drop the assumption, made for convenience of exposition, that our wave is the first of its kind and that it not only starts from a neighborhood of equilibrium – through all qualifications we must hold on to this – but that it is entirely unaffected by the results of previous evolution' (ibid., p. 157). The implication here is that the *ab ovo* approach be dropped and that each business-cycle unit should be more explicitly set in historical time. 'Equilibrium' is to keep its role as the *theoretical and operational* 'centre of gravity' of all tendencies in the cycle. But, it is now a more complex concept to formulate clearly because 'we must take account of the fact that each neighborhood contains undigested elements of previous prosperities and depressions, innovations not yet completely worked out, results of faulty or otherwise imperfect adaptations and so on' (ibid.). He reiterated the point even more graphically later in *Cycles* when he referred to the 'second approximation' equilibrium as including 'all the underemployment, all the sloppiness, all the effects of indebtedness, all the undigested leavings of previous phases, all the imprints of chance events peculiar to the industry under study . . .' (ibid., p. 525). What we see here is a remarkable array of *disequilibrium* conditions creeping into the 'equilibrium' state – that is, the 'neighborhood' is

)eing enlarged almost beyond recognition. Schumpeter took some
:omfort from his claim that there 'is nothing in this to invalidate our
model. On the contrary, these facts are but a consequence of the process
lescribed by it.' However, he immediately recognized, even though he
ook little formal action to come to grips with the situation, that these
facts' could 'greatly increase the difficulties of analysis and complicate
he patterns of business situations we have to deal with' (ibid., p. 157).
The analytical task that he now posited, but did not face up to, is one in
which each prosperity traverse begins from a state of *disequilibrium* and
eturns via the other cycle phases to a *new and different disequilibrium*.
This really is *the* task for business-cycle analysis, although its degree of
heoretical intractability is inversely proportional to the amount of
reatment it has received in the literature. Here Schumpeter can
)erhaps be forgiven for not having tackled it, either.

It will be recalled that one of the key methodological principles upon
which Schumpeter based his theory of motion was that the dimensions
•f economic development and business cycles could be isolated for
analytical purposes from any consideration of 'pure' growth flowing
rom capital accumulation and population increases (see Chapter 4,
ection 4.1 above). His intention now was to add in the 'fact' of saving as
a source of finance capital thus only *partially* taking account of growth
ffects *per se* (*Cycles*, p. 158). Saving serves as an alternative source of
unding to the creation of credit and facilitates the repayment of credit
oans. Therefore, it interacts with the role of credit in the cycle as it was
•utlined in the previous section of this chapter and modifies the
raverses involved. To the extent that an expansion is funded by the
nternal savings of firms or by transfers from household savings rather
han by credit creation, the 'overheating' of the boom period is
mitigated as demand growth cannot be as great (ibid., p. 593). Here
•chumpeter concluded that 'depressions may be expected to be milder,
he more, other things being equal, the expenditure of preceding
•rosperities has been financed by saving and accumulation' (ibid.,
•. 588). We see here, incidentally, a further suggestion that the
oundations of the depression path are already laid down during the
xpansion phase and that, therefore, the notion that depression 'comes
fter' a recession is not an adequate representation of the relationship
•etween the two contraction phase types. Savings have two sorts of
ffects in contraction periods: one is that they can accelerate the
utodeflation as firms repay short-term credits by borrowing from other
avers and the other is that their presence can alleviate a depression by
llowing additional expenditures through dis-saving (ibid., pp. 588–9,
93).

It is clear, however, that this treatment of saving as a mere modifying factor in shaping the cycle did not take Schumpeter to the nub of the growth problem. He constructed his theory of the cycle in isolation from saving as finance capital accumulation used to fund net investment in durable means of production. This dimension of motion, independent of innovations in its 'pure' form, was then to be reintegrated into the theory. This would enable the empirically-relevant, *competitively-moti vated union of net investment and innovation decisions by the manageria agents of existing firms* to be given its proper role in the cycle traverses No such extension of the cycle theory was ever attempted and it is an ironical twist that the form of competition that carries Schumpeter' name in modern economic analysis, so-called 'Schumpeterian Compe tition', was never an integral part of his own formal analysis. His focus remained on *new* firms with *new* plant and equipment as the manifes tation of innovative activity. The more complex traverse puzzles pose by *existing firms forced to innovate by competitive threat* and th accompanying need to restructure and rebuild the *existing means o production stock* was not a part of Schumpeter's theory of motion (cf. e.g., Nelson and Winter, 1982, pp. 29–30, 39–40, 275).

It serves to compound the irony that what has come to be known a the 'Schumpeterian Hypothesis' – 'the claim that a market structur involving large firms with a considerable degree of market power is th price that society must pay for rapid technological advances' (ibid p. 278) – also cannot be found in Schumpeter's mainline theory c development and the business cycle. It is, of course, present i *Capitalism* (especially pp. 87ff.), but this belated recognition of th force of monopoly power in relation to the innovation process was neve incorporated into the *theory* of motion. This is clear from his treatmen of the next additional 'fact' that he wanted to include in his analysi namely the existence of imperfect competition (*Cycles*, p. 160). I inten to consider this suggestion of Schumpeter's at some length because represents one of the most glaring lacunae in his theory, especially in th light of the emphasis given to monopoly power in *Capitalism* (see als Chapter 2, section 2.3 above on this theme). His persistent focus o cycle traverses that are dominated by a flexible price-quantity marke mechanism, that originates in the perfectly-competitive view of capita list structures and operations, enabled him to side-step much of th analytical difficulty that must be contended with when innovating agen already have monopoly power and inhabit large-scale enterprises bui around massive commitments to a particular and inflexible physica technical structure of production.

Schumpeter referred to this fifth of his additional 'facts' quite candid as the need to recognize that 'the entrepreneurial impulse impinges upon an imperfectly competitive world . . . [and] also that entrepreneurs and their satellites almost always find themselves in imperfectly competitive short-time situations even in an otherwise perfectly competitive world' (*Cycles*, p. 160). Now it should be emphasized immediately that this piece includes two very different perceptions of the involvement of monopoly power in the process motion. One that is not at issue here is that entrepreneurs depend upon *temporary* monopoly positions in order to appropriate the profit returns that flow from their innovations. This aspect of monopoly power *is* an integral part of Schumpeter's theory, but it emerges, as he indicated, quite independently of the market structures that surround the *new* firms established to implement the innovations. The aspect to be dealt with here is the notion that the innovation process 'impinges upon an imperfectly competitive world'. That is to say, the traverses that make up the phases of the business cycle that is induced by a wave of innovations must focus on the reactions and adaptations by agents and firms with explicit monopoly power over their market situations.

One matter of analytical strategy that Schumpeter overlooked in his apparent desire to emphasize imperfect competition as the context of the wave of innovations, is that this 'modification' cannot legitimately be simply added onto the established competitive version of the theory. The inclusion of a market structure characterized by monopoly power demands a complete reformulation of the steady circular-flow model from where everything about motion 'begins' in Schumpeter's theory as well as a reformulation of the associated 'equilibrium' that forms the 'centre of gravity' of the fluctuations traverses. It is quite apparent that his perception of the circular-flow model just cannot be 'modified' to the extent necessary to encompass the quite different nature of equilibrium where monopoly-power firms make up some or all of the industries represented. The mix of unilateral and inter-firm strategic behaviours that now controls price and quantity outcomes is not adequately represented as a modification to price-taking market responses. However, Schumpeter's appreciation of the need for this radical reconstruction of his theoretical framework was incomplete. He made the *carte blanche* statement that 'we now drop the assumption of perfect competition altogether', but the changes to his analysis that he envisaged making as a consequence were quite superficial (ibid.).

In this regard, he wrote that 'we must expect our system – particularly its equilibrium tendency – to function much less promptly and effectively than it otherwise would and everywhere points to be replaced by zones' (ibid., p. 66). Moreover, 'propositions and proofs will be less stringent, zones of indeterminateness will emerge, sequences of events will be less prompt, and buffers will be inserted between the parts of our mechanism so that its gears will be slower to mesh' (ibid., p. 160). These sorts of analytical changes imply that monopoly power brings only sluggishness and imprecision to the existing market-adjustment mechanism. Schumpeter came closer to what is really required when he recognized that within such markets 'there will be more room for individual strategy, moves and countermoves which may impede, although they may also facilitate, the system's struggle toward equilibrium' (ibid.). In this same vein, he also saw that operations under monopoly power conditions involve 'a different technique of adjustment characterized by many movements that seem, and sometimes are, erratic, . . . [and] possibly also a different equilibrium, *if indeed any equilibrium be reached*' (ibid., p. 67, emphasis added). Regardless of these potentially insightful passages, however, he proceeded to 'shoot the messenger', so to say, by arguing that in response to these 'many freakish patterns . . . the economist's engine for the production of paradoxa will be worked up to, and perhaps beyond, capacity' (ibid., p. 160). The hint here was, it seems that such modifications and difficulties as those to which he alluded should not be perceived as paradoxical characteristics of capitalism, but rather as readily soluble aspects of analysis. Any 'paradoxa' that economists are wont to emphasize are of their own making in this context, as elsewhere, although no examples were given. Schumpeter's attitude in such situations was, though, made evident again later in *Cycles* when he criticized Michal Kalecki's work along the same lines. He quoted Kalecki (1937) to the effect that investment brings both prosperity and problems for the capitalist economy in motion. But he went on: 'In case the reader should think this a "paradox", Mr. Kalecki has the reply to offer, which has before him brought comfort to so many economists faced with impossible results of their own making, namely, that "it is not the theory which is paradoxical but its subject – the capitalist economy".' (p. 187).

One particular implication of monopoly power to which Schumpeter did give some attention was the existence of spare productive capacity and unemployed labour power under its disequilibrating influence. He attributed the excess capacity to two aspects of decision making by managerial agents: one being to ensure that capacity is available to provide for peaks of demand in the prosperity-boom phase of cycles especially where the industry is a 'cyclical' one (e.g. most means of production producing industries); and the other being 'to build ahead of demand' in a longer-term (trend) sense such that in any particular cyclical expansion, excess capacity may exist (ibid., p. 158 and n). A further, more 'accidental', source of excess capacity cited was that rapid technological change can make some perfectly operational means of production obsolete for economic reasons and these means may be retained as physically perfectly-sound spare capacity (ibid., p. 509). The most obvious and significant impact of such excess capacity on Schumpeter's analysis was stated thus: 'Output will much more readily expand in prosperity than we should expect from the Pure Model and costs and prices will rise less than they otherwise would.' (ibid., p. 158). Again, here, we find him emphasizing a monopoly power effect as just a modification to the 'pure models' operations. However, as I will return to show in a moment, he was aware that the general subject of price determination in the cycle where agents have monopoly power requires considerable reworking of the 'pure model' if it is to be dealt with effectively.

In the interim, I want to make some reference to the question of the effects of unemployed labour power and other resources in the mono-poly-power context. Schumpeter summarized his view quite clearly when he argued that 'since our process itself produces both imperfections of competition and disequilibria which account for underemployment that may outlast the cyclical unit that produced it, we include, by recognizing that every cycle is heir to preceding cycles, also what this course may contribute to the total unemployment with which any given unit starts' (ibid., p. 161). His point was that while unemployment increases during contraction phases, especially where depression is involved, the traverse to a restored 'equilibrium' should show how it is eliminated. But under the influence of monopoly power in labour-power and resource markets, some of the unemployment may remain such that *full employment ceases to be a property of equilibrium states and instead indicates – paradoxical though this may sound – disequilibrium of a certain type'* (ibid., original emphasis). Schumpeter did not explain the precise 'disequilibrium' nature of full employment under such conditions, or any other aspects of this issue, being content simply to declare that none of the implications is 'an obstacle to accepting our analysis' (ibid.). His only further consideration of the employment-unemployment issue comprised some empirical description of their quantitative movements during particular cycles (ibid., pp. 509ff.).

To return to the subject of commodity prices and monopoly power, we have seen that the immediate implication to which Schumpeter referred was that prices are likely to be relatively less volatile in such circumstances. He linked this consequence in part to the existence of excess capacity: the 'tendency of monopoloid situations to produce stable prices is reinforced, even if there is no cartel or monopoly in strict sense, by the practice of providing capacity for cyclical pea demands' (*Cycles*, p. 539). The effect comes about because, for much o the cycle, firms operate to the 'left' of their minimum average cos optimum so that during expansions unit costs may decline for some tim and delay the upward pressure on prices (ibid., p. 160 and n). Tw other considerations may also mitigate against price fluctuations in th cycle. One is the existence or threat of intervention by public authori ties, for it 'requires spectacular emergencies – inflation may not b sufficient – to "justify" an increase [in a particular price] in the eyes c an invariably hostile public opinion' (ibid., p. 537). And, as well, 'an reduction of prices will be looked upon as a proof of past exploitation and [mean] that it may be impossible or difficult to increase price agair (ibid., p. 539).

The other related consideration that is pertinent here is that unde 'monopoloid' conditions, 'price cannot impersonally rise as does th price of wheat. Somebody who can be identified has got to do the thin . . . .' (ibid., p. 537). The sanction that may be applied to the agen involved is that he or she 'risks losing custom' largely because he or sh cannot predict the strategic reaction of others in the industry unless 'th thing' is done from a position of price leadership or within a situation c overt or tacit collusion. Other price-setting agents may or may nc follow suit, with the latter reaction more likely if they perceive a opportunity to gain an increase in market share (ibid.). The effects of price decrease are similarly uncertain. Any gain that is expected fror such a decision may not be realized if other agents follow the indivi dual's lead. Moreover, the incentive to reduce price will not be great i the commodity price elasticity of demand is known to be so low that th quantity sold may respond less than is required actually to increas revenue (ibid., pp. 537, 539). Under these circumstances, Schumpete saw that there may be an inclination for agents to collude, but he playe down the significance of such a procedure, especially at the overt formalized level. Collusive practice 'requires machinery which is diffi cult and sometimes costly to set into motion' and may involve 'difficul ties of taking action in the face of divergent interests of members' (ibid. pp. 538, 539; cf. pp. 539–40). Price inflexibility from this latter sourc he considered to be of limited significance.

Schumpeter's inclination was, in general, to portray the implication of monopoly power for business-cycle analysis as being of minima concern. He was prepared to assert that monopoloid conditions mak 'not so much a difference in ultimate results as a difference in the way b which they are reached' which, while it 'is to be sure, quite sufficient t upset our expectations as to the behavior of price-quantity pairs in the short run . . . it is not sufficient to upset the working of our process' (ibid., p. 543). Furthermore, he pointed to the contrary possibility that monopoly power positions can assist in the price-quantity adjustment processes of the cycle. Their value to economic agents, he argued, consists, rather than in any power to follow a long-run policy of restriction of output, in the facilities they afford for steering safely through difficult situations and for undisturbed planning'. That is, monopoly power rather 'mitigates than intensifies cyclical difficulties' (ibid., pp. 543, 539). In all this argument, what is cried out for is some detailed traverse analysis that demonstrates how in the cycle monopoloid conditions bring about the positive and/or negative consequences so baldly asserted. Here we have in Schumpeter's own work a clear example of the very problem of economists' neglect of monopoly power analysis that he complained of in his Preface to Zeuthen's 1930 book (see above, Chapter 2, section 2.3).

In not responding to this analytical challenge, Schumpeter used the escape route of claiming that monopoly power was empirically insignificant in the historical period that his theory was designed to address, namely capitalism up to about the mid 1930s. It remained a force 'as yet not great enough to dominate the picture in any country' (*Cycles*, p. 97). And, with respect to the market manifestations of such power, his perception was that 'there is little reason to believe that . . . stability or rigidity [of prices] has been on the increase during the last fifty years, and that it really merits the attention which has been paid to it of late . . .'. That is, as far as he was concerned, there 'is less genuine rigidity, and what there is of it is less dislocating, than is widely assumed' (ibid., pp. 536, 543). However, it should be noticed that in the present context of his formalized cycle theory, Schumpeter had an incentive to play down the complicating effects that monopoly power would have had for his analysis should he have taken its presence seriously. Clearly the same concerns did not trouble him in *Capitalism* where its structural and operational effects were, in fact, emphasized as the most relevant state of capitalism upon which to focus. And, what is more, the vital Part II of the later work containing this emphasis seems to have occupied a separate 'compartment' in his mind because the original presentation of the thesis dates from a 1936 lecture delivered at the US Department of Agriculture Graduate School (*Capitalism*, p. xiv; cf. the reference to 1935, p. 163). No documentary evidence of what the lecture contained is extant, so it is not possible to know whether it gave the same emphasis to monopoly-power capitalism as did the later version. What seems unlikely is that there was a total shift in Schumpeter's attitude towards the relevance of this form of the system between the drafting of the two works. There are other suggestions, too, in *Capitalism* that more of it dated from the 1930s, comprising references to 1932, (p. 224) and 1938 (p. 231) in the text.

I think it is worth considering Schumpeter's much richer treatment of the implications of monopoly power in *Capitalism*, even if it is only to reflect on what might have been had he taken the trouble to rework this theory using a model in which imperfect competition dominates market activity.

One immediate casualty in any elaboration of this alternative perspective is the readily accessible explanation of price-theoretic equilibrium. Schumpeter now expressed strong scepticism about what was in his cycle theory a central tenet, albeit one hedged around with all sorts of qualifications. A more extreme argument was used in the present context to suggest that in the case of oligopolistic industries 'there is in fact no determinate equilibrium at all and the possibility presents itself that there may be an endless sequence of moves and countermoves, an indefinite state of warfare between firms'. Only in special theoretical cases can an equilibrium be shown to exist under conditions that are unlikely ever to rule in reality. Equilibrium will therefore, be 'much harder to attain . . . and still harder to preserve' than where market-price competitive forces are dominant (*Capitalism* pp. 79–80). The form of competition indulged in by firms with monopoly power is more likely to be 'predatory' or 'cut throat' and linked to socially wasteful processes such as advertising and the suppression of new methods of production. Any realistic 'equilibrium' state of such an industry, should it be established by some accident, is also unlikely to bring full employment or maximum output (ibid., p. 80). It should be noted in passing, though, that this emphasis on negative aspects of monopoly power could be misleading if it is not kept in mind that Schumpeter firmly believed in the *net* economic and social benefits of the *'unfettered'* dominance of the phenomenon. Indeed, in the present work he was of the opinion that the vital force of 'creative destruction' central to his whole analysis of motion, including the cycle theory would be much less effective in generating 'progress' in a price competitive environment.

It became apparent to him, too, that under monopoloid conditions the *ab ovo* methodology could not legitimately be applied in the explanation of motion. No longer can innovations be introduced only by virgin entrepreneurs through new firms and plants. Instead, the focus now had to be on the activities of managerial and research agents in established large-scale enterprises. Indeed, one of his key empirically ased defences of 'unfettered' monopoly power was that *this* mode of innovation is most effective (e.g., ibid., p. 81). One effect of such a source of innovations is that the process of motion takes on a degree of continuity that is absent in the earlier model. The introduction of innovations is here an integral part of the overall operations of the firms instead of being a process that is just added on by virtue of other agents' decisions. And, at the same time, the nature of the mobilizing incentive for innovation strategies is changed from one of choice by individual entrepreneurs to one of necessity where it becomes a mode of competitive defence against the constant threat of losses of market share (e.g., ibid., pp. 84, 85, 102). As I have already indicated, this 'Schumpeterian competition' never became part of his own theory of the cycle.

A side effect of this focus upon innovation as a competitive process implemented by large-scale firms is that it led Schumpeter to give more attention to its implications for the physical-technical structure of production. Decisions to innovate that involve the production of new means of production and their installation within established production structures pose some quite complex adjustment requirements for both the individual firm and the economy as a whole (ibid., pp. 96ff.). By comparison, the adding on of new productive capacity that facilitates new combinations can be handled analytically with somewhat less complicated traverse argument.

Price dynamics under monopoly-power conditions were also considered further in *Capitalism* (pp. 92ff.). Schumpeter now gave much more emphasis to the merits of price inflexibility as a general stabilizing force in capitalist motion (ibid., p. 95). He realized, though, that this inflexibility robs capitalism of its central co-ordinating and equilibrating mechanism so that, by implication, the price of less severe fluctuations is a continuous state of industry supply and demand maladjustments. In spite of this, his belief remained that monopoly power brings a net benefit to the system (ibid., pp. 186, 194).

Taken together, this set of characteristics of monopoly-power capitalism has profound implications for the way the business cycle is to be explained. It must have been quite apparent to Schumpeter that even at the primary level of his theory, taking full account of the structures and operations of this empirically-relevant form of capitalism would present formidable analytical difficulties. He certainly showed no inclination to take up the challenge in any extant work.

.4 The three-cycle schema

Schumpeter saw his idea for a 'third approximation' in business-cycle theory, in which three simultaneously-operating cycle units were modelled, as a significant and distinctive advance over other theories (*Essays*, pp. 139–40; *Cycles*, pp. 161ff., 212ff.). He could see 'no reason why the cyclical process of evolution should give rise to just one wavelike movement'. It is more probable that waves of innovations 'will set into motion an indefinite number of wavelike fluctuations which will roll on simultaneously and interfere with one another in the process' (*Cycles*, p. 161). The result of this 'interference' process is an observed time series of the selected cycle-indicator variable that exhibits an irregular temporal profile (as the chart on p. 213 of *Cycles* shows so clearly, at least as a matter of geometry or trigonometry). Thus, 'the impression we derive from any graph of economic time series [does not] lend support to a single-cycle hypothesis . . . [and] the reader need only inspect any of the charts in this book in order to satisfy himself that it is much more natural to assume the presence of many fluctuations of different span and intensity, which seem to be superimposed on each other' (ibid., pp. 161–2).

There are two related aspects of this multicycle empirical perception that should be emphasized in order to clarify its links to the theoretical three-cycle schema. First, the analytical dissection of a time-series into its constituent cyclical components is not to be considered as merely the result of the application of certain statistical techniques (ibid., pp. 165, 168–9). He argued emphatically that 'there is a theoretically indefinite number of fluctuations present in our [time-series] material at any time, [where] the word *present* . . . [means] that there are real factors at work to produce them and *not merely that the material may be decomposed into them by formal methods* . . .' (ibid., p. 168, original emphasis). In this passage, Schumpeter set himself the challenge of actually accounting for the different cycles as an extension of his theory, albeit with the practical limitation of a three-cycle format. The second aspect of the multiple-cycle notion gives emphasis to its status as an extension of his single-cycle approach. Multiple cycles are *implied by* his theory in either its 'first-' or 'second-approximation' versions in that the empirical cycle forms can all be traced to the causal effects of different new combinations in the innovation wave. They must, then, be shown to be *explained by* the theory. Thus, there is no 'problem of different causation' posed in this 'third approximation' and all the cycle components are 'to be explained in terms of the process of economic evolution as described in our model'. So it was that he considered innovations, along with 'their immediate and ulterior effects and the response to them by the system, . . . [to be] the common "cause" of them all, although different types of innovations and different kinds of effects may play different roles in each' (ibid., p. 172).

Analytical tractability demanded that Schumpeter simplify the multiple-cycle pattern that emerges from the decomposition of empirical
time-series. As indicated already, he chose to limit himself to three
simultaneous units with different periods and, probably, different
amplitudes. This choice had 'no particular virtues' and he thought at
first that five 'would perhaps be better, although after some experiment-
ing, . . . [he] came to the conclusion that the improvement in the picture
would not warrant the increase in cumbersomeness'. Moreover, it
stands to reason that as we draw away from the single-cycle hypothesis
we shall reap the bulk of the harvest to be hoped for at the first steps and
that then these returns will be rapidly decreasing' (ibid., p. 169). He was
also adamant that 'it cannot be emphasized too strongly that the three-
cycle schema does not follow from our model – although multiplicity of
cycles does . . .' and that 'nothing in . . . [it] implies a hypothesis' about
cycles (ibid.). What was most important was simply that the three-cycle
choice gave Schumpeter 'a convenient descriptive device' and one which
he 'found . . . useful in his own work and in marshaling his facts' (ibid.,
p. 170).

The key characteristic of each cycle category in the schema is its
periodicity. Schumpeter also found the three-cycle choice convenient
because he could readily identify three empirically-established cycles
with a range of durations that more or less accorded with his theoretical
basis for arguing the multiple-cycle idea. Each was then named in
honour of its 'discoverer' (see above Chapter 8, section 8.2). There was
a short cycle, of 40 months, named after Joseph *Kitchin*, a medium cycle
of some nine to ten years, named after Clément *Juglar* and a long-wave
cycle of about 54 to 60 years, named after N. D. *Kondratieff* (*Cycles*,
p. 170). Further to this convenience, Schumpeter found that while there
may be no 'rational justification' for it, 'the integral number of Kitchins
in a Juglar or of Juglars in a Kondratieff' is always the same. The 'rough
impression' from the relevant time-series was that 'it is possible to count
off, historically as well as statistically, six Juglars to a Kondratieff and
three Kitchins to a Juglar – not as an average but in every individual
case' (ibid., pp. 173–4; cf. pp. 172–3). He went on, though, to soften
the rigidity that is apparent in this observation at first sight (ibid.,
p. 174n), as well as to emphasize that this empirical regularity had no
basis in his theory and that nothing in his theory depended upon it –
indeed he observed that his theory would suggest irregularity in the
relative periodicities of the three cycles (ibid., p. 174).

What, then, was Schumpeter's theoretical rationale for the multiple-
cycle hypothesis? Most immediately it is provided by the fact that by
their nature, the different innovations that comprise any wave have

different periods and quantitative profiles of gestation, diffusion and absorption. The interference and compounding of the effects of the individual innovations results in a highly irregular observed time-series of any appropriate indicator variable (ibid., pp. 166–7). It was to these irregular fluctuations that he applied his schema in order that some theoretical coherence could be realized. He granted, though, that 'why' innovations which differ so much in period of gestation and in the time it takes to absorb them into the system should always produce cycles respectively somewhat less than 60 years, somewhat less than 10 years, and somewhat less than 40 months, is indeed difficult to see' (ibid., p. 174).

Such difficulty is compounded by the complications introduced in Schumpeter's second rationale for the existence of multiple cycles, namely his argument that the diffusion and absorption processes of individual innovations may themselves generate sequences of interdependent cycle units before their effects are fully worked out. Thus: 'Major innovations hardly ever emerge in their final form or cover in one throw the whole field that will ultimately be their own.' (ibid., p. 167). This may well be the case and the examples of railroads, motor cars and electric power that he cited in passing might lend themselves readily to the idea that each innovation was 'carried out in steps each of which constitutes a cycle' (ibid.). However, the accompanying generalized argument that the *sequential* interdependence and interference of these cycle steps 'tends to weld them into a higher unit that will stand out as a historical individual' and that 'the cycle of higher order is but a product or composite of these [cycles] and has no existence of its own' (ibid., p. 167–8) defies explanation. It is a *non sequitur* in that according to Schumpeter's own reasoning, what generates the compound outcome of separate cycles is their interference with each other as *simultaneous* and somehow *additive* events. Recall that the separate cycles 'roll on simultaneously and interfere with one another in the process', with their consequent 'superimposition' requiring temporal coincidence (ibid., pp. 161, 162). A *sequence* of cycles cannot conform to this mode of interference and superimposition. Only the separate sequences themselves with their common origins in particular innovations can be compounded by virtue of their temporal juxtaposition, but this is not what Schumpeter argued.

The third rationale that he gave for the multiple-cycle idea had more plausibility but added little to the first and fundamental one. He argued that the simultaneous cycles that result directly from the various innovations in the wave may generate secondary effects of their own that are manifested as cycles of the same indicator variable. This vague notion was illustrated by examples in which the diffusion of the effects of railroadization and 'the Industrial Revolution' were said to take on a cyclical form. The latter phenomenon 'consisted of a cluster of cycles of various span that were superimposed on each other. But these together wrought a fundamental change in the economic and social structure of society which in itself also had some obviously cyclical characteristics.' (ibid., p. 168). These secondary cyclical reflections of the original cycles that flow from each innovation contribute further to the complex multiple of cycles within the observed time-series fluctuations.

As was indicated above, the interference between the constituent cycles of different periods will manifest itself as a compounding of their individual amplitudes. 'These cycles', wrote Schumpeter, 'will displace each other's peaks and troughs and between them produce contour lines that are completely ununderstandable [sic] without due recognition of the phases of the others into which the phase of any given cycle happens to fall' (ibid., p. 167). Any phase 'may be entirely blotted out or even reversed' by this interference of simultaneous cycles (ibid., p. 463; cf. p. 503). It is an integral part of this argument that 'the sweep of any cycle is the trend of the cycles of next lower order' (ibid., p. 173). For instance, the Juglar cycle's units centre themselves around the trend path of the indicator variable that comprises the phases of the contemporaneous Kondratieff long-wave (ibid., p. 205). This means necessarily that these so-called trends will have regular and sustained positive and negative periods, as well as 'horizontal' periods of 'equilibrium'. Moreover, they are not the same as constant or variable rate growth trends that are often argued to form the core of business cycles because in Schumpeter's thesis, each cycle in the schema originates in the same wave of innovations independently of any argument about the 'pure' growth that may accompany it. It should be noticed that this form of cycle-on-trend superimposition is not what Schumpeter illustrated in his three-cycle chart (ibid., p. 213). Instead, this chart shows the three cycles as compounding around a common horizontal 'axis' with arithmetic scales. The outcome is a complex and irregular contour of fluctuations, but these cannot be the same as those that would emerge if each cycle were compounded with the others by superimposing it on the phase path of the cycle of 'the next lowest order'. The distinction between the two perceptions of cycle interference is illustrated in a very simplified format in Figures 9.1 and 9.2 using two cycles only.

There is one analytical consequence of Schumpeter's three-cycle schema that warranted more attention that it received. Where a particular time-series is argued to result from the compounding of three cycles with different periodicities, the involvement of the 'equilibrium'

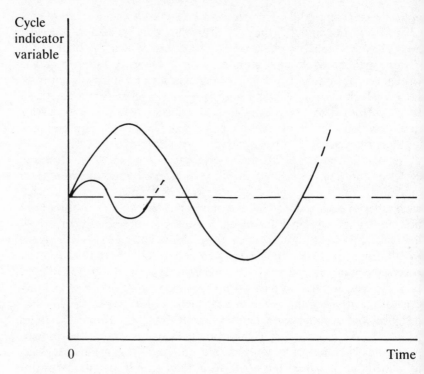

Figure 9.1   Schumpeter's chart – simplified

period in the analysis requires reconsideration and modification. This comes about because only at points (strictly, periods) in history where the three cycles pass through 'equilibrium' in 'the same direction' can the cycle units all be argued to start from an 'equilibrium' state in Schumpeter's original sense. That is, 'the sweep of each longer wave supplies neighborhoods of equilibrium for the wave of the next lower order' (*Cycles*, p. 173). Given the numerical relations between the periodicities of the three cycles, this can occur in an *overall* sense only at the beginning of each Kondratieff long-wave prosperity every 54 to 60 years. In the interim, innovations that induce shorter cycles must be argued to begin from much more approximate 'equilibria'. As Schumpeter put it, because 'shorter waves must in most cases rise from a situation which is not a neighborhood of equilibrium but [one that is] disturbed by the effects of the longer waves in progress at this time, we must now modify our previous proposition that the process of innovation starts from such neighborhoods only, as well as our concept of neighborhood of equilibrium itself' (ibid.). Just what modifications

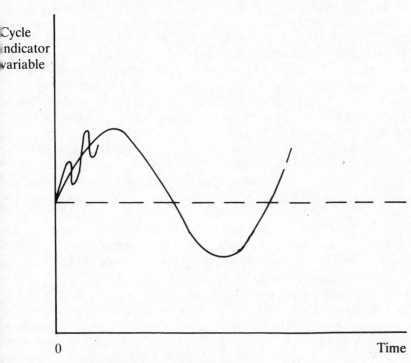

Figure 9.2   Phase-'trend' superimposition

would be required to make allowance for this complication were not made evident. But, it is clear that they would be considerable because the very essence of Schumpeter's thesis is that the wave of entrepreneurial activity can only be engendered by the tranquil and relatively certain conditions of an 'equilibrium' period. As was the case with the monopoly power 'extension' of the theory, there was no explanation here of how agent motivations and behaviours must alter to enable a wave of innovations to flow from a state of radical disequilibrium. The three-cycle schema was, therefore, left with only a loose connection to its theoretical roots and it became more of an empirical framework of analysis in *Cycles* than an integral part of the theoretical explanation of business cycles.

Amongst the few business-cycle analysts who took the trouble to comment on Schumpeter's business-cycle analyses, the three-cycle schema found little favour. Gottfried Haberler did not agree with the general principle of regular cycle periodicity in the first place, so it was not surprising that he dissented from the three-cycle idea. He concluded in his 1937 book that 'it is not possible to interpret the succession of cycles of different length and amplitude as resulting from the superimposition of independent or interdependent cycles of different length (Schumpeter's three-cycle schema)' for the reason that observed business-cycle fluctuations comprise 'a complicated chemical compound and not a mechanical mixture whose constituent parts are separable by more or less mechanical statistical devices' (1964, pp. 457, 458). Simon Kuznets's perception was similar in his substantial and generally critical review article on *Cycles* published in 1940 (1954, pp. 105ff.). He concentrated on the empirical evidence elicited by Schumpeter in support of the three-cycle schema and found it to be seriously deficient in both method and substance, although he granted, *contra* Haberler, that a case probably could be made for the existence of more than one-cycle category, defined by periodicity – at least a 'long' one and a 'short' one (ibid. pp. 116ff., 121). But, the fact remained in his view that the 'three-cycle schema and the rather rigid relationship claimed to have been established among the three groups of cycles cannot be considered, on the basis of the evidence submitted, even tolerably valid; . . . nor could such validity be established without a serviceable statistical procedure' (ibid., p. 122). As the occasion demanded, Alvin Hansen's obituary reflections on Schumpeter's contributions to business-cycle theory included a more circumspect reading of the limitations of the three-cycle schema (1951, p. 82). The message remained, though, that while he agreed that there was some substance in the idea of a 'long' and a 'short' cycle periodicity, he felt that Schumpeter had formulated too rigid and definite a schema to be supported by the evidence elicited. At least, he concluded, the analysis remained 'a matter of controversy' (ibid.).

9.5   Statistical and historical analyses

As I indicated in the opening chapter of my study, I do not intend to provide any detailed exposition or reassessment of Schumpeter's use of statistical and historical 'techniques'. The purpose of this section is confined to drawing together a number of contemporary critiques of his endeavours to give his theory some empirical complement. These critiques are useful because they were undertaken by analysts competent in the business-cycle field who read Schumpeter's work from a contemporary analytical perspective. As is well known, most of his empirical work appeared in *Cycles*, where the bulk of the book, indeed all but about 200 of its more than 1000 pages, is devoted to statistical and historical description of business-cycle phenomena. He dealt with data from England, Germany and the USA covering a period from the late eighteenth century until the late 1930s. The critical pieces that I will summarize below all comprise reviews of *Cycles* that appeared in various journals after the book was published. Each reviewer, in his own way, drew conclusions about Schumpeter's empirical analyses and the extent to which they complemented the cycle theory to which they were juxtaposed.

Oscar Lange (1940) chose largely to avoid trying to come to grips with the more than 800-page morass of data and description, claiming that it defied adequate representation in the space of a review. However, he did manage to conclude that the historical chapters were 'the climax of the work' and 'a real work of art' (p. 190). He found in these chapters 'the only treatment of the history of business cycles available in English' and he felt that this gave the whole book 'a value quite independent of the correctness of Professor Schumpeter's theoretical model . . . [and] even should the theory . . . presented prove to be a complete failure . . .', that value would remain intact. And, while Lange did not judge the theory to be a 'complete failure', he clearly signalled the need to keep the theoretical and empirical parts of the book separate.

The review by Simon Kuznets, also from 1940, was more technically incisive and he was critical of Schumpeter's work on more specific counts (1954). He tackled both the theoretical and empirical dimensions of the book, concentrating on the 'bunching' of innovations as the root cause of cycles, the four-phase model and the three-cycle schema. In the case of each of these elements, he centred his critique on their potential as empirically relevant means of understanding observed cyclical phenomena. To put things bluntly, Kuznets found little to praise and much to condemn in Schumpeter's project. I will not work through all of his objections here. The point to be made concerns only his assessment of the statistical-historical content of the book in its claimed role of illustrating and complementing the theoretical arguments that preceded it. Far from the analytical consistency and complementarity that Schumpeter sought, Kuznets coud not 'escape the impression that . . . [the] theoretical model in its present state cannot be linked directly and clearly with statistically observed realities; that the extreme paucity of statistical analysis in the treatise is an inevitable result of the type of theoretical model adopted . . .' (p. 116). He objected to the substitution of impressionistic and qualitative historical discussion for hard statistical analysis, a limitation that was attributed to 'the difficulty of devising statistical procedures that would correspond to the theoretical model' (p. 116). With particular reference to Schumpeter's claims about the empirical status of the Kondratieff long-wave cycles, Kuznets was especially harsh in his comments. He found a 'failure to follow articulate methods of time series analysis [which] reduces the statistical methods to a mere recording of impressions of charts . . .', circumstances under which disagreement over interpretation 'is easily possible; and such ease is an eloquent testimony to the insufficiency of the crude statistical procedures followed in the treatise to provide a basis for establishing cycle types of so elusive a character as the Kondratieffs' (pp. 120, 121). Such overdependence on casual chart readings as empirical evidence also characterized Schumpeter's handling of the shorter-cycle categories, especially in the case of the Kitchin where Kuznets found the support for it to be meagre, at best (pp. 121–2). And, as far as he could see, the 'core of the difficulty seems to lie in the failure to forge the necessary links between the primary factors and concepts (entrepreneur, innovation, equilibrium line) and the observable cyclical fluctuations in economic activity' such that 'no proper link is established between the theoretical model and statistical procedure . . .' (pp. 122–3). Given the sort of complementarity that Schumpeter had hoped to establish between his three 'techniques', all of this was strong condemnation indeed.

The review written by Erwin Rothbarth (1942) was rather more circumspect than that of Kuznets, even though he came to similar conclusions. He found theoretical and empirical weaknesses in the book, too, with the two dimensions of the argument left without sufficient articulation. Thus, the 'argument is frequently impressionistic, the statistics and historical facts appealed to bear very often a much too indeterminate relation to the theory they are meant to prove . . .' (p. 223). Leaving aside the overstatement 'meant to prove', the message here is the same as Kuznets's. Later in the same review he wrote that 'I find it impossible to hide my sense of disappointment at the more empirical parts of Professor Schumpeter's book. One could have wished that he had been able to adduce evidence more directly relevant to his main thesis . . . .' (pp. 228–9). To this he added the telling remark, although again we should duly temper the 'to prove' demand, that '[p]erhaps it is impossible, from existing historical and statistical data, to prove or disprove . . . Schumpeter's theory. *In that case what is the relevance of the empirical parts of the book?*' (p. 229, emphasis added). Perhaps here Lange has provided the best answer.

Jacob Marschak (1940) expressed similar sympathies to those of Lange in his review: 'any economist who like the reviewer can never dare to judge but is sometimes able to enjoy the writings of professional economic historians will not fail to enjoy even more Schumpeter's interpretation of the history of capitalism. That and nothing less is the actual goal of the book.' (p. 893). At the same time, he, too, expressed some limited misgivings about the theoretical-empirical links: 'The method used and possibly the material available exclude the applicability of strict statistical tests which might show whether and which coincidences or discrepancies between fact and hypothesis have been due to chance or to recognized systematic causes.' He further tempered this view by noting 'the author's own cautiousness and skepticism [that] must disarm any critic not entirely deprived of a sense of measure. It is not claimed by Schumpeter that any of the hypotheses is strictly true or more than merely plausible.' (p. 893). Kuznets, especially, would not find quite so much in this assertion with which to sympathize as Marschak did and would certainly have been surprised to read the latter's opening claim as far as *Cycles* is concerned, at least: 'What is more important: the making or testing of hypotheses? Professor Schumpeter has made a major contribution to both these branches of economics, with equal enthusiasm and industry, with equal perspicacity, and with equal sense of measure.' (p. 889).

Readers, now familiar with Schumpeter's theory of motion, may like to turn to the empirical chapters of *Cycles* and decide for themselves how many of the reviewers' observations they find cogent.[1]

9.6 Summary
The analysis in this chapter moved from Schumpeter's abstracted core dimensions of the business cycle to a consideration of the more empirically-oriented influences that he claimed affect its observed form.

1. The particular secondary factors that superimpose themselves on the primary cycle include the psychological reactions of agents and the overextension of credit. The prosperity and boom phase now ends in a crisis in which the seeds of an ensuing depression may already be sown.

2. In the contraction phase that follows, the 'normality' of the primary recession is compounded and overwhelmed by the pathological secondary collapse which Schumpeter attributed to a less than fully explained 'Vicious Spiral' of 'Abnormal Liquidations'. It is to be noticed that his four-phase cycle effectively turned out to have three phases only as no intertemporal separation of the recession and depression characteristics is possible.

3. Because of the complex and variable nature of the secondary factors that could be involved in the depression, Schumpeter chose only to suggest some of the forces that could bring it to an end. These included an ultimate end to the spiral of liquidations and the recognition of 'depression-business' opportunities by some agents, but *not* in the form of innovations at this stage of the cycle. He even

allowed that some policy intervention by the government may be needed to break the depression. Once again, though, the analysis provided lacked precision and conviction and the nature of the lower turning point into recovery was left in vague terms, albeit this time with the mitigation that, given the empirical variability of depressions, it could all hardly have been otherwise.

4. The recovery phase itself that was to end in a new 'neighborhood' of equilibrium turned out to be another traverse about which Schumpeter had little of substance to say.

5. Further, more general secondary complications were added by Schumpeter in an endeavour to increase the empirical content of his argument. These included a more extensive spread of demand for created credit, a more explicit inter-industry diffusion of innovation effects, the extension of the disequilibrium content of the 'neighborhood' of equilibrium, the explicit recognition of the need to reintegrate pure growth phenomena into the business cycle traverses and a recognition that imperfect competition dominates in a modern capitalist economic system. In none of these cases, though, was he moved to make any formal amendments to his established theoretical analyses.

6. The lack of any theoretical endeavours to take account of imperfect competition and the monopoly power of firms in their markets represented a serious shortcoming in Schumpeter's analyses. It led him grossly to understate the complex nature of the real-world fluctuations that his theory was supposed to help explain.

7. The three-cycle schema that Schumpeter devised enabled him to represent at the theoretical level the empirical phenomenon of the multiplicity of simultaneous cycles imbedded in any observed time series. Its inclusion added little to the explanatory power of his theory.

8. Finally, Schumpeter's efforts to situate his theoretical arguments in their statistical and historical contexts left most of his contemporary critics unimpressed. In spite of the massive proportions of this aspect of his work, it was found that his approach lacked rigour and failed to elicit much contact with his theory. Here again, this extension of his analyses added little to reinforce the merits or negate the limitations of his theory of motion.

Note
1. In the light of the above critical commentary, especially that of Kuznets, it is interesting to recall and *to ponder on* the fact that Schumpeter was the elected President of the Econometric Society from 1937 to 1941!

10 Concluding reflections

10.1 Preamble

It is now time to establish in a summary form the main terms of reassessment that have emerged during this study. To this end, in the next two sections of this chapter, I assemble the most significant methodological and substantive points of critique that I have elicited and then go on to set out those dimensions of Schumpeter's theoretical analyses that I consider to represent his immediately positive legacy to analysts of motion who came after him.

The two sections are complementary in that my arguments in both are intended to point towards future directions for the analysis of motion in economic systems. This applies as much to the critical tenets as it does to the direct contributions, for it seems to me that much can be gained from critique that makes evident the need for and merits of alternative analytical premises and directions. And, what is more, in Schumpeter's case, he intended that his work should be read critically with a view to elaborating and improving it. We should recall his valedictory words on leaving Bonn for Harvard in 1932: 'I never wish to say anything definitive, if I have a function it is to open doors not to close them.' (quoted by Haberler, 1951a, p. 46). In this same vein, as we saw earlier on, he explicitly recognized the 'many glaring lacunae and . . . many unfulfilled desiderata' of *Cycles* and advised his readers accordingly: 'The younger generation of economists should look upon this book merely as something to shoot at and to start from – as a motivated program for further research. Nothing, at any rate, could please me more.' (p. v). My concluding reflections in the next section will re-emphasize several key 'lacunae' and 'unfulfilled desiderata' of which Schumpeter was so aware, but there is perhaps more to 'shoot at' than he imagined when exposing himself as a 'target'.

As I foreshadowed in the Introduction, I have certainly done quite a bit of 'shooting' along the way and my critique has gone beyond the 'lacunae' and 'desiderata' to penetrate rather more into the methodological and substantive core of the theory of economic development and business cycles, a core that I suspect Schumpeter expected would be accepted as sufficiently orthodox to keep it out of the 'firing line'. In this respect, I have built onto the crucial critical insights formulated by Paul Sweezy in 1943 and that have, since then, been virtually ignored. Sweezy posed three key questions about the *substance* of Schumpeter's

theory – not about its *logic* as presented on its own assumptions: 'Ha
. . . [Schumpeter] really isolated and abstracted for analysis the *primum
mobile* of change? Is the picture of the circular flow fully satisfactory? Is
the result of joining the two elements a correct representation of the
essentials of capitalist reality?' (1943, p. 93). In each of these respects,
he found Schumpeter's analysis wanting and concluded that the
questions must be answered in the negative. (Cf. the critical arguments
and conclusions drawn by Oscar Lange in his 1935 paper – Lange, 1968.)
It will be readily apparent that I agree with the terms of Sweezy's
critique and that, in part, my study has endeavoured to elaborate upon
them, while at the same time adding terms of my own.

However, I am also aware, to continue Schumpeter's analogies, that
the study's expositional journey has taken us past many 'doors' that
have been left ajar by his endeavours and that, on the other side of these
'doors' are to be found powerful insights into some particulars of the
nature of capitalist motion and the way we should go about analysing
and explaining it. Schumpeter has received little recognition for opening
some of these 'doors' even though, over the years and from other
sources, many of the ideas have taken their place in the body of
accepted economic analysis.

As I emphasized earlier in the study, it is not a legitimate line of
critique simply to point to the incomplete nature of Schumpeter's theory
of motion. Any such reading should be tempered by giving due weight
to the fact that his own intentions and ambitions were consciously
delimited. He did not seek to provide a complete explanation of
business cycles in any sense because he was all too aware of the complex
and ever changing substance of the objects with which he was dealing.
His aim was rather to identify the most essential of the causal factors
involved in order to formulate a core of explanation upon which can be
superimposed other, less universally relevant influences. These latter
influences then act to modify the core processes and give the cycle its
empirical form. Schumpeter thereby implicitly accepted that no theory
could ever be comprehensive enough totally to account for all the details
of observed fluctuations or to make accurate predictions about their
future course.

These considerations led him to the important methodological and
substantive distinction between his primary business-cycle model and
the secondary wave of factors that impinge upon it. My reading is that
Schumpeter had high hopes for the general acceptance of his primary
model as a piece of 'pure' theory even though he referred to it as a 'first
approximation' in his total analysis. He saw it as a necessary 'skeleton'
or 'chassis' that must be there to support any more comprehensive

theorizing about cycles. As such, it is not unreasonable to expect that the model should be logically and substantively complete so that the 'flesh' or 'construction' that is to be built up around it can take a definite and meaningful shape. My critique has been largely directed at this level of Schumpeter's theoretical analyses in order to establish the extent to which the 'chassis' can take the analytical weight that he and others after him may want to put on it. It should already be apparent that I do not consider it to be made of the appropriate material to have the strength and rigidity required for any extensive use. In the next section, I reiterate why.

10.2 A selective critique

Here I outline those elements in the construction of Schumpeter's theoretical analyses that most seriously limit their capacity to provide understanding of the capitalist motion. As indicated in the preamble above, my focus is upon the primary business-cycle model and its foundations in the steady circular-flow conditions and the theory of economic development. My critical premises are that the model should, as far as it goes, be logically complete and provide a coherent and faithful abstract representation and explanation of capitalism undergoing unstable motion. I intrude into the secondary dimensions of the business cycle only to the extent of checking on their logical bona fides as extensions of the primary model. Substantive matters beyond the primary model are not at issue in this summary critique.

10.2.1 Capitalism and the circular-flow model

When Schumpeter set out to define capitalism as an economic system, some of the characteristics that he cited were those that are necessary for a system to be so classified in a generally accepted sense. Most particularly, such a system must be built up around the premises that physical means of production are owned by a delimited group of agents who engage in production by employing other agents to work with those means for a pre-agreed wage income. Means of production ownership combines with a legally established and defended system of property rights that enable owners to claim as profit income, *by virtue of that ownership alone*, the residual of sales revenue after meeting all contractual outlays for inputs. Now while these premises were more or less present in Schumpeter's vision of the system *per se*, they were *not* part of the construction of the circular-flow model upon which the remainder of his theoretical analyses depended so heavily.

In the circular-flow model, Schumpeter's formulation of his vision of capitalism as a pre-analytic cognitive act had its origins in his readings of received 'static' theory. His representation of the system for the purposes of theoretical analysis was oriented more towards expositional convenience and tractability than towards empirical consistency with real-world characteristics,~even in the most abstracted sense. The resource base of the system is confined to labour power and 'land' and no class of agent possesses the produced means of production that are such an obvious and significant part of the production structure of capitalism. Indeed, there is no production *structure* as such and no capitalist means of production owners amongst the system's constituent agents. Income generation and distribution procedures do not allow any scope for a surplus payable as profit, for all income payments are exhausted by the market-determined values of labour power and 'land' service flows. All this was designed to be consistent with the 'Austrian' conception of production that Schumpeter adopted. He portrayed production as a fully vertically-integrated 'straight-line' process that takes place in isolated and independent economic entities. The only class of outputs is final consumer commodities. Produced means of production comprise only transitory intermediate goods that are wholly internal to the entities concerned. Schumpeter did not ascribe any working capital status to the intermediate goods 'stock' and the circular flow requires no *advances* of funds in order to operate.

The circular-flow model worked up by Schumpeter, then, included no produced means of production beyond intermediate goods, no means of production owners as capitalists, no capital even in its finance form as advances and no profit income. Clearly such a model could not be claimed to represent a capitalist economic system, for it lacked all of the key features of such a system.

It seems that his rationale for constructing such a model, beyond that provided by his admiration for Walras's general equilibrium framework, was that no steady-state circular-flow from which change is absent can be capitalist. A 'stationary' capitalism in this sense is a contradiction of terms as capital and profit, and the capitalist agents who possess and appropriate them, are strictly 'dynamic' phenomena. They can be part of an economic system only once motion is underway. These considerations also provide the rationale for excluding 'externally' produced means of production, especially durable forms that must be carried through more than one production period. For with no advances of finance capital, no capitalists and no scope for profit, there is just no place for such means in the model as Schumpeter chose to construct it. However, the obvious existence of solid plant and equipment troubled Schumpeter from a common-sense perspective throughout his analyses. We find his discourse frequently straying into argument that includes produced means of production, but he never really came to grips with how they could be included in his theory. He sensed, too, that the traverses of motion would be affected by the need to contend with durable production structures in processes of change. It is my view that this ambivalence can be attributed to Schumpeter's failure to give due attention and definitude to production structures when formulating the circular-flow model in the first place.

As I argued in the text above, there was readily available and known to Schumpeter an alternative analytical framework which, had he chosen to utilize it, could have enabled him immediately to transcend all these limitations. Its construction includes *from the outset* capital as advances, capitalists as owners of produced means of production and employers of labour power, and a surplus that can be appropriated as profit, together with durable and non-durable produced means of production as an integral and necessary part of the production processes. These processes remain vertically sequential with the associated working capital needs made explicit. But, at the same time, each line of production is shown to require produced inputs from other sectors of the economy such that the production sectors exist in a pattern of mutual interdependence. This perception of production implies two evident characteristics of industrialized capitalism, namely that some firms specialize in producing means of production for industrial consumption and that there will be a circulation and exchange pattern of produced means of production. Moreover, the explicit inclusion of a physical production structure enables part of technology to be represented as *embodied* in means of production with obvious ramifications for any endeavour to analyse technological change.

This alternative model is also explicitly a reproduction schema. That is, the set of conditions for the circular-flow to proceed period by period without disruption are an integral part of the model's construction. Included in these conditions is some uniform rate of profits or equilibrium vector of rates of profit in the several sectors. Because of this presence of profit, the model can be readily extended to include saving and capital accumulation. The conditions for expanding reproduction and balanced economic growth can then be made explicit in terms of the additional production of produced means of production and of consumer commodities required. And, apropos this last point, it can and has been argued with good reason that the most essential source of motion in a capitalist economic system, and logically prior to any accompanying innovations, is just this capital accumulation process. If this argument is accepted, then the appropriate 'centre of gravity' for a

model of instability is a steadily expanding reproduction path o
balanced economic growth path. More on this in item *10.2.2* below.

In the present context, it is also appropriate to draw attention t(
Schumpeter's neglect of monopoly power and its associated marke
structures in his *theoretical analysis* of economic development and th(
business cycle. The steady circular-flow model that he constructed wa:
one in which supply and demand based market-price competition rul(
the events, including the processes of adjustment to any change tha
may be introduced. In its 'purest' state, the model would be perfectly
competitive, but Schumpeter's representation was not confined to tha
extreme in that he made due allowance for various impediments to th(
'perfect' operation of markets. Although, from time to time, he showe(
some awareness of the need to allow for monopoly power forces, th(
discussions were generally digressions from the mainline of his analysis
Where the forces were linked into the analysis, they were treated as jus
another impediment to the smooth working of free competition. N(
attempt was made to build the appropriate agency, structures anc
operations into the circular-flow model from the outset as a prope*
treatment would require. It was only in *Capitalism* that Schumpete*
really gave monopoly power the importance that it warranted as a forc(
shaping the temporal path of capitalism. This was amongst his mor(
significant insights and I will refer to it again in the next section. The fac*
remains, though, that his main theory of capitalist instability was neve*
reworked to take full account of the implications of monopoly power.

10.2.2   *The generation of motion by innovations*

When Schumpeter weighed up the endogenous causes of motion that he
intended to emphasize as the essential explanation for economic
development and its unstable form as the business cycle, he decided that
capital accumulation and investment should have no immediate role to
play. They are the source of purely quantitative economic growth, a
process that he considered to involve merely adjustments and adaptations that managerial agents could handle within the bounds of the
pre-existing structures and operations of the circular flow. This meant
that the forces of economic growth could not be responsible for
instability of the degree that Schumpeter wanted to explain. Such
disruptions, he argued, can only arise from waves of innovations or new
combinations undertaken by entrepreneurial agents with the necessary
special talents to implement them successfully. He therefore constructed his theory of motion in isolation from any growth considerations, but he always carried forward the idea that they could readily be

added back into the analysis at some appropriate time. Such an analytical reintegration was never carried out.

The result of this analytical strategy was that Schumpeter failed to give due priority to the forces of capital accumulation and investment as the essential core of capitalist motion. It may well be that these processes rarely take place in the absence of innovations and that, therefore, innovations have the vital role in any proper understanding of motion that Schumpeter attributed to them anyway. It is probably also the case that the need to innovate is a competitive force that capitalist means of production owners and their producing agents cannot avoid confronting or economically resist. Both of these considerations appear to put innovations in the front line of the causes of motion and to encourage their analysis as such in isolation from other forces. What this approach misses is the equally important fact that the capacity to innovate is more often than not *preconditioned* by the capacity to accumulate finance capital within the system and by the scope for investment in the sense that the productive capacity is or can be made available to produce additional and/or qualitatively different means of production. These preconditions are by no means trivial in their implications once the structure of production is allowed to take on its pattern of sector interdependencies and to involve commitments to fixed and durable means of production in which particular technologies are embodied.

Schumpeter's steady circular-flow model enabled him to detour around such potential complications. New combinations were so designed that they could be added into the system and only elicit the requirement that the existing highly mobile and adaptable resource base be *reallocated* by means of relative price adjustments. Free competitive markets ensure that this is carried out and once the wave of innovations ceases and its effects have been fully diffused and absorbed, a return to a new steady circular-flow 'equilibrium' is assured. It is readily apparent that this fiction, with its new entrepreneurs, new plants, new firms and new credit finance simply added into Schumpeter's perception of the circular-flow conditions, led him grossly to understate the complexity of the traverses that comprise economic development and the business cycle. The image of the system used is too 'fluid' and 'pliable' adequately to represent the sequential, time- and resource-consuming processes that are set in train by most decisions to innovate. And, it must be said that these limitations that Schumpeter inflicted upon his analyses could have been so readily obviated had he chosen a circular-flow construction more immediately consistent with the obvious realities of industrial capitalism. The alternative was available, but this was not to be.

10.2.3   Treatment of new combinations

There are four aspects of Schumpeter's treatment of new combinations that warrant some critical comment: first, the classification of new combinations and their various implications for understanding motion; secondly, the causal origins of these various forms of new combinations; thirdly, the mode and means by which the new combinations were argued to be implemented; and fourthly, the associated claim that the new combinations will appear discontinuously in time in waves or clusters. Each of these aspects takes some part in the generation of and form taken by motion in Schumpeter's analyses.

His broad coverage of new combination types will appear again in the next section as one of his contributions to the theory of motion that has significant explanatory potential. What is at issue here is that having set up this broad and carefully defined classification, Schumpeter applied it in a very casual manner to his analyses and certainly failed to make the best use of its potential. Specifically, he did not carry each category into his core model as a distinct form of innovation with its own implications for the way it is to be implemented and diffused, and hence for the traverse pattern that ensues. Perhaps there is a sense in which this coverage was too wide ranging for the purposes of the core model that Schumpeter sought to establish. For this reason, it may be argued that it was quite appropriate for him to have focused only upon the two forms that he did, namely product innovation and process innovation. This is a not unreasonable suggestion, but it does leave the requirement in place that the two chosen forms be kept distinct in the analysis. For even though *in operation* there are interdependencies between them – product innovations usually require process innovations and process innovations may require qualitatively new inputs that effectively give rise to product innovations – they remain very different as far as their origins, implementation and diffusion are concerned. That is, they generate quite different traverses in the expansion phase of the business cycle and leave different legacies to be realized in the contraction phase that follows. Schumpeter's treatment fell well short of either drawing the distinction fully enough or of ensuring that its implications for the primary traverses were adequately detailed.

Further to this first aspect of the treatment of new combinations, it will be recalled that Schumpeter casually mentioned in passing that each involved the setting up of a 'new production function'. The formal implications of this mode of representation were not pursued any further and no attempt was made to distinguish the relative resource use and displacement patterns of innovations. This is especially significant for any understanding of how product and process innovations will be involved in motion and what economic and social effects will ensue as the cycle proceeds. It is clear that, e.g., a relatively capital (real means of production) -attracting and labour power-displacing innovation will generate quite different traverses from a labour power attracting and capital displacing innovation (cf. the detailed analysis of this issue in Lowe, 1976, Part IV).

A second aspect of innovations to which Schumpeter gave inadequate explanatory attention had two dimensions: the source of opportunities to carry them out and the conditions that would actually bring about their implementation. Both of these issues arise because of his claim that innovations are to be treated as an endogenous cause of motion. Examples of the particular questions to be answered here are: Do potential entrepreneurs pursue opportunities on the demand or output side or do they pursue them on the supply or input side of their calculus (or both)? That is, are innovations 'demand pulled' or 'technologically pushed'? Do potential entrepreneurs seek out pre-existing opportunities and/or to what extent are they instrumental in creating opportunities for themselves? What are the agency and other links between research, invention and innovation? And how are innovations related to firm size and/or the degree of monopoly power in markets? Some of these issues were attended to by Schumpeter in his later works, especially in *Capitalism*. However, they were not part of the theory of economic development and the business cycle where innovation opportunities were simply assumed to be available in an always sufficient supply and potential entrepreneurs were simply assumed to respond in the tranquil conditions of the steady circular-flow 'equilibrium'.

Thirdly, we have seen that Schumpeter's analysis of the mode and means of implementing new combinations had three dimensions: Who carries out the innovations? What resources do they use to set up the new production processes? And what is the source of finance capital that they use in order to obtain command over those resources?

Schumpeter's perception of the need to be specific about the organization of human agency in his analyses was another potential contribution of note that will be referred to again in the next section. The only critical comment to be made here is that he probably gave undue emphasis to the fiction of the 'virgin' entrepreneur in his theoretical analyses. His recognition of 'corporate' entrepreneurs came only later in his career and as was the case with monopoly power, the mainline of his theory was never reworked in the light of this recognition. The second question concerning resource use was addressed under *10.2.2* above and nothing more need be said about it now.

There remains the matter of finance capital for innovations to consider. Here Schumpeter's primary model depended very heavily upon the facility of bank credit created *ad hoc* in response to the demand for it by intending entrepreneurs. His perception that the real process of innovation should be kept in direct contact with its monetary-financial implications was an insight of some significance. It shifted attention to finance as a means of facilitating and, possibly, constraining waves of innovations without any implication that the monetary sector could cause fluctuations in an independent way. Moreover, Schumpeter's use of banks (and bankers) as the institutional mediation in the financing process was not the *deus ex machina* that it may appear to be at first sight in his theory where saving and capital accumulation are initially absent. Banks have always been providers of, especially, short-term credit in capitalist economies and Schumpeter made correct use of this fact in his theory. The issue that warranted more careful attention in this argument, though, was the practical one of the extent to which bankers should be represented as providers of high-risk 'venture' finance under the sorts of conditions posited in the core model – entrepreneurs with no experience, no equity, assets or collateral and demanding new everything to set up their new combinations. Under such circumstances, budding entrepreneurs could be expected to meet stiff resistance to their approaches except from the most adventurous of bankers. On the basis of Schumpeter's own recognition of an alleged nine out of ten failure rate of new entrepreneurs, it might have been expected that he would paint a more cautious picture of bankers' responses. Bankers, as he well knew, are inclined to be a conservative and prudent lot, especially in the face of such evident lender risk. Of course, the whole issue was made excessively artificial by Schumpeter's choice of a steady circular-flow model in which entrepreneurs have no capacity to save and provide themselves with an equity base and no access to savings of others that may be borrowed on explicitly 'venture-capital' terms as a supplement or alternative to bank credit.

Once again, Schumpeter's idea was that saving and savings could be added onto his initial arguments at the appropriate time. In this case his claim was that as profit is the main source of saving, and as profit is only generated once development is underway, saving could not legitimately be part of the means by which development is explained. This logic becomes a *non sequitur* when it is realized that as profit is a necessary condition for any realistic portrayal of capitalism, the capacity to save will always be present to lift some of the explanatory burden from bank credit in the innovation process.

Finally, there is the question of whether it is legitimate to model innovations as appearing in discontinuous waves. Schumpeter's argument concerning this matter was rather casual given his heavy reliance on the idea in the 'shaping' of business cycles. If innovations have a more continuous time profile, the business-cycle traverse to be explicated will be somewhat different from that posited in the primary model where innovative activity comes to an end during the expansion phase. Moreover, continuous innovations, as Schumpeter recognized, are more likely to be absorbed without the disruptive pressures that waves of them bring. Now there is a sense in which it is reasonable to argue that innovative activity is self-reinforcing and cumulative through imitation. And there is, too, reason to believe that a build-up of such activity may wane as economic expansion proceeds and the risks of failure are perceived by potential entrepreneurs to increase. However, the fact remains that *a priori* reasoning can only take us so far in this matter. What Schumpeter needed to do here was to reinforce his argument with some empirical evidence that such waves have occurred in history other than in association with long waves. As things turned out, probably due to a paucity of data, the evidence that he elicited about innovations in short and medium cycles generally was sketchy and inconclusive.

10.2.4 *The analytical representation of motion*

I have maintained throughout this study that any explanation of motion should be by means of traverses that are as detailed and rigorously argued as possible. Traverses are the only way of representing what motion actually involves, namely changes that impinge upon an economic system and are followed by the several dimensions of reaction to them that take place in strictly temporal sequences with a definable causal logic. There were places in Schumpeter's analyses where he seemed to sense what is required in this respect, but the traverse idea was not applied as a consistent methodological principle.

The details of the various traverse phases that merge into one another in sequence to constitute the business cycle were never presented with sufficient precision for Schumpeter to claim that he had formulated a closed and logically-coherent explanation of the phenomenon, even at the primary-core theoretical level. It was really only the expansion phase of the primary cycle that he considered in any substantively specific way. The upper turning point was left with no explanation at all and the recession return to 'equilibrium' was asserted to be such an obvious process that it required no specification. In particular, regarding the recession phase, Schumpeter's unusual claims that it is non-pathological and comprises the working out of all of the economic benefits that are ultimately to flow from the previous wave of innovations were not defended with any definite analysis.

Regarding the 'second approximation' business-cycle analysis that emerges with the secondary-wave effects, only two critical comments of a methodological nature are appropriate here. Schumpeter argued that the secondary-wave effects are to be superimposed upon the primary model in order to represent the secondary business-cycle. Having done so, he was then rather cavalier in his treatment of the logical form to be taken by this superimposition. He was vague about the point in the primary cycle at which the secondary-wave may begin to take effect, but it is evident that this must most often be during the prosperity phase and result in an aggravated boom. Once this is argued, though, the status of the recession phase with its very special characteristics is brought into question. It cannot be that any depression that may occur is just a phase that follows the recession, i.e. that the recession 'turns into' a depression, because with the secondary-wave effects already in train at the upper turning point, there will be no recession in the primary sense. In effect, this makes Schumpeter's four-phase cycle a misnomer, for the cumulative build up of the depression phase *replaces* the recession phase as the form taken by contraction. If 'recession' is intended to convey that contraction goes from bad to worse when a depression appears, then another name should have been used for the early stage of contraction in order to avoid confusion with the particular recession format in the primary cycle.

A further piece of logic that Schumpeter left in the air concerned the essential nature of the recovery phase of the secondary cycle. He drew the analogy with the 'equilibration' processes of a primary recession, because both phases in their respective contexts must bring about a restoration of 'equilibrium' at the end of the cycle unit, but this approach explains nothing. The disequilibria from which the two phases begin are totally different and, consequently, so must be the traverses through which the system passes on its way to the new 'equilibrium'. So, even though Schumpeter understandably did not want to commit himself to a particular theory of the secondary cycle, the overall impact of his analysis would have been enhanced by more attention to these logical rather than substantive issues.

As I pointed out in my preamble to this chapter, these several critical observations are intended to have a positive thrust. From the limitations of Schumpeter's analyses, we can identify some future directions for improving our understanding of motion. To a large extent these remain unexplored to their full potential.

10.3 Contributions reassessed

The legacy of Schumpeter's positive contributions to our understanding and analytical treatment of capitalist motion comprises both methodological and substantive aspects. Some of these he made explicit and pointed to as merits of his work. Others of them he left implicit and without the emphasis that is warranted by their potential. The order of the list set out below reflects no 'grading' of the contributions and each should be assessed only in relation to the implications that it has for the further development of motion analyses. (Cf. the similar lists prepared by Michael Reclam, 1984, p. 195 and Gunther Tichy, 1984a, pp. 86–7.)

1. Schumpeter worked on the premise that capitalism is an *inherently unstable system* and thus reaffirmed Marx's notion that the explanation for such instability must be found within the logic of the system itself. External factors have an important role in shaping the instability, but they cannot explain its essential origins.

2. The three methodological principles that Schumpeter implicitly adopted in his theoretical analysis of motion enabled him to work it out in a logically coherent sequence. To reiterate, first, he founded his theory upon a model of the economy in circular-flow 'equilibrium' in the absence of any change-induced motion. This allowed him, secondly, to introduce selectively and progressively those factors of change that cause motion and to present a delimited and controlled analysis of their individual and cumulative consequences. The third principle complemented this controlled presentation in that the totality of motion is taken to be separable into several distinct dimensions that can be traced to specific causes. This analytical dissection requires that for a complete theory, these component dimensions be reintegrated into an interdependent whole. For Schumpeter, the importance of these three principles is to be found in his isolation of economic development generated by discontinuous waves of innovations as the most fundamental dimension of motion. He went on from there to argue that the primary business-cycle is the temporal form taken by motion that is founded on development and then to imply that ever more empirically relevant aspects of motion can be added in as required – in particular, the secondary-wave effects and economic growth trends. The effect that this analytical strategy has is to lift Schumpeter's theory above any charge of eclecticism in that he gives causal priority to one particular element of change. At the same time, though, he makes due allowance for all other elements that contribute to the explanation of unstable motion in such a

way that their relative priorities can also be made apparent. What is more, the strategy also precludes any reading of monocausality into his theory.

3. Schumpeter made judicious use of the concept of equilibrium. In particular, his construction of the steady circular-flow 'equilibrium' state served three interdependent theoretical purposes. First, it provided a means of bringing some order, coherence and simplification to observed reality, albeit by way of some assumptions that diverge significantly from that reality, as we have seen. The effect was to generate a framework of relevant variables and their functional relations that is analytically tractable. Secondly, the formulation of an 'equilibrium' state facilitates the formalized expression of disequilibrium states as definable patterns of deviations from the 'equilibrium' conditions. Thirdly, the tenets of the 'equilibrium' state provide insights into the logic of responses that can be argued when disruptions to that state generate a disequilibrium. In Schumpeter's words, the 'equilibrium' provides an '*apparatus of response*'. And, in his case, the construction of the 'apparatus' was such as to ensure that any disequilibrium engenders the responses by constituent agents that will ensure the restoration of 'equilibrium'. (Cf. here the arguments of Cowen and Fink, 1985). In Schumpeter's theory of motion, then, the 'equilibrium' state provided a 'centre of gravity' around which to represent instability of the system over time. He saw this notion as of more than theoretical significance, for he held that such significance depends in the first place upon 'equilibrium' having a real-world counterpart. While his idea of a 'normal business situation' may not have corresponded precisely to the empirical equivalent that he sought, it is clear that capitalism's motion has not been characterized by any continuous 'explosion' into chaos over time. Periods of, perhaps extreme, disequilibrium have always been followed by a return to more 'normal' conditions. It follows that at least in an ill-defined sense, some empirical *centre of gravity* must exist. The extent to which it can be analytically defined and applied must remain a moot point.

4. In formulating his analyses, Schumpeter revealed a distrust of purely aggregate theoretical reasoning. He made some effort to be specific about the particular sectors and classes of agents that are relevant to the explanation of motion, although he never really set out clearly a meso-level economic structure and organization that he could apply consistently.

5. Schumpeter couched his 'equilibrium' concept in terms of the circular flow rather than using the timeless 'static' form. That is to say, he recognized that in the steady circular-flow state, motion through time

is still the centre of attention. Agents still act in time, albeit as automaton-like beings and time-consuming economic events and sequences take place in maintaining the circular flow. Motion in this limited sense is, then, not absent, but it is not motion that is induced by change and the troublesome aspects of elapsing time are assumed away by the perfect certainty of exact repetitions. Motion induced by change is the ultimate focus of Schumpeter's analyses, but he remained sensitive to the need for such motion to be shown not totally to destroy the steady circular-flow potential of the system.

6. In constructing his circular-flow model, Schumpeter gave production its appropriate status as the foundation piece of the economic system. This followed from his common-sense perception that what such systems 'do' most essentially is to mediate between human material needs and Nature in order to ensure that 'adequate' provisioning is realized. Whatever else the systems and their attached socio-political orders 'do', 'adequate' material provisioning is a mandatory precondition. Founding the circular flow on production focused attention directly upon the most significant site of the generation of motion through change and facilitated Schumpeter's emphasis on the supply side in his theoretical analyses.

7. One of Schumpeter's most significant potential contributions to our understanding of motion in all economic systems was the emphasis he gave to the role of innovations. His 'isolation' methodology, in which he excluded the capital accumulation and investment that usually accompanies and facilitates innovations, may have exaggerated the significance of innovations and understated the complexity of the motion that they generate, but to have insisted that they must be given a '*front-line*' role was an insight of lasting relevance. Moreover, in his conception of innovations, he included a wide range of 'novelty' that would have to find a place in any comprehensive theory of motion that argues innovations as its essential cause. His five categories of new combinations covered technology on the input side of production, qualitative dimensions of commodity output, organizational and managerial facets of production, geographic and other aspects of the search for input supplies and markets for output. Such variety would be difficult to handle in any formal analysis and Schumpeter concentrated upon the first two. However, the fact remains that each of the five can provide firms with innovation-based economic advantages and they all should be given due weight in a complete analysis.

8. In conjunction with his focus on innovations, Schumpeter also endeavoured to provide some analysis of the human agency aspects of the processes involved. This required him to broach issues in economic

sociology and to identify the characteristics and functions of key agent groups in the implementation and diffusion of innovations. In particular, he separated the function of ownership of means of production from the function of controlling them in production by means of 'directing' labour power. Then he introduced a duality into the 'directing' processes themselves, whether they are carried out by working capitalist owners or salaried executive workers: one set of tasks demands routine administration and management skills, but there is another set that requires additional and rarer talents, namely the initiation, supervision and control of 'enterprise' that involves doing new things that disrupt established structures and operations. Only a relatively small, élite group has the necessary leadership and other talents to carry through the latter processes of 'creative destruction' and the pattern of their participation in economic activity is, as Schumpeter so clearly recognized, a vital determinant of what happens to economic motion. The presence, dimensions and activities of the entrepreneurial group of agents affects both motion through time in one country and the relativities of motion between countries over any comparable historical period.

9. The monetary complement of the real forces of motion played a significant and proper role in Schumpeter's theoretical analyses. He was conscious from the construction of his circular-flow model onwards that money must take its appropriate place in the argument, with its particular forms and roles being specified at each analytical stage. Of particular significance is his emphasis upon the financial sector's key role as the provider of the means of facilitating real economic activity, including innovations, and upon the fact that as a private sector of the economy, its revenue flows and interest yield depend upon it doing so successfully. And, to the extent that the financial institutions create what is recognized as money by means of their credit operations, the money supply becomes endogenously linked to real activity. For Schumpeter, the main institutions involved here were banks and their banker agents were argued to act in a more or less regulated environment to 'shape' the flow of credit to borrowers. In a 'dynamic' setting, then, the idea of a fixed or given money supply is rendered meaningless as both the supply and demand sides of the money market become integral parts of the motion itself. In this analytical context, Schumpeter inevitably regarded interest as a monetary phenomenon. However, his emphasis was not upon 'liquidity preference' notions, but rather upon the roots that interest has in the real dimensions of economic activity that give rise to the state of the money market. This latter focus

represents, at least, an appropriate complement to portfolio views of interest determination.

10. Once motion is underway, Schumpeter recognized that economic decision-making by agents becomes a more or less hazardous affair. He argued that during business-cycle fluctuations, varying degrees of uncertainty and economic insecurity would have to be faced by economic agents and that these conditions could only be handled by the agents forming expectations. It was to his credit that he insisted that any satisfactory analytical treatment of such expectations would have to explain their formation within the terms of the model being used. That is, expectations would become another component of the traverse that constitutes a phase of motion. This insight has recently risen to prominence as the general principle behind the various versions of 'rational' expectations-formation theory.

11. The aspect of Schumpeter's work that has enjoyed most recognition, other than his emphasis upon the role of innovations in economic motion *per se*, is his treatment of their relation to monopoly power and market structure generally. It is in association with this aspect that his name is still most explicitly registered in economic literature through the concept of 'Schumpeterian competition' and the 'Schumpeterian hypotheses' about the generation of innovations. The former concept concerns that form of competitive strategy that is adopted by market participants who have monopoly power over the characteristics of their commodities, including price. In such situations, the only means of access to a sustainable increase in firm size and/or market share comprises product innovation and the only means of access to a sustainable increase in unit profit return comprises cost-reducing process innovation. The 'Schumpeterian hypotheses' have been devised to suggest that the 'volumes' of such innovations (however measured) are positively correlated with the degree of monopoly power and/or firm size in an industry (see, e.g., Kamien and Schwartz, 1982). These associations suggested by Schumpeter, albeit only clearly in his late works, have led to a resurgence in concern to model capitalist motion as a simultaneously quantitative and qualitatively-evolutionary process (see, e.g., Nelson and Winter, 1982). Perhaps as much remains to be done with the other insights that Schumpeter left us.

References

Bauer, O. (1986) 'The accumulation of capital' [1913], trans. J. E. King, *History of Political Economy*, 18.

Bellofiore, R. (1985a) 'Money and development in Schumpeter', *Review of Radical Political Economics*, 17.

Bellofiore, R. (1985b) 'From Wicksell to Keynes through Schumpeter: the conceptual roots of the monetary theory of production', mimeograph.

Boehm, S. (1989) 'The Austrian tradition: Schumpeter and Mises', in K. Hennings and W. J. Samuels (eds), *Neoclassical Economic Theory, 1870–1930*, Kluwer Academic, Boston.

Bronfenbrenner, M. (1986) 'Schumpeter and Keynes as "rich man's Karl Marxes" ', in Wagener and Drukker (eds) (1986).

Burchardt, F. A. (1931–32) 'Die Schemata des stationären Kreislaufs bei Böhm-Bawerk und Marx', zwei Teile, *Weltwirtschaftliches Archiv*, 34, 35.

Clemence, R. V. and F. S. Doody (1966) *The Schumpeterian System* [1950], Augustus M. Kelley, New York.

Cowen, T. and R. Fink (1985) 'Inconsistent equilibrium constructs: the evenly rotating economy of Mises and Rothbard', *American Economic Review*, 75.

Crum, W. L. (1946) *Rudimentary Mathematics for Economists and Statisticians*, with J. A. Schumpeter, McGraw-Hill, New York.

Dobb, M. (1973) *Theories of Value and Distribution Since Adam Smith: Ideology and Economic Theory*, Cambridge University Press, Cambridge.

Earley, J. S. (1981) 'Schumpeter as "anti-Monetarist" ', mimeograph.

Earley, J. S. (1983) 'Schumpeter's theories of money and credit: a second approximation', Working Paper Series, Department of Economics, University of California, Riverside.

Earley, J. S. (1987) 'Schumpeter's theory of credit and his concepts of capital and interest', mimeograph.

Frisch, H. (ed.). (1982) *Schumpeterian Economics*, Praeger, Eastbourne, East Sussex.

Frisch, R. (1951) 'Some personal reminiscences on a great man', in Harris (ed.) (1951).

Frisch, R. (1966) 'Propagation problems and impulse problems in dynamic economics' [1933], in R. A. Gordon and L. R. Klein, *Readings in Business Cycles*, Allen & Unwin, London.

Giddens, A. (1977) *Studies in Social and Political Theory*, Hutchinson, London.

Goodwin, R. M. (1986) 'The M-K-S system: the functioning and evolution of capitalism', in Wagener and Drukker (eds) (1986).

Goodwin, R. M. (1988) 'Walras and Schumpeter: the vision reaffirmed', mimeograph.

Haberler, G. (1951a) 'Joseph Alois Schumpeter, 1883–1950', in Harris (ed.) (1951).

Haberler, G. (1951b) 'Schumpeter's theory of interest', in Harris (ed.) (1951).

Haberler, G. (1964) *Prosperity and Depression: A Theoretical Analysis of Cyclical Movements* [1937], new edition, Allen & Unwin, London.

Hansen, A. H. (1927) *Business Cycle Theory: Its Development and Present Status*, Ginn & Co., Boston.

Hansen, A. H. (1951) 'Schumpeter's contribution to business cycle theory', in Harris (ed.) (1951).

Hanusch, H. (ed.) (1988) *Evolutionary Economics: Applications of Schumpeter's Ideas*, Cambridge University Press, Cambridge.

Harris, S. E. (ed.) (1951) *Schumpeter, Social Scientist*, Harvard University Press, Cambridge, Mass.

Heertje, A. (ed.) (1981) *Schumpeter's Vision: "Capitalism, Socialism and Democracy" after 40 years*, Praeger, New York.

Heilbroner, R. L. (1986) *The Worldly Philosophers: The Lives, Times and Ideas of the Great Economic Thinkers* [1953], 6th edition, Simon & Schuster, New York.

Heilbroner, R. L. (1988) *Behind the Veil of Economics: Essays in the Worldly Philosophy*, Norton & Co., New York.

Hilferding, R. (1981) *Finance Capital: A study of the latest phase of capitalist development* [1910], ed. T. Bottomore, trans. M. Watnick and S. Gordon, Routledge & Kegan Paul, London.

Jensen, H. E. (1987) 'New lights on J. A. Schumpeter's theory of the history of economics?' *Research in the History of Economic Thought and Methodology*, 5.

Kalecki, M. (1937) 'A theory of the business cycle', *Review of Economic Studies*, 4.

Kamien, M. I. and N. L. Schwartz (1982) *Market Structure and Innovation*, Cambridge University Press, Cambridge.

Keynes, J. M. (1936) *The General Theory of Employment, Interest and Money*, Macmillan, London.

246 *Schumpeter's Theory of Capitalist Motion*

Khan, M. S. (1957) *Schumpeter's Theory of Capitalist Development*, Muslim University Press, Aligarh, India.

Kuznets, S. (1954) *Economic Change: Selected Essays in Business Cycles, National Income and Economic Growth*, Heinemann, London.

Lange, O. (1940) 'Review of *Business Cycles* by Joseph A. Schumpeter', *Review of Economic Statistics*, 22.

Lange, O. (1968) 'Marxian economics and modern economic theory' [1935], in D. Horowitz (ed.), *Marx and Modern Economics*, MacGibbon & Kee, London.

Löwe, A. (1925) 'Der gegenwärtige Stand der Konjunkturforschung in Deutschland', in M. J. Bonn and M. Palyi (eds), *Die Wirtschaftswissenschaft nach dem Kriege: Festgabe für Lujo Brentano zum 80. Geburtstag*, Bd. 2, Duncker & Humblot, München.

Löwe, A. (1926) 'Wie ist Konjunkturtheorie überhaupt möglich?', *Weltwirtschaftliches Archiv*, 24.

Lowe, A. (supra Löwe) (1976) *The Path of Economic Growth*, assisted by S. Pulrang, Cambridge University Press, Cambridge.

Lowe, A. (supra Löwe) (1987) *Essays in Political Economics: Public Control in a Democratic Society*, ed. A. Oakley, Wheatsheaf, Brighton, and New York University Press, New York.

Luxemburg, R. (1951) *The Accumulation of Capital* [1913], trans. A. Schwartzschild, Routledge & Kegan Paul, London.

Machlup, F. (1951) 'Schumpeter's economic methodology', in Harris (ed.) (1951).

Marget, A. W. (1951) 'The monetary aspects of the Schumpeterian system', in Harris (ed.) (1951).

Marschak, J. (1940) 'Review of *Business Cycles* by Joseph A. Schumpeter', *Journal of Political Economy*, 48.

Marx, K. (1971) *Capital: A Critique of Political Economy*, volume II [1885], ed. F. Engels, Progress Publishers, Moscow.

März, E. (1965) 'Zur Genesis der Schumpeterschen Theorie der wirtschaftlichen Entwicklung', in *On Political Economy and Econometrics: Essays in Honour of Oskar Lange*, ed. anon., Pergamon Press, Oxford.

Meek, R. L. (1967) *Economics and Ideology and Other Essays: Studies in the Development of Economic Thought*, Chapman & Hall, London.

Minsky, H. P. (1986) 'Money and crisis in Schumpeter and Keynes', in Wagener and Drukker (eds) (1986).

Minsky, H. P. (1988) 'Schumpeter: finance and evolution', mimeograph.

Morishima, M. and G. Catephores (1988) 'Anti-Say's Law versus Say's Law: a change in paradigm', in Hanusch (ed.) (1988).

Nell, E. J. (1967) 'Theories of growth and theories of value', *Economic Development and Cultural Change*, 16.

Nelson, R. R. and S. G. Winter (1982) *An Evolutionary Theory of Economic Change*, Harvard University Press, Cambridge, Mass.

Nurkse, R. (1934–35) 'The schematic representation of the structure of production', *Review of Economic Studies*, 2.

Popper, K. R. (1960) *The Poverty of Historicism* [1957], 2nd ed., Routledge & Kegan Paul, London.

Reclam, M. (1984) 'J. A. Schumpeter's "Credit" theory of money', unpublished PhD dissertation, University of California, Riverside.

Rothbarth, E. (1942) 'Review of *Business Cycles* by Joseph A. Schumpeter', *Economic Journal*, 52.

Samuels, W. J. (1983) 'The influence of Friedrich von Wieser on Joseph A. Schumpeter', *The History of Economics Society Bulletin*, 4.

Schneider, E. (1975) *Joseph A. Schumpeter: Life and Work of a Great Social Scientist* [1970], trans. W. E. Kuhn, Bureau of Business Research Monograph No. 1, University of Nebraska-Lincoln.

Schumpeter, J. A. (1908) *Das Wesen und der Hauptinhalt der theoretischen Nationalökonomie*, Duncker & Humblot, Berlin.

Schumpeter, J. A. (1910) 'Die neuere Wirtschaftstheorie in den Vereinigten Staaten', *Schmollers Jahrbuch*, XXXIV.

Schumpeter, J. A. (1912) *Theorie der wirtschaftlichen Entwicklung*, 1st ed., Duncker & Humblot, Leipzig,

Schumpeter, J. A. (1915) *Vergangenheit und Zukunft der Sozialwissenschaften*, Duncker & Humblot, München.

Schumpeter, J. A. (1930) Preface to Zeuthen (1930).

Schumpeter, J. A. (1934) *The Theory of Economic Development: An Inquiry into Profits, Capital, Credit, Interest and the Business Cycle* [1912, 1926], trans. R. Opie, Harvard University Press, Cambridge, Mass.

Schumpeter, J. A. (1935) *Theorie der wirtschaftlichen Entwicklung: Eine Untersuchung über Unternehmergewinn, Kapital, Kredit, Zins und den Konjunkturzyklus*, 4th edn., Duncker & Humblot, München.

Schumpeter, J. A. (1939) *Business Cycles: A Theoretical, Historical and Statistical Analysis of the Capitalist Process*, 2 volumes, McGraw-Hill, New York.

Schumpeter, J. A. (with W. L. Crum), see Crum (1946).

Schumpeter, J. A. (1948) 'Some questions of principle', in L. Allen (ed.), *Research in the History of Economic Thought and Methodology*, 5, 1987.

Schumpeter, J. A. (1951) *Essays on Economic Topics of J. A. Schumpeter*, ed. R. V. Clemence, Kennikat Press, Port Washington, NY.

Schumpeter, J. A. (1952a) *Aufsätze zur ökonomischen Theorie*, J. C. B. Mohr (Paul Siebeck), Tübingen.

Schumpeter, J. A. (1952b) *Ten Great Economists: From Marx to Keynes*, Allen & Unwin, London.

Schumpeter, J. A. (1954) *Economic Doctrine and Method: An Historical Sketch* [1914], trans. R. Aris, Allen & Unwin, London.

Schumpeter, J. A. (1954a) *Capitalism, Socialism and Democracy*, 4th edn. [1942], Allen & Unwin, London.

Schumpeter, J. A. (1954b) *History of Economic Analysis*, ed. E. B. Schumpeter, Allen & Unwin, London.

Schumpeter, J. A. (1955) *Imperialism and Social Classes* [1919, 1927], ed. B. Hoselitz, Meridian Books, New York.

Schumpeter, J. A. (1956) 'Money and the social product', trans. A. W. Marget, *International Economic Papers*, 6.

Schumpeter, J. A. (1970) *Das Wesen des Geldes*, ed. F. K. Mann, Vandenhoeck & Ruprecht, Göttingen.

Schumpeter, J. A. (1985) *Aufsätze zur Wirtschaftspolitik*, ed. W. Stolper and C. Seidl, J. C. B. Mohr (Paul Siebeck), Tübingen.

Schumpeter, J. A. (1987) *Beiträge zur Sozialökonomik*, ed. and trans. S. Böhm, Böhlau Verlag, Vienna.

Seidl, C. (ed.) (1984a) *Lectures on Schumpeterian Economics: Schumpeter Centenary Memorial Lectures, Graz 1983*, Springer-Verlag, Berlin.

Seidl, C. (1984b) 'Schumpeter versus Keynes: supply side economics or demand management?', in Seidl (ed.) (1984a).

Seidl, C. (1984c) 'Joseph Alois Schumpeter: character, life, and particulars of his Graz period', in Seidl (ed.) (1984a).

Smithies, A. (1951) 'Schumpeter and Keynes', in Harris (ed.) (1951).

Stolper, W. F. (1943) 'Monetary, equilibrium, and business-cycle theory', *Review of Economic Statistics*, 25.

Streissler, E. (1982) 'Schumpeter's Vienna and the role of credit in innovation', in Frisch (ed.) (1982).

Sweezy, P. M. (1943) 'Professor Schumpeter's theory of innovation', *Review of Economic Statistics*, 25.

Sweezy, P. M. (1951) 'Schumpeter on Imperialism and Social Classes', in Harris (ed.) (1951).

Tichy, G. (1984a) 'Schumpeter's business cycle theory: its importance for our time', in Seidl (ed.) (1984a).

Tichy, G. (1984b) 'Schumpeter's monetary theory: An unjustly neglected part of his work', in Seidl (ed.) (1984a).

Tinbergen, J. (1951) 'Schumpeter and quantitative research in economics', in Harris (ed.) (1951).

Vercelli, A. (1985) 'Money and production in Schumpeter and Keynes: two dichotomies', in anon. ed., *Production, Circulation et Monnaie*, Presses Universitaires de France, Paris.

Wagener, H. J. and J. W. Drukker (eds) (1986) *The Economic Law of Motion of Modern Society: A Marx-Keynes-Schumpeter Centennial*, Cambridge University Press, Cambridge.

Walras, L. (1954) *Elements of Pure Economics or the Theory of Social Wealth* [1874], trans. W. Jaffé, Allen & Unwin, London.

Walsh, V. and H. Gram (1980) *Classical and Neoclassical Theories of General Equilibrium: Historical Origins and Mathematical Structure*, Oxford University Press, New York.

Warburton, C. (1953) 'Money and business fluctuations in the Schumpeterian system', *Journal of Political Economy*, 61.

Wieser, F. von (1911) 'Das Wesen und der Hauptinhalt der theoretischen Nationalökonomie, Kritische Glossen', *Jahrbuch für Gesetzgebung, Verwaltung und Volkswirtschaft im Deutschen Reich*, 35.

Wright, D. McC. (1950) 'Schumpeter and Keynes', *Weltwirtschaftliches Archiv*, 65.

Zarnowitz, V. (1985) 'Recent work on business cycles in historical perspective: a review of theories and evidence', *Journal of Economic Literature*, 23.

Zeuthen, F. (1930) *Problems of Monopoly and Economic Warfare*, with a Preface by J. A. Schumpeter, Routledge & Sons, London.

Index

agents, *see* economic agents
'animal spirits', 150, 180
Austrians, 32
Austrian Marxists, 19, 56, 70
autodeflation, *see* credit deflation

bank credit, *see* credit
Bauer, O., 19, 56
Böhm, S., 2, 4, 5, 13
Böhm-Bawerk, E. von, 2, 32, 68, 70,
   125, 144
  stages model of production of, 19
Burchardt, F., 19, 70
business, 'normal' state of, 62–3, 85,
   86, 240
business cycle
  classical and growth forms, 163–4
  core variables in, 164
  credit in, 205–6, 226
  and credit deflation, 180–82, 192
  and debt, 197–8
  depression phase of, 5, 199–200
  and employment, 189–90, 190–91
  excess production capacity in,
   210–11
  existing firms in, 177, 178–9,
   184–5, 189, 192, 197
  and full employment, 205, 211
  and income redistribution, 188–9,
   190–91
  indicator variables for, 163–4, 165
  leading and lagging variables in,
   164–5
  monopoly power in, 209–15, 221,
   226
  and 'neighborhood' of equilibrium,
   167, 168–93 *passim*, 206–7
  new firms in, 177–8, 185, 192
  phases of, 168–73, 174–5, 192
  price determination in, 211–13, 215
  primary version of, 175–93, 197
  pulse charts of, 165
  recovery in, 200–205, 226, 238
  and savings, 207–8

  secondary wave in, 169, 194–205,
   225, 238
  three-cycle schema of, 174,
   215–22, 226
  as traverse process, 162, 167, 168,
   169–73, 182–3, 184, 185–6,
   187, 191, 192, 237–8
  see also traverses and trend, 164,
   171–2, 219, 239
  unemployment in, 206, 211
  vicious spiral of, 198, 225
business cycle theory
  as endogenous theory, 166–7
  erosion of entrepreneurial profit
   in, 175–6
  essentials of, 168–75, 192
  method of, 162–7, 175, 192
  monetary, 135, 145, 159–60
  waves of innovations in, 166,
   170–71, 175

Cantillon, R., 55
capital
  defined, 29–32, 107
  dimensions of, 29–30
  finance, 16, 23, 29, 30, 32, 75, 105,
   121, 136, 138, 139, 142, 145–8
   passim, 153–5 *passim*, 186,
   207, 208, 230, 233, 235, 236
  as means of production, 29–30, 31
  as mode of organizing production
   and income distribution, 30
  monetary theory of, 32
  working, 32, 75, 133, 230, 231
capitalism
  bizarre version of, 65
  circular-flow model of, 15, 64–5,
   229–32
  competitive, 32–8
  defined, 26–9, 229–30
  dual perception of, 81–2
  essentials of, 23, 32
  fate of, 13–14
  and large-scale firms, 37–8

vision concept, 22, 26
and Walras, 3, 15
    see also Walras, L.
'Schumpeterian' competition, 38,
    208, 215, 243
'Schumpeterian' hypotheses, 208, 243
Schwartz, N. L., 243
Simiand, F., 40
social classes, 12, 49–52, 105, 120–21
stock-flow distinction, 60
structure, duality of, 48
Sweezy, P. M., 18–19, 227–8

Tichy, G., 239
traverses, 23, 32, 35, 69, 73, 84–5,
    89, 96, 97, 99, 103, 118, 120,
    123–5 *passim*, 128–32 *passim*,
    135, 142, 145, 159, 160, 162,
    167–73 *passim*, 182–7 *passim*,
    191, 192, 198–209 *passim*, 211,
    213, 215, 226, 231–8 *passim*, 243

uncertainty, 59, 61, 87–9, 111, 112,
131, 150, 176–7, 179, 180, 182,
    187, 191, 197, 243
unemployment, 211
USA
    Department of Agriculture Gradu-
        ate School of, 213
    economic theory in, 4

Vienna, 1, 2, 56
vision concept, 229–30
    see also Schumpeter, J. A.

Walras, L., 2, 3, 7, 15, 19, 23, 55,
    56, 76, 77, 78, 87, 230
Walras-Edgeworth schema, 86
Wieser, F. von, 2, 4
Winter, S. G., 208, 243
workers, salaried, 27, 29

Zarnowitz, V., 163, 164
Zeuthen, F., 34, 213